QUALITY VENISON III

ALL NEW WILD GAME RECIPES AND HUNTING TALES TOO...

AUTHORS
STEVE AND GALE LODER

MEMBER

PENNSYLVANIA OUTDOOR WRITERS ASSOCIATION

QUALITY VENISON III

Published by
Loders' Game Publications, Inc.
P.O. Box 1615
Cranberry Township, Pennsylvania 16066
Phone: (724) 779-8320 Fax: (724) 779-9533

1st Printing, 4,000 copies

ISBN: 0-9662284-2-1

WIMMER
COOKBOOKS
ConsolidatedGraphics
1-800-548-2537

Dedicated to Mom and Dad Flack

Doris Flack: June 11, 1920 to February 12, 2001
Richard Flack: May 11, 1920 to August 30, 2001

Thanks Mom and Dad for shaping me into the person I am today…for bringing me up as a caring Christian, guiding me and being there for me always…then for letting me "go" to make life's journey on my own…but still being there…always…just in case I needed you. As a parent of a young lady, I know just how difficult that can be.

I feel blessed for having had you both for parents. You were not only there for me before you passed on but the love and caring did not end there. Just when Steve and I thought we would have to delay the publishing of this book until the economy turned around, you gave me one last gift…an inheritance that I never expected, just large enough to back our publishing expenses. Now that's true love!

Steve and I feel privileged to have been able to enjoy many wild game meals with you both. We always appreciated your visits, most times from several states away, so the least we could do is to serve you our very own wild game dishes, sometimes at your request. When we asked what you preferred, your preference was always "your wild game, of course." Remember, Dad, you would delve into the meal without asking any questions? Mom, you, on the other hand, learned to ask what you were about to eat so as to not be shocked later on? You always enjoyed it, you just had to know what you were going to eat first.

We can no longer share our wild game dishes with you, but we both thank you for all the wonderful memories we made together. We will cherish them forever.

On The Cover: "First Hunt"
Limited Edition Print
Painted by Jack Paluh

The thoughts from "First Hunt:"

"The evening was a crisp calm. My sixth sense felt the presence of someone or something staring at me. I rolled my eyes to see a buck, a nice one, looking up at me. He came following the path that paralleled my treestand. My movements had betrayed my hiding spot. I was frozen in place. My heart was pounding so loud, I was sure that he heard it."

Jack Paluh captures this experience that most hunters can identify with, in **"First Hunt."** **"First Hunt,"** designed to promote youth hunting, is a refreshing outlook for both novice and seasoned hunters. Jack's model for **"First Hunt"** was his own son, Adam.

Jack Paluh, Artist

Whitetail deer have always been Jack's passion. If you have a good hunting story, Jack always has the time to listen. He is an avid bow hunter and each October you will not find him in his home studio, but rather twenty-five feet up above in his treestand. To the trained eye, the woods are full of activity. In your treestand, away from life's distractions, *"there is peace."* Most of Jack's ideas are inspired as he patiently awaits and observes nature at its best. The family tradition continues as Jack's young family matures to legal hunting age. This long awaited tradition is passed onto another generation.

Perhaps one of Jack's whitetail images may evoke one of your whitetail memories.

Jack Paluh resides in northwestern Pennsylvania in a small borough called Waterford. It is here in this historical one-street-light town that Jack, his wife Marian, and their three children call home. He was a "doodler" from the time he could hold a pencil. Jack's only formal art education was that of a local trade high school. It was there under the guiding hands of local talented art teachers that he excelled and was encouraged to pursue the art field.

Twenty some years later, Jack recognizes his highest honor by meeting and talking with people who have bought his artwork. He is never too busy to swap stories or discuss the newest ideas in hunting. Whether it be painting, hunting or photography, Jack's natural sense of humor is ever present as well as his strong faith in God. "God has truly blessed me with a job I love," states Paluh. "I encourage others to find their talents and develop them. It is my privilege and honor to share my artwork, to inspire others, especially our youth, to the wonders of the outdoors."

For more information on Jack Paluh's artwork, please contact his studio at Jack Paluh Arts, Inc., 2869 Old Wattsburg Rd., Waterford, PA 16441, 814-796-4400, phone and fax. E-mail: JPA@erie.net or visit our website at www.jackpaluh.com.

Canvas prints of "First Hunt" with your young hunter's image on the hunter may be available in the future.

In Appreciation

We want to stop here to thank and give credit to those individuals who have shared their time and especially talent with us to make the self-publishing of our third book possible. Again, we have to thank our Lord for giving us the health, time and all the following people who supported us in the writing of *Quality Venison III.*

Once again, a big time thanks goes out to our artist friend, Jack Paluh, who allowed us to use another one of his beautiful art prints, "First Hunt" on the cover of our book. Jack's art is truly exceptional in our home and would be in yours, too. We also thank Bob Mitchell, Editor of *Pennsylvania Game News* magazine, for taking the time out of his busy schedule to give us two article reprint permissions and our hunting article contributors, Jerry Zeidler, Dennis Russell, Ron Wilson, Tom Mitchell, Joel Marvin, Ken Hunter, Gordon Krause, John Zent, and Karl Power for their permission to reprint their hunting articles and wild game recipes in our very special hunting tales section for you. To all, we wish you much continued success in your outdoors writing efforts, and let's all remember to make our next generation of our youth a part of our outdoor experiences with mother nature.

A special thanks goes out to all of the Arliss family on Lock Pit Road in Clyde, New York, where we spent over thirty-five years with them hunting, fishing, camping, celebrating weddings, and our kids' graduations. Without their lifelong friendship and sharing their appreciation for wildlife and God's outdoors, none of our three *Quality Venison* cookbooks could have been written. Their home, and especially their family, has enriched our lives greatly, to say the least. Please take a moment to read our thoughtful remembrances of Bill Arliss, Sr. who passed in 2000 and his grandson, Billy Arliss, who tragically passed in 2001, because they were very good, hard working people, and they will be surely missed by all of us who knew them.

In Remembrance of
William Arliss, Sr. and Billy S. Arliss

This page is in remembrance of only two special people who make up the Arliss family in Clyde, New York, who are my life long friends. Their family lost Bill Arliss, Sr. on 3/26/2000. Bill's hard, to say the least, work ethics were taught to all of his sons, and that is their legacy as seen in their own individual work ethic and business success. You are gone, but not forgotten, Bill.... Steve

William B. Arliss, Sr., age 79 of 895 Lockpit Rd., Clyde, New York, died Sunday, March 26, 2000 at ViaHealth of Wayne, Newark Campus surrounded by his family.

Friends and family were invited to attend a gathering in his honor on Wednesday, March 29, 2000 at the V.F.W. Post 947 in Clyde, New York. Memorial contributions were asked to be made to the Clyde Volunteer Ambulance Corporation.

Mr. Arliss was born in Savannah, New York on March 3, 1921. He served his country in the United States Army during World War II while stationed in Japan. He was a member of the Clyde V.F.W. Post 947 and served as Post Commander in 1977. Mr. Arliss was employed and retired from Local 832 out of Rochester, New York as an Operating Engineer. He also worked on the family farm and was an avid fisherman. He is survived by his wife of 59 years, Ella Holt Arliss; 6 sons, Fred (Rhayna), Roger, Larry (Denise), William Jr. (Susan), Randy (Tina), Philip (Bobbi Jo) all of Clyde, New York; 2 daughters, Ida (David) Hartman of Philadelphia, Pennsylvania, Shelley (Douglas) Lecher of Gastonia, North Carolina; 18 grandchildren; 2 great grandchildren. Mr. Arliss was predeceased by his brothers, Adelbert, Frederick, Robert, Alden; a sister, Ruth Fulmer; half brother, Thomas Breen.

The Arliss family also faced another grievous loss in Clyde, New York when May 29, 2001 a tragic vehicle accident took the life of young Billy S. Arliss. I was friends of Billy for over twenty-five years and to anyone who knew Billy, liked him for the person he was. I will never understand why God called him home at such a young age, but there are many things in God's plan for us that I will never understand until later. You are gone, but certainly not forgotten, Billy... Steve

Billy S. Arliss died on May 29, 2001 as the result of injuries sustained in a motor vehicle accident in Plattekill, New York. Billy was born on January 19, 1969 in Newark, New York. He was the son of Frederick and Rhayna Tompkins Arliss. He was a graduate of Clyde-Savannah High School class of 1987, where he was an All-Star athlete playing on their golf, football and basketball teams. Billy continued his education at Methodist College in Fayetteville, North Carolina, graduating in the class of 1991 with a Bachelor of Science degree in Business Administration. He was a member of their NCAA Div. 3 All American Golf Team for four years. Billy was a former member of Wayne Hills Country Club, and served as assistant golf pro at Bristol Harbor Golf Club in Canandaigua and Sodus Bay Heights Golf Club in Sodus Point. He was employed by the Park Lane Construction Company in Clyde, New York. Billy had just married the former Laurie Ufholz on May 19, 2001.

Billy is also survived by a step daughter, Erica Kerr, one sister, Kathryn Ann Arliss, his paternal grandmother, Ella Arliss, one nephew, Brian Arliss, his in-laws, and many other relatives. His memory will live on forever.

Introduction

For the sportsman hunter, it all starts from the field to the dinner table, whether your wild game or fish is enjoyed with your family and friends or if the wild game is donated to food banks feeding our less fortunate people in our communities, there is a great deal of personal satisfaction we feel for making a difference. It is the sportsman hunters that are making a difference in controlling our wildlife population and often helping to feed the hungry people in our communities across North America by their donations of wild game to their local food banks through programs such as Farmers and Hunters Feeding the Hungry and Hunters Sharing the Harvest.

Carrying on the hunting tradition from one generation to another is extremely important in keeping our outdoor sports of hunting and fishing alive. The theme from our book's cover and throughout our hunting tales' section is to make a difference in a kid's life by taking him or her with you when you hunt or fish. You will not only be making memories that will last a lifetime, but you just might spark enough interest to introduce yet another young person to the wonders of spending time in God's outdoors and the importance of outdoor sports.

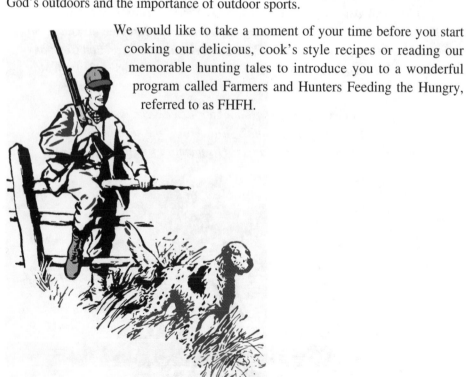

We would like to take a moment of your time before you start cooking our delicious, cook's style recipes or reading our memorable hunting tales to introduce you to a wonderful program called Farmers and Hunters Feeding the Hungry, referred to as FHFH.

Ministering With A Meal

By Gordon Krause

Funny the things that stick with you. Back when I started college some twenty odd years ago, students were forced to take mandatory elective classes in addition to their major, mine being Computer Science. Searching the catalog, I hit upon "Psychology 101." Great! Sounded like an easy to pass course that might even provide some secrets about how people think. Well, I did pass the class, but sorry to say, have forgotten most of what I learned. However, one lesson stuck with me after all those years. It was about the Pyramid of Needs that all men and women have. Roughly stated, everyone has a pyramid of various needs, the lower layers necessary before the upper layers can be built upon. The lower layers contain things like food, shelter, clothing and security, the basic daily needs we all take for granted. The upper layers are concepts like love and spiritual fulfillment. The premise is that it is impossible to reach the upper layers if there are serious problems with the lower ones. In other words, you probably will not be putting much thought into your spiritual growth path when you are cold, hungry, homeless and afraid of being harmed on the streets.

That made good sense and recently it occurred to me that Jesus probably knew all about this concept long before the word Psychology had even been invented. Take a look at how food played a big part in many of the situations that Jesus found himself in with his followers. The loaves and fish that he fed to the multitudes, the wedding feast of Cana and of course The Last Supper. It's as if Jesus knew that a person free from hunger was going to be much more open to the "Word." At FHFH, we can help to do the same. No, we don't require anyone to listen to a sermon before venison chili is served for lunch. But by helping to fulfill the basic needs of the people that receive our venison donations, we build up the lower layers of their pyramids, allowing them to climb up to where they can hear whatever ministry they are exposed to. By supporting FHFH in time, talents and treasures, we can all be indirect ministers of the healing "Word." The "Word" we all so desperately need to hear! (For information about this program call 301-739-3000 or log onto their Website at www.fhfh.org.)

Contents

Welcome, Once Again To Our "Country Kitchen"

Grilling, Frying, and Broiling Venison 13

Italian Style and Crockery Cooking Venison 31

Cooking Venison Traditional Style 51

Let's Cook The "Other" Wild Game 67

Appetizers and Side Dishes 97

Welcome To Our Hunting Tales Contents, "It's Tradition"

When It Is Time To Hunt In God's Great Outdoors 120

The Family That Hunts Together
by John Zent, *American Hunter* 121

The Quality Hunter by Gordon L. Krause 122

Dad Flack's Treasured A.H. Fox Double Barrel 12-Gauge 123

This Teenager's First Cottontail Rabbit - 1964 125

Take a Kid Hunting
by Dennis Russell, *Pennsylvania Game News* 128

A Fond Waterfowling Memory - 1966 130

This Teenager's "First Ruffed Grouse" - 1967 132

Firsts and Fond Memories by Jerry Zeidler Jr. 134

My Duck Hunt With Tennessee Dan 137

Our Daughter's First Wild Turkey Hunt 141

First Gun by Tom Mitchell, *Pennsylvania Game News* 146

In Memory of Sherman 149

It Was To Be Ella's Last Buck - 1987 155

It Was Ella's Deer Tale To Tell 160

A Duck Hunt I Remember Very Well 163

Sometimes "Bird Huntin' Ain't Easy" 166

Finally A Canadian Goose Success - 1988 169

The Once In A Lifetime Buck by Ron Wilson 174

Pheasant Hunting "Mississippi Style" 181

Waterfowling On Pennsylvania's Lake Pymatuning - 1994 184

My First Deer by Ken Hunter 187

A Deer Season - Short But Oh, So Memorable 191

My First 10-Point Buck by Joel Marvin 194

Days of Yore With Bill Arliss, Sr. 198

A Tale Of Yore Because Of Our Friend Ella! 200

Maggie's First Buck by Karl J. Power 202

Nature Laughs In God's Outdoors 208

Welcome, Once Again, To Our "Country Kitchen"

When I met Steve over twenty-five years ago it did not take a week for me to see his love of hunting, fishing and his love of exercise in the outdoors. Once I started eating the delicious wild game or fish he would prepare for me how could I say "no" to his outdoors adventures? After we were married I would even help him set two alarm clocks to be sure he was "up and at-um" on hunt day. I enjoyed his wild game so much that I began to cook it even if it was squirrel or rabbit for my own mother, God rest her soul. Mom, if you only knew what you ate when you came to our house. Well, I guess most of the time you did know!

We are certain that you will find our "cook's style" wild game recipes very tasty as well as easy to prepare for your family and friends. Enjoy... Gale

Our Spiritual Acknowledgment

When we look back over the way our first two venison cookbooks were conceived, and the way they have been marketed and sold, we see our Lord's guiding hand. With our books' successful sales we will continue to give a tithe amount back to the Catholic Church, Catholic Charities, and other Christian organizations who are helping the less fortunate children of God here in our country and around the world.

We thank you oh Lord, for all you continue to do for our family!

GRILLING, FRYING, AND BROILING VENISON

My friend, hunter and dog lover, Jim Trotta says, "when charcoaling or gas grilling, all kinds of venison, whether it is caribou, elk, moose, or other red meat big game, it is best medium rare. Basting with Steve's barbecue sauces or marinades, while grilling or oven broiling, will keep all big game steaks flavorful and from drying out, too." Gale and I recommend steaks be seared to medium rare while turning occasionally for basting, turned with a spatula or tong so you do not lose any game steak juices. Serve hot off the grill or out of the oven, too, depending on your weather or time allowed for cooking, and may we suggest preparing one of our side dishes to accompany your scrumptious big game meal, too?

Zesty Venison and Broccoli Stir-Fry

2	tablespoons olive oil	1	teaspoon salt
1	pound venison steak, sliced thin	½	teaspoon dried oregano
2	cloves garlic, minced	1	(10-ounce) package frozen chopped broccoli, thawed
½	teaspoon red pepper, crushed		
1	(14½-ounce) can beef both	1	(16-ounce) package your favorite pasta, cooked to package directions, drained
1	tablespoon cornstarch		

In large skillet heat olive oil over medium-high heat. Add venison, garlic, and crushed red pepper; sauté 8 minutes or until venison is browned. In small bowl mix broth, cornstarch, salt and oregano; add to skillet. Stir in broccoli. Bring to boil over medium heat and boil 1 minute. Reduce heat to low; cook 4 minutes longer or until heated through. Toss with your favorite pasta.

Herb Grilled Venisonburgers

1½	pounds venisonburger	½	cup chopped green onions
⅓	cup Italian bread crumbs	¼	cup salsa
1	teaspoon dried parsley flakes	½	teaspoon dried basil or oregano
3	teaspoons spicy mustard	½	teaspoon black pepper
1	teaspoon salt	½	teaspoon Italian seasoning

Mix all above in large bowl by hand. Shape into patties and cook on grill to desired doneness. Serve venisonburgers on your favorite buns topped with a tasty favorite sliced cheese or topped with sliced fresh tomato or even grilled sliced onions!

You will be pleasantly surprised at how delicious these burgers are, and so easy to make. We enjoyed them with our "Delightfully Different Summertime Salad," which you will find in the "sides" section of this book.

Easy and Cheesy Venisonburgers

1	pound venisonburger	1	teaspoon dried diced onions
⅓	cup Parmesan shaker cheese	½	teaspoon salt
⅓	cup of a jar of roasted (red) peppers, drained and diced small	½	teaspoon black or cayenne pepper
		1	teaspoon Italian seasoning

In a large bowl add venisonburger and your remaining ingredients. Now use clean hands to kneed your venisonburgers to blend and season completely. Roll it into 4 round balls and then put each on a dinner plate. Flatten each ball into a seasoned venisonburger. Now bake, fry, or barbecue grill them to desired doneness, depending on your venisonburger mixture and preference.

Barbecued "Buck" Burgers

1	pound venisonburger or sausage	1	tablespoon sugar
¼	cup finely chopped onion	1	cup catsup or salsa
1	teaspoon salt	¼	cup vinegar
½	teaspoon black pepper	½	teaspoon powdered mustard
1	tablespoon olive oil		

Mix together venisonburger or sausage, onion, salt, and black pepper. Shape into 4 patties. Pan fry in hot oil to brown on both sides. Combine remaining ingredients in a bowl. Pour over venison patties in frying pan. Cover and simmer 20 minutes. Serve on hamburger buns with a tossed salad and your favorite beverage, or by themselves with hot buttered rice and a favorite vegetable side.

This easy 1 frying pan lunch or dinner can be enjoyed by 3 to 4 people at home or deer camp. Cooking nutritious venison should be easy and enjoyable for hunters young, old, men and moms alike!

Mom's Easy Venison and Veggies

1	cup of your favorite rice, cooked to package directions	16	ounces of your choice frozen mixed vegetables
1	tablespoon butter or olive oil	1	(14½-ounce) can beef broth
1	pound venison steak, cubed and thinly sliced	⅓-½	cup of any prepared salad dressing
		½	teaspoon each salt and black pepper

Prepare rice to package directions. Heat 1 tablespoon of butter or olive oil in a medium size frying pan. Brown your venison by stirring constantly for 5 to 10 minutes. Now add your vegetables, cook 3 to 5 minutes over medium heat until tender crisp. Add beef broth and bring frying pan mixture to a boil and then stir in cooked rice, salad dressing, salt and black pepper and simmer on low heat 5 minutes or until thoroughly heated.

Mushroom Stuffed Loin Steaks

2	pounds venison loin steaks, cut 1¼-1½ inches thick	2	cups soft bread cubes
½	stick (¼ cup) butter or olive oil	½	teaspoon salt
¼	cup finely sliced celery	1	teaspoon black pepper
2	tablespoons chopped onion	1	teaspoon dried leaf thyme
1	cup sliced fresh mushrooms	½	teaspoon dried leaf marjoram

Cut a 2-inch slit in the side of each steak. Insert the knife in the slit and make a pocket by fanning the knife. Do not cut through. Heat butter or oil in large skillet. Sauté celery, onion, and mushrooms about 5 minutes. Combine bread cubes and seasonings with vegetables in skillet. Toss lightly. Fill each pocket in steak with ½ cup stuffing. Place on broiler rack in pan so tops of steaks are 3 to 4 inches from heat. For medium doneness, broil 6 to 8 minutes on first side and 6 to 8 minutes on other side. Do not overcook!

We recently had this tasty venison chop luncheon for 2 and we en-joyed the differently spiced grilled flavor our venison had; kind of like blackened beef steak or pork loin chops. This recipe "is some-thing to write home about." Try it and you will see!

Father's Day Venison Loin Chops

½	cup soy sauce	1	teaspoon chili powder
¼	cup Worcestershire sauce	½	teaspoon garlic salt
¼	cup firmly pack brown sugar	½	teaspoon black pepper
¼	cup good red wine, (not cooking wine)	1-1¼	pounds venison loin chops, about 1-inch thick

In a small bowl combine the above 7 marinade ingredients and stir. Pour ½ into a small baking dish. Arrange your venison chops in the baking dish and pour the remaining marinade over them. Now cover and marinate overnight. In the morning turn the loin chops to marinate until grilling for lunch.

Grill your special venison loin chops over medium coals for 4 to 6 minutes per side or medium to medium rare doneness for pink, juicy and delicious chops. We suggest turning chops with a tong so as not to "poke" and lose precious chop juices. Add a pasta salad for a deliciously, nutritious venison chop dinner.

2 to 3 servings (depending; you may need to double it)

Tip: You may want to use enough marinade to coat your chops and save remaining in another dish for your next venison steak dish or a topper for grilled steaks.

Broiled Venison Steak and Bacon

1½-2	pounds venison loin steaks	1	teaspoon garlic salt
	Prepared mustard	4	slices bacon

Score surface of the steak into diamond shapes. Spread top side with mustard and garlic salt. Place the steak on broiler rack in pan so top of steak is 3 to 4 inches from heat. Broil 5 to 6 minutes. Turn the steak. Spread with mustard. Place slices of bacon over top. Broil 5 minutes or until medium done to taste.

"Our Venison Loin Steaks with Garlicky Steak Sauce" teams steak sauce with garlic and green onions to make a sauce that deliciously complements grilling your favorite loin steaks. Add extra zesty flavor to the steaks by brushing them with steak sauce during grilling. A simple blend of steak sauce and butter does double-duty. Part is used as a baste for the steak and part as a sauce when served.

Our Venison Loin Steaks with Garlicky Steak Sauce

4-6	**(1-1½ pounds) venison loin steaks, cut 1-inch thick**	**¼-½**	**cup spicy or regular steak sauce**

Garlicky Steak Sauce:

2	**tablespoons butter**	**½**	**cup thinly sliced green onions**
¼	**cup finely chopped garlic**	**½**	**cup spicy or regular steak sauce**

Place venison steaks on grid over medium, ash-covered coals. Grill, uncovered, 15 to 18 minutes for medium rare to medium doneness, turning and brushing occasionally with ¼ to ½ cup steak sauce. Meanwhile, heat butter in small saucepan over medium-low heat. Add garlic; cook 4 to 5 minutes or until tender, stirring occasionally. Add onions; continue cooking 4 to 5 minutes or until onions are tender. Stir in steak sauce; heat through. Serve steaks with "Garlicky Steak Sauce". You will enjoy!

Fourth of July Venison

1	**pound venison round steak, cut into 1½-inch cubes**	**¼**	**cup chili or picante sauce**
		2	**tablespoons tarragon vinegar**
¼	**cup olive oil**	**½**	**teaspoon salt**
1	**clove garlic, sliced**	**¼**	**teaspoon black pepper**

Place venison cubes in a bowl. In another bowl blend remaining ingredients for a marinade and pour over venison. Cover and refrigerate about 4 hours. Place venison cubes on metal skewers. Broil or grill 3 inches from heat about 10 to 15 minutes. Baste venison cubes with marinade before serving. Serve with baked potatoes and a favorite vegetable, like my neighbor, Mike's home grown fresh tomatoes, sliced, with a salad dressing topping. Thanks so much, Mike for your tomatoes...

Larry's Barbecue Venison Steak

½	cup water	3	tablespoons sugar
¼	cup red wine vinegar	1	cup catsup or salsa
½	teaspoon salt	1-1½	pounds venison steaks, cut ¾-inch thick
½	teaspoon powdered mustard		
½	teaspoon chili powder	2	tablespoons butter
2	tablespoons chili sauce		Cooked rice or noodles
½	teaspoon black pepper		Favorite bread
2	teaspoons celery seed		

Make barbecue sauce by combining first 10 ingredients in a large saucepan and simmer 15 minutes. While sauce is simmering, cut venison steak into 2 x 3-inch pieces. Brown venison in skillet in melted butter. Add barbecue sauce; cover and simmer 40 minutes or until tender. Serve over cooked rice or noodles. Add garlic or Italian bread. Enjoy!

Herb-Rubbed Venison Steaks

1-2	teaspoons dried leaf thyme	1	teaspoon salt
1-2	teaspoons basil	½	teaspoon black pepper
1-2	teaspoons oregano	2-3	pounds tenderloin of venison or sirloin steak, cut 1-1½ inches thick
1-2	teaspoons dried leaf rosemary or Italian seasoning, crushed		
4	cloves garlic, minced		Bottled barbecue sauce or Worcestershire sauce (optional)
½	cup finely chopped onion		

For seasoning mix: in a small bowl combine herb seasonings; thyme, basil, oregano, rosemary or Italian seasoning, garlic, onion, salt and black pepper. Rub seasoning mix onto both sides of the venison. Grill the steak on an uncovered grill directly over medium-hot coals to desired doneness. For medium doneness, allow 8 to 10 minutes total for a steak 1-inch thick; 15 to 20 minutes total for a steak 1½ inches thick. Turn the steak once during cooking. Brush the steak occasionally with bottled barbecue sauce or Worcestershire sauce, if desired. Or you could make your own sauce in minutes. Great steak with baked sweet potatoes and fresh corn.

Thank you so much, Jocelyne Mahler for giving us permission to sample and use one of your favorite venison recipes in our home and in our wild game cookbook. We followed your recipe carefully and our first meal was so delicious that we shared it with a friend, Renee, who said it was "awesome." We just had to have it again within a week, too! This recipe is actually a 2 step recipe, but the final meal is all worth the effort.

Jocelyne's Marinated Venison Swiss Steak

2-3   pounds venison hindquarter steaks, cut into small strips or cubes (Before cooking be sure to remove any bones or fat left by the butcher if you did not do it yourself before freezing). Ingredients vary some depending on the amount of steak.

¼-⅓   cup soy sauce

¼-⅓   cup cooking oil of your choice

2-3   tablespoons lemon juice

1-1½   teaspoons diced garlic clove

2-4   tablespoons red wine vinegar or good red wine

½-1   teaspoon black or cayenne pepper, (optional) will be spicy!

Combine the above ingredients in a large bowl. In the morning of your luncheon or dinner, add your venison to the marinade and turn all your venison to coat thoroughly and marinate for 3 to 4 hours. Then before preparing the Swiss steak drain venison on paper towels.

Preparing Swiss Steak:

2-3   tablespoons butter

1-2   tablespoons olive oil

½-¾   cup flour

1   cup diced onions

1   tablespoon oregano

1   tablespoon powdered mustard

2   (14½-ounce) cans stewed tomatoes

2   bay leaves

Salt to taste

In a large Dutch oven or large saucepan melt 2 tablespoons butter and add 1 tablespoon olive oil. Dredge venison steaks in flour and brown in Dutch oven or saucepan in the butter and olive oil. Brown the venison by stirring frequently adding more oil if necessary for 4 to 5 minutes. Then add the onions to pan and stir this mixture well for another 5 minutes or so. Sprinkle oregano and powdered mustard on steaks. Scrape bottom of pan or Dutch oven well to get browned bits loosened. Then

Jocelyne's Marinated Venison Swiss Steak continued

add stewed tomatoes, bay leaves, and salt to taste. Mix well, cover and let simmer on low heat 1 to 2 hours. This is all it will take to make the venison very tender and simply delicious! Serve this Swiss steak on a bed of wide noodles or with a side dish of boiled white or sweet potatoes with butter.

4 to 6 servings but do not count on there being any leftovers.

Jocelyne Mahler, Conesus, NY

Shotgun Venison Steak

2	pounds venison steak	1	teaspoon dried basil
	Salt and black pepper to taste	½	teaspoon dried oregano
1	tablespoon butter	½	teaspoon dried Italian seasoning
1	tablespoon olive oil	1	tablespoon Worcestershire sauce
½-1	bunch green onions and greens, finely chopped (about 1 cup)	1	(8-ounce) can tomato sauce
1	medium carrot, peeled and chopped	½	cup dry red wine (up to ½ cup additional, if needed) (not cooking wine)
1	large clove garlic, diced		Pasta or noodles of choice

Season venison steak on both sides with salt and black pepper. In a large, heavy frying pan over medium-high heat, melt the butter and add the olive oil. Add the venison steak in 1 piece and brown well on both sides. When the second side is nearly browned, add the green onion and carrot around venison. Stir and lightly brown. Add the garlic, basil, oregano, Italian seasoning, and Worcestershire sauce. Mix in the tomato sauce and wine. Bring to a boil, cover, and reduce heat to a simmer. Cook between 60 and 90 minutes, until the venison steak is very tender. (When venison steak is almost done, cook your chosen pasta or noodles to package directions; drain and cover to retain heat until meal time.) When venison steak is tender, remove venison from frying pan to a serving platter, cover to retain heat. Bring sauce to a boil, adding more wine if too thick. Taste and add more salt and pepper if necessary. Divide steak into serving pieces. Serve with pasta or noodles of your choice, pouring the sauce over top of venison steak and pasta or noodles. Add a green salad or vegetable side for a nutritiously delicious meal.

This recipe was going to be named "Dad's Special Venison Steak For You Two," named after Steve's dad who passed away in 1993, because it reminded Steve of the delicious game meals that his dad used to make at his restaurant. This is a venison dish that his dad's customers, mostly hunters, would have loved to delve into. We renamed it "Dad Flack's Special Venison Steak For You Two" when we realized that Steve had created and prepared this recipe for the first time the very day that Gale's dad passed away in California where he and Gale's mom had lived, in the year 2001. Gale's dad had just celebrated his eighty-first birthday just three months prior to his death. Although we had not seen either Gale's mom or dad in several years because we live in the east and they had moved to California to retire, we remember dad especially, always liking to see the two of us come to visit or when we would camp or fish in the stream near the property where he and Gale's mom lived at the time in New York State. We reciprocated by welcoming them to our home and feeding them game dinners after we married. They both looked forward to Steve's cooking, but we could tell that Gale's dad especially enjoyed Steve's meals. We will miss him - thank God for our memories - they never die!

Dad Flack's Special
Venison Steak for You Two!!

1½   **pounds boneless venison steak, trimmed of all fat if not done already by butchering, sliced ½-inch thick**

This steak does not have to come from the loin or backstrap because tender boneless venison steak comes from the sirloin rump roast between the top and bottom round roasts on each hindquarter. The sirloin rump roast is shaped like a small football so you cannot miss it if you process your own deer. Top or bottom round roast, sliced thin, can also be used.

⅓	**cup butter or olive oil**	**1**	**teaspoon parsley flakes**
½	**cup finely chopped onion or green onions**	**1**	**teaspoon oregano flakes**
1	**cup washed and thinly sliced fresh mushrooms**	½	**teaspoon each salt and black pepper**
½	**cup of any favorite prepared salad dressing**	**1**	**cup beef broth**
½	**cup diced fresh or frozen green bell pepper**	½-1	**cup of a favorite shredded cheese, (optional)**
1	**cup diced fresh or canned tomatoes**	6-8	**ounces of long grain and wild rice, cooked to package directions, (optional)**

Dad Flack's Special Venison Steak For You Two!! continued

In a large coverable frying pan or skillet, over medium heat, brown venison steak in butter or olive oil with onions and mushrooms for 5 minutes or so, then turn to brown a few minutes more. Then to your skillet add salad dressing, bell pepper, and diced tomatoes and stir. Add the 4 seasonings along with the beef broth and stir. Heat to nearly boiling and then turn heat down to low or simmer, cover venison dish and simmer for 35 to 40 minutes so the venison is tender as well as tasty and nutritious. Serve over your rice or even a baked potato, sweet or Idaho, or even noodles, for another memorable meal. *If using the optional shredded cheese, 5 to 10 minutes before serving your skillet venison special, top your meal with 1½ cups of a favorite shredded cheese, then serve as above.

"Gotta Have It" Venison Marinade

¾	cup port wine	1	small onion, finely chopped
1¼	cup olive oil	½	teaspoon ground black or white pepper
3	tablespoons dried tarragon		
2	tablespoons parsley flakes	¼	teaspoon sage
1	large celery stalk, coarsely chopped	1	tablespoon lemon juice (fresh is better)

Mix marinade ingredients in large mixing bowl. Place deer steaks flat in a glass baking dish or a marinade container. Do not overlap the deer steaks. Marinate deer steaks for a minimum of 4 hours, but not longer than overnight. Generally, the thicker the deer steak, the longer the steak should marinate. Prepare grill in normal fashion (charcoal grilling is best.) Remove deer steaks from marinade and place on grill (you can pour some of the extra marinade over steaks, but be careful not to put out coals.) Turn steaks over once during cooking. Again, you can pour a little of the marinade on the steaks. Discard any unused marinade. Cooking time will depend on thickness of deer steaks. (I prefer my steaks cut to ¾ inches.) Cook deer steaks to rare or medium rare (Do not overcook.) Steaks will be very, very tender and tasty. There is no need for any other sauces (for example; catsup, Worcestershire sauce, pepper sauce, etc.)

Leo Stepanian II

Three Favorite Marinades for Venison Steaks or Roasts up to 2 pounds

Venison Italiano Marinade:

1	cup tomato juice	1	teaspoon black pepper
1	teaspoon garlic salt or powder	1	teaspoon Italian seasoning
1	teaspoon onion powder	1	teaspoon parsley flakes
1	teaspoon salt	½	cup olive oil

In a medium bowl mix all ingredients for the marinade. Place up to 2 pounds of venison steaks in a marinade container or any other large food container with a tightly fitted lid. Pour the prepared marinade over the steaks and turn to thoroughly coat the steaks. Cover and marinate the steaks in the refrigerator 4 to 12 hours, turning occasionally.

Venison Teriyaki Marinade:

1	teaspoon ground ginger	½	cup soy sauce
2	cloves garlic, finely chopped	¼	cup red wine
1	medium onion, finely chopped	¼	cup water
2	tablespoons sugar		

Follow the same instructions as for the "Venison Italiano Marinade" above.

Deer Hunter's Marinade:

½	cup salad oil	½	teaspoon leaf basil
½	cup cider vinegar	¼	teaspoon leaf marjoram
1	teaspoon finely chopped garlic	1	teaspoon salt
2	tablespoons finely chopped onion	½	teaspoon ground black pepper
1	bay leaf, crushed		

Follow the same instructions as the "Venison Italiano Marinade" above.

You have several options when it is time to cook your steak or roast. You can grill, pan fry, or oven broil your steak; or oven bake if you chose to marinate a roast, basting with the marinade while cooking no matter which way you prefer to cook your nutritious venison. Remember to not overcook; medium rare to medium or pink in the middle is best. Add a baked sweet or Idaho potato of choice and a fresh or frozen vegetable for a scrumptious steak dinner.

Fire up your grill! Start with a trimmed, boneless venison round steak and add 1 of our savory sauces for basting and to serve along-side from **Quality Venison II**, *and you are on your way to a deliciously, nutritious venison steak dinner. Just add a vegetable of your choice. Even if you want to hold the onions, your steak will still be great! Just ask our daughter, Kelly, and her boyfriend, Jeff.*

Our Spicy Venison Steak and Onions

Spicy Rub:

1	teaspoon garlic powder	½	teaspoon cayenne pepper
1	teaspoon onion powder	1	boneless hindquarter steak, cut
1	teaspoon ground black pepper		1-inch thick (about 1¼ pounds)

Grilling Steak:

½	cup steak sauce, bottled or made up fresh	2	large onions, cut crosswise into ½-inch thick slices
¼	cup butter, melted		Vegetable oil
			Salt to taste

In a bowl combine rub ingredients; press evenly onto both sides of steak. Combine steak sauce and butter in small bowl. Measure ¼ cup for basting; reserve remaining mixture. Brush onion slices lightly with oil. Place steak and onion slices on grid over medium, ash-covered coals. Grill, uncovered, 12 to 15 minutes until steak is medium rare to medium done and onions are tender, turning occasionally and basting steak with ¼ cup steak sauce mixture. Season with salt, as desired. Discard any unused basting mixture. Carve steak into thin slices; serve with onions and reserved steak sauce mixture.

*We have been grilling and smoking our wild game meats for over twenty years using "the water smoker," both charcoal and electric, and have enjoyed grilled meats from gas grills. For <u>our taste buds</u> and money, too, the charcoal water smoker produces the most memorable wild game and other meat meals, too. See our **<u>Quality Venison</u>** cookbook for more smoking venison tips, and our **<u>Quality Venison II</u>** cookbook for lots of delicious marinades and tasty sauces. Enjoy!*

Penn's Woods Labor Day Picnic Smoked Venison Roast

For Charcoal or Electric Water Smoker:

1	(3 to 4-pound) venison roast	1	tablespoon lemon juice
½	cup good Burgundy or any favorite good red wine, (not cooking wine), or your on-hand prepared salad dressing	½	cup cider vinegar or water
		1	teaspoon sugar
		1	teaspoon each salt and black pepper
3	tablespoons Worcestershire sauce	1	teaspoon garlic powder or garlic salt
2	tablespoons spicy brown mustard	½	cup catsup or salsa

In a large Dutch oven with a lid add venison roast. In a medium size bowl add remaining ingredients and stir well to blend. Then pour ½ of the marinade over venison roast. With a sharp knife poke roast 10 to 12 times to allow marinade to penetrate the meat. Turn your roast over and also poke it 10 to 12 times and pour remaining marinade over your roast and cover. Over the 12 to 14 hour marinating period turn venison occasionally. Then smoke over charcoal or lava rocks adding water soaked hickory or mesquite wood chips for 3 to 4 hours, depending on amount of charcoal used and outside air temperature. Be careful "<u>not to overcook</u>." Medium rare venison is best!

We recommend your venison roast being boned out and fat removed, also, before freezing this nutritiously, lean meat and certainly before smoking or grilling. You can use your marinade 1 last time after placing your roast on your smoking grill. Pour over your roast and into your water filled drip pan for extra moist flavor. Or cut your roast into steaks to desired thickness and baste your steaks with marinade if grilling. Add our barbecue beans or other side dishes for a memorable wild game meal.

You can buy jars of Cajun spices at your grocery store, but when time and opportunity allows you will want to use our Cajun spice blend recipe to season your next venison meal for family, friends or at deer camp, even. The only problem with cooking this recipe for everyone at your deer camp is you will not have any leftovers and everyone will also ask you to be the camp cook until further notice! Just keep it coming. Cook, your reply should be "Glad ya'll like it, I know from years of experience I'm a good cook, but I am not cheap. Tips are welcomed!! Expect my answer to your request in the morning. The tip jar is on the kitchen table. Just a suggestion!"

Cajun Spiced Venison Steak or Roast

Our Cajun Spiced Seasonings:

5-6	pounds venison hindquarter roast or steaks	2	tablespoons cayenne pepper
4	tablespoons salt	1½	teaspoons black pepper
2	tablespoons sugar	2	teaspoons chili powder
1	tablespoon onion powder	2	teaspoons oregano
¼	cup fresh chives or parsley flakes	2	teaspoons Italian seasoning
¼	cup basil	1	cup good red table wine

Yields approximately 2 to 2¼ cups of marinade, which is enough for 5 to 6 pounds of venison. Prepare the marinade by combining all spices and wine in a bowl and mix well. Pour ½ of the marinade in a large baking dish. Place your venison roast or steaks in baking dish to marinate. Pour the remaining ½ of the marinade over the top of the steaks. Cover and place in the refrigerator. Turn after 8 to 12 hours. Marinate in the refrigerator another 8 to 12 hours.

Now that you have painstakingly marinated your prized, expensive venison to perfection, you can't wait to serve it to family or friends who will be coming over to dine with you and yours. Depending on the weather you will have 2 cooking choices. Grill the 5 to 6 pounds of marinated venison on your grill to perfection (medium rare is juicy and best) or you may choose to bake your roast or steaks in a large size plastic cooking bag, following cooking bag package directions, in ½ the original marinade for 2 to 3 hours at 325 to 350 degrees, (depending on the age of the deer), or until tender. Add your favorite vegetable side dishes and everyone will enjoy a memorable venison meal.

A day or two before your next family or friend get together inside or out, you have to prepare this easy can't miss barbecue sauce for your venison meal. Then grill, broil or even bake your venison steaks or roasts using this sauce as needed during cooking and with your meal. Smiles all around are guaranteed if your "quality cared" for venison was taken care of from field to freezer!

Our Country Kitchen Barbecue Sauce

½   cup chopped green onions

½   cup finely diced green pepper

1   large clove garlic or 2 small cloves garlic, diced

3   tablespoons olive oil

½   teaspoon dried oregano

½   teaspoon basil

½   teaspoon each salt and black pepper

2   cups of your favorite salsa

1   cup catsup or water

⅓   cup good red wine, optional

3   tablespoons lemon juice

4   tablespoons Worcestershire sauce

2   teaspoons liquid smoke

4-6   drops bottled hot pepper sauce, (and you can always add more hot sauce or cayenne pepper to spice up individual barbecue servings.

In a medium saucepan add all ingredients and heat to nearly boiling. Stir and turn down heat to simmer, uncovered, and time for 30 minutes or so, stirring occasionally if desired. Store this "treasured" barbecue sauce in the covered saucepan that it was cooked in, in the refrigerator until you use it for basting venison, moose, elk, or whatever game red meat steaks you are grilling, broiling or baking. Add your favorite vegetable dish, depending on how you choose to prepare your game with this sauce. You may want to use ½ the sauce for cooking, and save the remaining sauce for a gravy or add on with dinner, or save leftover ½ for the next picnic grilling, broiling, or smoking opportunity! You will certainly be glad you did!!!

Makes 3 to 4 cups, and is good for up to 3 pounds of smoked, grilled or baked venison.

Our Country Kitchen Barbecue Sauce continued

Our daughter, Kelly and her friend, Jeff were coming to celebrate my birthday with us on a cold Pittsburgh, Pennsylvania day in February. Since we were delighted with our new "Country Kitchen Barbecue Sauce" that we just made up, we wanted to try it on 2 to 3 pounds of venison round steak. It could have simmered in our Dutch oven, but we chose to use our crockpot to prepare our venison round steak using "Our Country Kitchen Barbecue Sauce." We suggest you make "Our Country Kitchen Barbecue Sauce" the day before or the morning of your evening meal.

Our Crockpot Venison Barbecue:

To your crockpot add 2 to 3 pounds of venison round steak or similar size roast (boneless and of course carefully trimmed of all fat if not done already). We recommend using cooking spray on the bowl of the crockpot for easy clean-up; then add your venison. Top with "Our Country Kitchen Barbecue Sauce" to nearly cover the venison. Save unused sauce for another meal of choice. Slow cook on high for 4 to 5 hours. This barbecue is truly memorable, so you may want to add favorite vegetables and beverages. Just a suggestion. Enjoy!

Grilling, Frying, or Broiling?

Here's a handy tip: BEFORE lighting your barbecue grill, spray your grill with any non-stick cooking spray to help keep your lean game from sticking to it. This way both game and vegetables will come off the grill or skewers, that should also be sprayed before threading, easily. Also, spray your barbecue spatula with non-stick spray for easy clean up. If you are frying any kind of wild game indoors or even baking it, too, spray your pan or baking dish with non-stick spray of choice and enjoy easier clean-up.

Leo's Spicy Venison Kabobs

3	tablespoons cooking oil	1	teaspoon red pepper flakes (optional)
2	tablespoons pickapepper sauce or pepper sauce of your choice (1 teaspoon hot pepper sauce may be substituted, if necessary)	1	teaspoon black pepper
		¼	teaspoon basil
		¼	teaspoon oregano
2	tablespoons strawberry or grape jelly	¼	teaspoon parsley flakes
2	tablespoons honey or maple syrup	1	teaspoon minced garlic
		1	pound venison tenderloin, cut in 1-inch cubes

In a bowl stir together oil, pickapeppa sauce or pepper sauce of choice, jelly, honey or syrup, red pepper, if using, black pepper, basil, oregano, parsley flakes and garlic. Stir in venison cubes. Cover and chill at least 2 hours. Drain venison cubes, reserve marinade. Thread venison on skewers and barbecue over medium heat. Try not to overcook. Venison is best when cooked rare to medium rare, or pink in the middle so it is juicy and very flavorful.

Deliciously Glazed Venison Kabobs

¼	cup honey	1	medium sweet onion, quartered and separated into 4 pieces
¼	cup grape or apple jelly		
½	cup bottled barbecue sauce	8-12	whole large fresh mushrooms
1	tablespoon prepared mustard	1	large bell pepper of your choice, cut into 1-inch pieces
1	pound venison loin or round steak, cubed, 1 to 2 inches thick		

In a small saucepan, combine honey, jelly, barbecue sauce and mustard. Heat until jelly melts (about 1 to 2 minutes), stirring constantly. Before grilling or broiling brush ½ of the glaze on venison cubes, saving ½ of the glaze for later use. On 4 long metal skewers alternate venison, onions, mushrooms and peppers. Cook venison kabobs on grill rack over charcoal (or in your broiler in oven about 4 inches from your heat source) for 8 to 10 minutes total grilling time or until venison is medium rare to medium done. Turn once and baste with glaze halfway through cooking time. This special venison dish goes great over rice any time of the year. Add a fresh green salad and enjoy!

ITALIAN STYLE AND CROCKERY COOKING VENISON

Photo is of "Mom's Luscious Venison Lasagna"
*page 85 in **Quality Venison II**.*

We recently had an urgent phone call from a customer who was given a copy of our first *Quality Venison* cookbook as a Christmas present and her husband and sons had put four Pennsylvania whitetails in her freezer. She said "I am not a big venison eater and 'Ella's Hunters Stew' calls for a ½ cup of parsley but does not say if it is fresh or dried." We told her that if you have quality cared for venison, where the deer's fat has not spoiled or freezer burn has not "tainted your venison" then either parsley spice is great. She said "I wanted to be sure because right now I am still not sure about cooking venison for our family." We then encouraged her to try some other great recipes from *Quality Venison* that were sure to please anyone and everyone at her dinner table. Cooking wild game is meant to be fun, so experiment and enjoy.

We particularly enjoy cooking and eating "Italian" and "Crockery" style recipes with venison because they are so flavorful, and our house smells scrumptious for hours. Any Italian dish is good, but when it is prepared with tasty venison, it tastes fantastic! And wait until you lift the lid of a venison crockpot meal; you will be lucky if the neighbors don't come knocking to have dinner with you if you happen to have your windows open. Don't be surprised if neighbors ask "smell's great, what's for dinner?"

Steve's Peppery Venison Meatballs

This Italian dish is fun to make and even easier to eat.
The only problem is, no leftovers!

1¼-1½	pounds venisonburger or venison sausage	½	cup green pepper, chopped, or 1 (4-ounce) can chopped green chili peppers
2	teaspoons garlic powder or 3 cloves garlic, diced	1	tablespoon parsley flakes
½	teaspoon onion powder	1	tablespoon Italian seasoning
1	cup bread crumbs	½	cup milk, optional
½	cup Parmesan or Romano shaker cheese	2	(26 to 32-ounce) jars of a favorite pasta sauce
2	eggs, beaten		Up to 1 pound your favorite pasta, cooked to package directions
1½	teaspoons salt		
½	teaspoon black pepper		Parmesan or Romano shaker cheese to taste

Preheat your oven to 350 degrees. In a large bowl add ½ of your venison and ½ of your remaining ingredients and seasonings, <u>except</u> pasta sauce, pasta and cheese. With a large spoon mix well. Add remaining ½ venison and the other ½ of the remaining ingredients and seasonings, <u>except</u> pasta sauce, pasta and cheese. Mix well again by spoon or hand and roll into meatballs approximately 2 inches in diameter. Place your meatballs on a baking sheet or 9x13x2-inch baking dish and bake in your preheated oven 30 to 35 minutes. While your meatballs are baking, start simmering your pasta sauce in a Dutch oven on top of your stove. After your meatballs are finished browning add them to your pasta sauce in the Dutch oven and simmer covered 45 to 60 minutes. While sauce and meatballs are simmering, cook up to 1 pound of your favorite pasta, cooked to package directions. Spoon meatballs and sauce over individual dishes of pasta and top with Parmesan or Romano shaker cheese to taste. Add buttered French or garlic bread for a very tasty Italian meal.

This recipe ought to have your spouse hugging your neck. We doubt there will be any leftovers, but they will be gone soon if there are any, and they will not likely even make it to your freezer.

Easy Venison Sausage Skillet For Two

6-8	ounces of pasta, your choice
1	pound venison Italian sweet or hot sausage, your choice
1-2	teaspoons olive oil or real butter
1	(14½-ounce) can diced tomatoes, your choice
1	(6-ounce) can tomato paste
1	(8-ounce) cup beef broth
1	(14½-ounce) can garbanzo beans or chickpeas
½	cup shredded cheese of choice

Cook pasta according to package directions and allow to drain. Set aside in same pan cooked in and cover to keep pasta warm and from drying out. Meanwhile, brown venison sausage in a large skillet of hot oil or butter for 5 minutes or so. Then stir in tomatoes, tomato paste, broth and beans. Bring to a boil, then reduce heat. Simmer 20 minutes and add cooked pasta. Sprinkle with your shredded cheese of choice and simmer 10 to 12 minutes to thoroughly heat. This is a complete meal by itself, but may we suggest you add a fresh green salad and/or French or Italian bread fixed your own special way for an "extra special" meal for 2.

What a meal deal for even young cooks to make at home for family or the crew at deer camp. This dish is sure to please!! Remember, everyone "loves" the cook whether at home or camp. Enjoy as we did.

Uncle Dom's Cheesy Sausage Casserole

8	ounces egg noodles or any small shaped pasta	½	cup good Burgundy or dry red wine, optional or add ½ cup water
1-2	tablespoons butter		
1	pound venison sausage, hot or mild	2	cups of either picante or pepper sauce, (not hot) of choice
8	ounces fresh mushrooms, sliced	⅓	cup shaker type Parmesan or Romano cheese
1	teaspoon garlic powder		
1	(15-ounce) can tomato sauce	4-8	ounces shredded mozzarella cheese (topper)

Cook pasta according to package directions. Preheat oven to 400 degrees. Meanwhile, in a large frying pan melt enough butter to brown venison sausage with mushrooms until sausage is not pink, and the mushrooms are tender; drain. Spray a 3-quart casserole dish with non-stick cooking spray for easy clean-up. Add frying pan of sausage and mushrooms, garlic powder, and tomato sauce, and wine if using, or water to casserole dish; stir. Add picante or pepper sauce and stir. Add in the cooked noodles or pasta; stir and sprinkle top of casserole with shaker Parmesan or Romano cheese and top with mozzarella cheese. Now bake uncovered for 10 to 15 minutes so the cheese is nicely melted, or microwave for 7 to 8 minutes. This Italian dish deliciously serves 8 or maybe only 6 hungry hunters who went back for seconds.

This easy lasagna-like casserole aims to please and will. We want to suggest young hunters at camp or at home prepare this recipe. For doing their fair share they will get a lot of "compliments to the chef."

Mom's Favorite Venison Italian Casserole

4-6 ounces of small pasta of your choice, cooked to package directions

1 pound venisonburger or sausage

1 (6-ounce) can tomato paste

1 (14½-ounce) can diced tomatoes

1 (14½-ounce) can garbanzo beans/chickpeas, or Italian green beans

¼ cup of a good Burgundy or red wine (not cooking wine)

1 teaspoon garlic powder

1 teaspoon Italian seasoning

⅓-½ cup catsup

1 (15-ounce) container of ricotta cheese

1 egg, beaten

1 cup or 4 ounces shredded mozzarella cheese or a cheese of your choice

Preheat oven to 350 degrees. Cook pasta according to package directions. Meanwhile, in a large frying pan or Dutch oven cook venisonburger or bulk sausage (hot or mild) 10 to 12 minutes. Stir occasionally. Now stir in tomato paste, diced tomatoes, garbanzo beans or Italian green beans. Stir well to blend. Add wine, garlic powder, Italian seasoning, catsup, ricotta cheese and the beaten egg. Stir well to blend. Spray a 3-quart casserole dish with cover with a non-stick spray product for easier clean-up. Add your venison mixture to the casserole dish and add your pasta. Blend well; top with your shredded cheese. Bake covered for 30 to 40 minutes.

Just a suggestion: Bake a loaf of French or Italian bread along with this tasty pasta dish and you will be glad you did.

Jerry tells us this recipe is a family favorite. We agree, so share it with family or friends soon and you will see, too.

Jerry Molettiere's Venison Steak Italiano

8	ounces spaghetti of choice	1	(26 to 28-ounce) jar of a favorite pasta sauce
1	pound venison or elk round steak, cut in thin strips	⅔	cup water
½	cup chopped green onions	¾	cup dry red wine, (not cooking wine) or catsup
1	(4-ounce) can mushrooms, drained	1	teaspoon instant beef flavor bouillon
2	fresh garlic cloves, minced small		Shredded mozzarella or Parmesan cheese
3	tablespoons olive oil or butter		

Cook your spaghetti as package directs, drain and set aside. In a large pan or Dutch oven, over medium heat, cook and stir steak strips, onions, mushrooms and garlic in oil or butter, until steak is browned, and the vegetables are tender. Now add jar of past sauce, water, wine or catsup, and bouillon. Bring pan to a boil and then turn down to simmer for 1 to 2 hours. Before serving add more water to your desired consistency if needed. Serve over spaghetti and top with shredded mozzarella or Parmesan cheese.

I can't tell you how many times over the years of our marriage that "Gale could not take it any more." She would just have to yell down to me from her upstairs home office, "hey, Steve, you have it smelling awfully good up here. I'm finding it really hard to concentrate on my work. I sure hope you wrote down the ingredients and any preparation tips so we can prepare it again." Wild game is nutritiously delicious, so let's enjoy every meal we can with family and friends. Thank you, Lord, for your wildlife bounty.

As I frequently do, I brought this freshly prepared lasagna dish by for my barber friends to sample at Harry Spohn's, Cranberry Township, Pennsylvania. Despite having had hoagies delivered, they found room for "Gale's Cheesy Venison Sausage Lasagna." Compliments were coming from everywhere in the shop. Harry, Rich, and Anthony said "it is wonderful, delicious, wow!" The best compliment had to come from one barber. He said "my wife is from Italy and she still makes homemade pasta for our Italian dishes. This lasagna is as good as any Italian pasta that she had made for me."

Gale's Cheesy Venison Sausage Lasagna

9	lasagna noodles	½	teaspoon garlic powder
1	pound of your favorite venison sausage, (more or less)	½	teaspoon each salt and black pepper
4	cups (32 ounces) of your favorite store bought pasta sauce		Red pepper to taste, (optional)
1	teaspoon basil	1	(15-ounce) container ricotta cheese
1	teaspoon Italian seasoning	2	cups shredded mozzarella cheese
½	teaspoon onion powder	1	cup shaker Parmesan cheese

(All ingredients are divided, in order to layer.)

Prepare lasagna noodles according to package directions. While the noodles are boiling brown venison sausage in a large skillet for 5 to 6 minutes on medium heat. Preheat oven to 350 degrees. Now spread 1 cup pasta sauce in bottom of a 13x9x2-inch baking dish. You may want to spray the dish with non-stick cooking spray for easy clean-up. In a cup combine the seasonings and mix well. Arrange 3 of cooked noodles in dish, slightly overlapping on sauce. Spread ½ of the ricotta over noodles. Sprinkle with ½ mozzarella. Sprinkle ½ the venison sausage, ½ of the 6 spices and ½ cup Parmesan cheese. Top with 1 cup pasta sauce. Repeat layering starting with 3 noodles, 1 cup pasta sauce, ½ ricotta, ½ mozzarella, ½ venison sausage, ½ spices. Add the last 3 noodles and last cup of pasta sauce. Top with ½ cup Parmesan cheese. Cover tightly with foil and bake 1 hour. If you want to brown the lasagna, remove foil after 50 minutes. Remove from oven and let is set 5 to 10 minutes, cut and serve. To any Italian food lovers - guaranteed to be better than "restaurant quality!" Enjoy!!

Our family of 3 had this nutritious and especially delicious Italian dish a couple of times and that was all it took to make it a special meal. We have had several friends sample it since, and they also liked it very much. If you like Italian food like we do you have to give this lasagna a try. It will be well worth your effort!!! Leftovers, if there are any, are exceptional, of course even after being frozen.

Our Easy Venison and Pepperoni Lasagna

1	pound bulk venison sausage or burger	⅔	cup shredded Parmesan cheese, divided
¾-1	cup sliced pepperoni, diced small	6	lasagna noodles (uncooked), Time Saver…Here!
½	cup chopped onion		
1	(26 to 28-ounce) jar of a favorite pasta sauce	1½	cups shredded mozzarella cheese, divided
1	(15-ounce) carton ricotta cheese, divided	1	teaspoon Italian seasoning
		1	teaspoon garlic powder
1	egg, beaten		

Preheat oven to 375 degrees. Cook venison sausage or burger, pepperoni, and onion in a frying pan over medium-high heat until sausage or burger is browned. Spread 2 tablespoons of sauce in a 2-quart oblong baking dish. Stir remaining sauce into meat mixture; set aside. Combine ricotta, egg, and ¼ cup Parmesan cheese; blend well. Place 3 lasagna noodles over sauce in dish, breaking noodles if necessary. Spread ½ of ricotta mixture, ½ of sauce mixture and ½ cup of mozzarella over noodles. Repeat. Sprinkle with remaining Parmesan cheese and Italian seasoning and garlic powder. Cover. Bake for 55 minutes. Uncover, sprinkle with remaining ½ cup mozzarella cheese and continue baking until cheese is melted. Let stand for 10 minutes.

Serves 4 to 6

The following is a 2 part recipe, that if made all at one time is quite time consuming. We would like to suggest making the pasta sauce ahead of time and reheat it just before serving. Steve made these 2 recipes back to back, and I thought, 'this meal better be good! I'm hungry!' I was not disappointed. Words cannot describe just how delicious this venison meal was. The pasta sauce was perfect and the venison melted in my mouth.

Our Peppery Olive Pasta Sauce

1	cup sliced fresh mushrooms	1	(8-ounce) can tomato sauce
½	cup chopped onion	1	cup of either pepper or picante sauce
1	garlic clove, minced		
1	tablespoon olive oil	½	of a (6 ounce) can pitted black olives, sliced in ½
¼	cup good red wine		Salt and black or red pepper to taste
½	teaspoon oregano		
½	teaspoon Italian seasoning	8	ounces freshly cooked pasta
½	teaspoon basil		

In a medium saucepan with a lid, over medium heat, lightly brown mushrooms, onion and garlic in olive oil. Cook 5 minutes or so stirring lightly. Add red wine, oregano, Italian seasoning and basil; stir. Add tomato, pepper or picante sauce and sliced olives. Stir well, simmer on low heat covered, 1 hour or so. Add salt and pepper to taste. Serve over a side dish of your favorite pasta cooked to package directions, and our "Our Venison Loin Mozzarella" below. You will be very glad you did!!

Our Venison Loin Mozzarella:

½	cup Italian style bread crumbs	2	(8 ounce) venison loin steaks, about 2 inches thick
½	teaspoon salt		
½	teaspoon black pepper	2	tablespoons olive oil
		4	ounces sliced mozzarella cheese

Add bread crumbs, salt, and black pepper to a paper bag and shake to blend. Then add your loin steaks; shake well and press bread crumbs into the steak. In a large skillet that has a lid heat olive oil and add the venison steaks, frying over medium heat for 5 minutes, timed so as to brown but not burn. Turn your steaks and again time for another 5 minutes. Repeat turning procedure for 10 more minutes total. We are trying to keep your venison loin steaks medium rare for you. After 20 minutes total cooking time, top the steaks with the mozzarella cheese and cover for 2 more minutes so the cheese melts. Place steaks on serving dishes with a serving of pasta and top with "Our Peppery Olive Pasta Sauce." Enjoy!

My dad made a 5 gallon version of this pasta sauce recipe at our restaurant regularly. Our customers certainly liked it and our family often had it at home on Sundays after Catholic mass.

Loder's Restaurant Style Pasta Sauce

2   tablespoons olive oil or butter

1   pound venisonburger or sausage or even venison steak cut in small pieces

½-⅔   cup chopped green onions

2   garlic cloves, diced

1   cup sliced and diced pepperoni

1½   cups sliced fresh mushrooms

½   cup good red wine, (optional), or water

1   cup beef broth

2   cups water

3   tablespoons tomato paste

1   cup salsa or pepper sauce, (not hot) of choice

1   (15-ounce) can diced tomatoes

2   medium size fresh tomatoes, chopped

1   teaspoon oregano

1   teaspoon Italian seasoning

1   tablespoon basil

1   teaspoon each salt and black pepper

Pasta, your choice, cooked to package directions

To your large sauce pan or Dutch oven add olive oil or butter, chosen venison, onions, garlic, pepperoni, and mushrooms. Cook over medium heat for 10 minutes, stirring constantly. Add red wine, if using, broth, water, and tomato paste. Stir well and add salsa or pepper sauce, tomatoes and remaining seasonings. Stir and bring to a boil. Cover, then turn stove down to a simmer and cook for 1 hour. Then check to see if your pasta sauce has your preferred consistency and add more water if needed. Stir and simmer at least 1 more hour. 30 minutes before eating, prepare your pasta according to package directions and take out your large dinner plates. Pasta lovers will certainly be back for seconds.

Cooking Tip: We would like to suggest that you prepare this delicious, fresh pasta sauce a day ahead of time. Then it is easy to reheat and serve over your freshly made pasta, be it at home or deer camp. Enjoy!

As usual we have taste tested this recipe for you and have found it easy to prepare and even easier to enjoy. Give it a try and you will agree. We want to dedicate this recipe in memory of our long time friend, Bill Arliss, Sr. who God has called home. We have hunted his land with Bill and his sons for over thirty-five years. What his family and the great hunting tradition has meant to my family!!!

Bill's Favorite Venison and Pasta

8	ounces uncooked pasta of choice	¼-⅓	cup spicy prepared mustard
1-2	cups of beef broth	½	teaspoon garlic powder
1	cup milk	½	teaspoon onion powder
2	tablespoons flour	½	teaspoon oregano flakes or Italian seasoning
2	tablespoons olive oil or real butter		Salt and black pepper to taste
1	pound of thinly sliced venison steak		Romano or Monterey Jack cheese
2	cups of your favorite frozen vegetables, (succotash, carrots and peas)		

Cook pasta according to package directions. Meanwhile, in a small bowl, blend the broth, milk and flour well and set aside. In a large skillet (frying pan) add oil or butter and strips of venison steak and stir. Now lightly brown steak for 3 to 5 minutes; remove and set aside in a dish. In the same skillet, cook and stir vegetables 2 to 3 minutes, adding butter or water until tender-crispy and remove from heat. Pour broth mixture that was set aside to the skillet or frying pan with your vegetables and simmer on low heat for 3 to 4 minutes or until sauce is thickened, stirring constantly. Blend in the mustard, garlic and onion powder and oregano or Italian seasoning and stir in the venison steak to your skillet. Add salt and black pepper to taste. Heat on medium for 5 to 10 minutes and serve over your bowl of pasta. Sprinkle bowl or serving bowls with your Romano, Monterey Jack or other cheese of choice. Makes 2 to 3 servings depending on who is joining you for lunch or dinner. Delicious for sure!

Our Homemade Venison Manicotti

8	manicotti shells	1¼	teaspoon salt, divided
1	pound venison sausage		Black pepper to taste
2	cups water	2	eggs, beaten
2	(6-ounce) cans tomato paste	3	cups ricotta cheese
½	cup chopped onion	¾	cup grated Romano or Parmesan
⅓	cup parsley flakes, divided		cheese, divided
1	large clove garlic, minced		Dash of black pepper
1	tablespoon dried leaf oregano, crushed or 2 tablespoons fresh minced basil		

Preheat your oven to 350 degrees. In a large pot or Dutch oven, in boiling salted water, cook the manicotti shells according to package directions. Drain and rinse under cool water then drain again. Set cooked shells aside under plastic wrap. While the shells are cooking, cook the venison sausage until browned and cooked through in a large saucepan. Then stir in the water, tomato paste, onion, ½ the parsley flakes, and all the garlic and oregano or basil. Add 1 teaspoon salt and black pepper to taste. Mix together and return the pot to the heat. Bring the sauce to a boil. Reduce to a simmer and simmer uncovered for 30 minutes, stirring occasionally. In a medium bowl, combine the eggs, ricotta and ½ cup of the Romano or Parmesan cheese. Season with ¼ teaspoon salt, the dash of black pepper and the remaining parsley flakes. Mix together to blend then stuff the manicotti shells with this cheese mixture. Pour ½ of the meat mixture into a 12x7x2-inch baking dish. Place the stuffed manicotti in the dish, then top with the remaining sausage mixture. Sprinkle with the remaining grated cheese to top it off. Bake in a 350 degree oven, uncovered for 40 to 45 minutes or until just heated through. Let the manicotti "stand" for 10 minutes before serving. Don't forget the tossed salad and the garlic bread. That's Italian. Enjoy!

For years we have been writing down our ingredients when we make new wild game recipes. We prepared this new pasta sauce recipe for our cookbook signing and venison sampling for our customers at Soergel Orchards, Wexford, Pennsylvania. This recipe makes a ton, so plan to serve plenty of family, friends, or a few deer hunters at camp. Guaranteed deliciously Italian. Now, pass the garlic bread, please and thank you.

Dad's Venison and Pasta Italiano

2 pounds venison stew meat or shoulder steak, cut into small chunks

8 ounces fresh mushrooms, sliced

2 (14½-ounce) cans diced or stewed tomatoes

1 pound fresh tomatoes, chopped small

½ of 1 large green pepper, chopped

1 teaspoon garlic powder

1 teaspoon chili powder

1 teaspoon oregano

1 teaspoon basil or Italian seasoning

1½ teaspoons salt

1 teaspoon black pepper

1 cup Burgundy wine (not cooking wine)

2 cups catsup or salsa

½ pound smoked sausage or kielbasa, cubed in bite size pieces

4-5 cups water

1 (16-ounce) package of your favorite pasta cooked to package directions

To a 6-quart crockpot add pieced venison, sliced mushrooms, canned and fresh tomatoes. Stir well and add green pepper, spices, wine, catsup or salsa, sausage or kielbasa and water. Stir well to blend. Set crockpot to low and cook 7 to 8 hours or cook on high for 4 to 6 hours. Serve over your favorite pasta. Pass the Parmesan cheese, please.

Gale's Venison and Wild Rice Soup

2 cups sliced fresh mushrooms

¾ cup chopped onion

¾ cup chopped celery

2 (14½ ounce) cans beef broth

1 (6 ounce) package long grain and wild rice

1 (10¾ ounce) can golden mushroom soup

2 cups milk

1½ pounds venison roast or stew meat, cubed small

½ cup parsley flakes

¼ cup dry red wine (not cooking wine), optional

3 tablespoons soy sauce

1 cup of your favorite barbecue sauce

1 (15½-ounce) can corn and 1 can water

Spray your crockpot with non-stick cooking spray to prevent sticking. To the pot add sliced mushrooms, chopped onion, celery, and beef broth. Then add rice, soup, milk, cubed venison, and remaining ingredients. Stir well to blend. Set crockpot on high for 4 to 5 hours or low for 6 hours. Before serving add more water if needed for desired consistency.

Shirley's Italian Style Cooking Tip

Recently we were talking about how we have always enjoyed cooking venison in Italian style recipes, like "Venison Parmesan," "Venison Mozzarella," and "Mom's Venison Lasagna." I told her my dad, Harry, would always bake his hand seasoned meatballs on a tray for 25 to 30 minutes and drain them before adding them to his already prepared and simmering pasta sauce for our customers that evening. Shirley said "with lean nutritious venisonburger I just make my usual meatballs and carefully place them <u>uncooked</u> in my simmering pasta sauce that will cook for 2 hours or more. The meatballs turn out firm and delicious over pasta and I don't even have to clean up a frying pan or baking tray that was used for precooking my venison meatballs." Now that's a cooking tip!

What good cook does not have a favorite or several favorite stew or chili recipes? Well, this is one of our favorite stews and it will be one of yours, too. Give it a try soon for everyone to enjoy whether at home or at deer camp. Reheated and served a second time, it is even better, if that is possible.

Steve's Favorite Venison Stew with Roasted Peppers

1½-2 pounds venison stew meat, cubed
1 cup green onions, chopped
4 red potatoes (1 pound), peeled and chopped
2 carrots, chopped
2 celery stalks, chopped
2 fresh tomatoes, chopped
1 (14½-ounce) can beef broth
1 can of cream of "your favorite" soup
1 (12-ounce) jar roasted red peppers, drained and chopped
1 package dry onion soup mix
1½ cups chopped fresh mushrooms
4 cups water
4 teaspoons flour
2 teaspoons parsley flakes
½ teaspoon black pepper or to taste
1 teaspoon salt
2 tablespoons diced jalapeño peppers (optional)

In your 5-quart crockpot add cubed venison, green onions, potatoes, carrots, celery, tomatoes, beef broth and cream of soup. Stir to blend well. Add roasted peppers, dry onion soup mix, and mushrooms; stir. Pour 4 cups water into a large bowl, stir in 4 teaspoons flour and blend out lumps. Add flour and water mixture to crockpot along with parsley flakes, black pepper, salt and jalapeño peppers (hot), if using, and stir well. Cover and cook on low for 8 to 9 hours or on high 5 to 6 hours or until carrots and potatoes are soft and your venison is tender. Add garlic or buttered Italian bread or rolls and enjoy!

We asked our friends, Bill and Denny, to try samples of this delicious Italian style sausage and seafood dish. Our family likes recipes to be a little spicy on occasion and after living in the south this was one of our neighborhood favorites. Bill and Denny, who also like "spicy" food even called us to say how much they liked the sample we gave them. (We used 1 teaspoon of black pepper and "Hot Venison Sausage") So...so good too!!

Easy "Crocked" Venison Sausage Creole with Peppers and Beans

1	pound venison sausage, (hot or mild), pieced, if bulk sausage; or thinly sliced, if link sausage	¼	cup bread crumbs
1	cup chopped green onions	½	cup bottled clam juice
2-3	fresh garlic cloves, diced small	1	(15-ounce) can chickpeas, (garbanzo beans)
1	(10¼-ounce) can onion soup	1	(15-ounce) can cannellini or white kidney beans
1	(12-ounce) jar fried or roasted peppers, chopped	2	tablespoons spicy prepared mustard
1	(14½-ounce) can chicken or beef broth	2	(6½-ounce) cans chopped clams
1	(10 to 14½-ounce) can diced or stewed tomatoes	1	teaspoon each oregano and black pepper, (only ½ teaspoon each if using hot sausage)

Let's cook: Spray your 5 to 6-quart crockpot with non-stick cooking spray to help with easy clean-up. Sausage; to brown or not to brown before adding it to your crockpot is a good question. If you use cubed venison steak in this recipe instead of venison sausage there is no need to brown it in a frying pan before adding it to your crockpot. If you used our homemade lean venison sausage recipes from our first book, *Quality Venison, Homemade Recipes And Homespun Deer Tales,* on pages 72, 118, and 131, there is no need to brown this lean, healthy sausage first. However, if you use a butcher's shop lean pork or even their venison sausage you may want to brown it 10 to 15 minutes, drain if needed before adding it to your crockpot. It is a bit more healthy for you this way.

Easy "Crocked" Venison Sausage Creole continued

Add your cubed venison steak if you desire or the venison sausage that we recommend, to your crockpot. Add all your remaining ingredients and stir well. Then set your crockpot on high for 4 to 5 hours or on low for 7 to 8 hours. All crock pots are not created equal as far as heating, so you may need to add some water and stir well before serving. Add hot pepper sauce or shredded cheese to individual bowls and serve friends at home or deer camp. Enjoy, for sure!!

In A Hurry, Steve,
"The Venison Man" Made A Cooking Mistake...

After grilling some venison of ours to medium rare perfection, Steve was in a hurry to freeze our leftover steak for a future cold winter day. We would prepare one of our barbecue sauces to pour over it and let it simmer to desired tenderness to serve with rice or a potato, or even serve it as a holiday appetizer.

Because Steve was in a hurry, something went wrong. He did not take the time to wrap our venison steak in plastic freezer wrap and then put it in a good freezer bag like he always does with fresh venison. Instead he put the steak in a plastic container with a plastic lid and froze it with our usual big hopes of an easy and delicious venison dish for this winter. Wrong! Freezer burn ruined it!

Our very important wild game freezing tip: ALWAYS freeze cooked wild game in plastic freezer wrap before freezing it in a plastic storage container. Months later when you want to use the game in a recipe it could likely pick up freezer burn if just frozen in the hard plastic storage container. You can't get the freezer burn taste out of the meat no matter what recipe you use.

This is definitely one of our favorite Chili recipes. Steve prepared this chili in July of 2001 so we could taste test it for inclusion in this cookbook. But whether it is fixed in the summer, fall or winter, it's sure to please your family and or guests. They'll be asking what's in it, but don't tell them...let them guess!

Slow Cooker Chunky Wild Game Chili

1	pound venison stew meat, cubed small	¼	cup prepared spicy mustard
1	squirrel or rabbit, quartered at joints and back, cut into 2 or 3 pieces - if you have 1 large rabbit you may want to add 1 cup of water, too	1	(14-ounce) can beef bouillon
		1	teaspoon chives
		1	teaspoon horseradish sauce or hot pepper sauce
		1	teaspoon Italian seasoning
1	cup finely diced fresh tomatoes	½	cup finely chopped fresh onion
1	cup sliced fresh mushrooms	1	(15-ounce) can kidney beans
1	(12-ounce) jar of your favorite pepper sauce or fried or roasted peppers, drained and diced	1	(15-ounce) can chili beans
		1	cup water
		1	(14½-ounce) can stewed tomatoes

Spray a 5-quart crockpot with non-stick cooking spray for easy clean-up. Add cubed venison and cut up squirrel or rabbit and all remaining vegetables and seasonings; stir well. Cook on high 7 to 8 hours. While your whole house smells great, your meal will taste even better. Add hot pepper to taste and a bread of choice.

We are always talking cooking with our friend Shirley. We shared two memorable tips with her. First, her family should always eat their carefully, preferably hand processed, quality cared for venison, fried, baked, or broiled, medium rare, juicy and pink in the middle. Second, when she makes chili from venison try using small cubes of stew meat or even venison steak instead of ground venisonburger because cubed venison adds so much more flavor to the chili.

We were hungry for "a winter warmer" soup one day, so out we went for the few ingredients we did not have on hand. This easy to prepare recipe was delicious. Just ask our taste testing friends at Harry's Barber Shop here in Cranberry Township. After they enjoyed it they served samples to several of their customers and the pot was empty before you knew it. Add extra chili powder or (hot) cayenne pepper to individual bowls to taste, and crackers, too. Enjoy!

Home Style Italian Chili Soup

1½	pounds venisonburger or sausage	1	(10¾-ounce) can of any cream of soup
1	teaspoon basil		
1	teaspoon parsley flakes	1	(14½-ounce) can or 2 cups beef broth
1	teaspoon chili powder		
½	teaspoon Italian seasoning	1	(14½-ounce) can diced tomatoes
½	teaspoon ground sage	1	(8-ounce) can tomato sauce
½	teaspoon ground or prepared mustard	1	(15½-ounce) can cannellini beans
		1	(15½-ounce) can garbanzo beans
½	teaspoon garlic powder	2-3	teaspoons Italian style bread crumbs
½	teaspoon onion powder		
½	teaspoon each salt and black pepper	1	cup water
		½	teaspoon red pepper flakes, optional

Brown your venison in a large frying pan over medium heat for 10 to 15 minutes and add it to your 4 to 5-quart crockpot. (Tip) Spray the bowl with non-stick cooking oil for easy clean-up. To a cup add next 10 seasonings, stir. Sprinkle over venison that you added to the crockpot. Spoon in your cream of soup, add beef broth, diced tomatoes and tomato sauce. Stir the ingredients in the crockpot well to blend. Cook on high for 2 to 3 hours or low 4 to 5 hours. Add your beans, bread crumbs and water, if necessary. Stir well. Red pepper flakes are optional for a spicy dish for all. Cook another 2 hours on high or 3 hours on low. You and yours will enjoy this meal for sure! Thank God for Italians!

*Who would believe that this simple recipe could be so delicious?!
All our recipes are user friendly, but this is one of the easiest, and
definitely one of the tastiest. After smelling this wonderful aroma
for several hours I could hardly wait to delve into it! Thanks for this
recipe, Gerry.*

Gerry's Deer Huntin' Stroganoff

1½-2 pounds cubed venison stew meat   2   (10-ounce) cans mushroom soup
1   package dry onion soup mix   1   teaspoon garlic powder
2   (4-ounce) cans undrained   1   teaspoon black pepper
      mushrooms   1   pound package egg noodles

Place all ingredients <u>except</u> egg noodles in crockpot in above order and mix
well. Cook 6 to 8 hours on low heat or on high heat for 4 to 6 hours, or until venison
is very tender. Cook 1 pound package egg noodles, drain, and mix with venison
mixture. Great that day; better a day or two later.

Gerry Smerka, Hamburg, NY

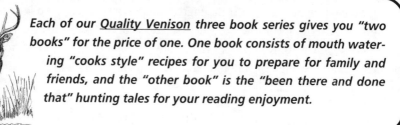

*Each of our <u>Quality Venison</u> three book series gives you "two
books" for the price of one. One book consists of mouth watering "cooks style" recipes for you to prepare for family and
friends, and the "other book" is the "been there and done
that" hunting tales for your reading enjoyment.*

COOKING VENISON TRADITIONAL STYLE

Here is Steve about to hand carve thinly sliced, medium rare cooked hind-quarter venison roast for our Easter special meal for our family. For this and other special venison and wild game recipes you will want to have all of our wild game cookbooks. Taste and see!!

We are dedicating our "Traditional Style" venison recipes to our good friend, Ella Arliss. She has shared a great deal of her wisdom about cooking the "other red meat" over the years. She recently confirmed what we have been saying all along, that when cooking with venison, if you are a hunter or farmer fortunate to take and feed your family from the deer of the mid-west or northeast where they are "farm fed" deer, if field dressed and butchered properly, including aging, there is not any better other "red meat" for your family's dinner table.

When Ella wrote to us recently to share her treasured venison recipe with us, her letter ended with, "this is the venison steak recipe I always used to feed our hungry deer hunters on the first day of gun season. Now I am getting too lazy to cook for them any more. Thank goodness that you, Steve, still come to deer hunt with us because for years now, we have enjoyed the wild game chili, stew, gumbo, or soup that you bring for all of us to enjoy. Like your dad, you have the gift for good cooking of all wild game, which we really look forward to on opening day of deer gun season!!" Some of those recipes are right here in this "Traditional Style" section. Steve spent many hours creating, preparing, and taste testing, so you can enjoy the "fruit of your harvest."

Guaranteed you are going to want to make this chili-like dish at deer camp or at home for special gatherings every year. It takes one person over 1 hour to prepare but it feeds so many, hard to say how many, because of seconds and maybe even third bowls to some, that it is worth all your effort!!

Venison and Bean "Hot" Pot

1	pound venison stew meat, cubed small	1	cup water
1	pound venison sausage (hot or mild)	1	teaspoon salt
		½	teaspoon black pepper
2	tablespoons flour	½-1	teaspoon cayenne pepper, to taste
1	cup chopped onions	1	teaspoon Italian seasoning
3	(15-ounce) cans chili beans, in sauce	½	teaspoon oregano
		½	teaspoon garlic powder
1	(15-ounce) can tomato sauce	1	bay leaf, whole

Preheat oven to 350 degrees. In a large frying pan brown venison stew meat along with your venison sausage over medium heat for 15 minutes or so, stirring occasionally. Drain, retaining drippings in frying pan and place venison into a 3-quart casserole dish that has been sprayed with non-stick cooking spray. To frying pan drippings add flour, stir well to blend and then add chopped onions. Stirring constantly, cook over low to medium heat until flour is dissolved and onions are clear. To your frying pan add remaining ingredients and heat to a boil. Pour ½ of beans and sauce mixture into the casserole dish with venison and stir well. Add remaining seasoned beans and sauce mixture to casserole and again stir well. Bake uncovered at 350 degrees for 1½ hours, stirring 1 to 2 times. Pass the bread and butter and please fill our bowls all around.

We asked our priests and office staff if they would like to sample this venison dish for lunch at our church and they were, of course, "game." Everyone who tried it like it according to the thank you note that we received. We cook venison meals for our priests out of sincere appreciation for their dedication to thousands of our Catholic Church parishioners. They deserve nutritious meals that are provided from God's blessing man with a renewable food resource provided through us whitetail deer hunters. We really believe that!!

Our "Oven Bagged" Priestly Venison Stew

1	large oven cooking bag		1	soup can water or (1 cup to 14½-ounce) can beef broth
2	pounds venison stew meat, carefully trimmed and cubed small		1	(4-ounce) can any type of mushrooms, undrained
⅓	cup flour		¼	cup steak sauce or catsup
2	tablespoons olive oil or butter		1½	cups chopped fresh celery
1	teaspoon each salt and black pepper		1½	cups chopped fresh carrots
1	teaspoon garlic powder		1	cup finely chopped fresh green pepper
1	teaspoon chili powder		1	cup finely chopped onion
1	teaspoon Italian seasoning		½	teaspoon parsley flakes
1	(10½-ounce) can cream of celery or mushroom soup, (save can to measure water, if using)			

Preheat your oven to 350 degrees. Place your large size cooking bag in a 13x9x2-inch baking dish. Add 1 tablespoon flour to bag and shake to protect it against bursting per instructions that came with the cooking bag. Add cubed venison stew meat, flour, and all remaining ingredients. Then turn bag to coat well. Return bag to pan and oven bag should not hang over your pan. Close bag with the nylon tie provided with bag. Cut 5 or 6 (½-inch) slits in the top of your bag. Place dish on your oven rack, allowing room for the cooking bag to expand while cooking. Bake your venison stew for only 1½ hours. Serve this tasty vegetable dish in bowls as is or better yet, bake some whole potatoes of choice in your oven along with your stew and serve them together for a complete and delicious meal! Enjoy…

After being blessed and taking two New York State deer within an hour of each other in 2000, upon returning to Pittsburgh, Pennsylvania, despite poor health, I managed to hand process my farm fed six point buck. I gave my quartered doe to our meat processor and had him process it as I requested. I have to admit, his venison "hot sausage" turned out great when used in this "from scratch" recipe in September, 2001. I guess venison and beans go together as well as steak and eggs, regardless of the time of day or the size of your group!

My Mom's Italian Style Sausage and Two Bean Stew

1	pound bulk venison sausage, broken into bite-size pieces, (if using mild sausage consider adding chili powder or adding spice to each bowl at serving)	1	(14½-ounce) can Italian style stewed tomatoes
		1	(10¾-ounce) can tomato soup
		1	(15 to 16-ounce) can garbanzo beans, (chick peas)
2	fresh garlic cloves, diced small	1	(15½-ounce) can kidney beans
½	cup minced fresh onions of choice, or dried onions	2	tablespoons prepared spicy mustard
2	tablespoons olive oil or real butter	¼	cup Italian style bread crumbs
2	cups finely diced fresh tomato	1½	cups fresh sliced mushrooms
1	(8-ounce) can tomato sauce		

To your Dutch oven or large saucepan with a lid or top add small pieces of bulk venison sausage, diced garlic, onions of choice and 2 tablespoons of olive oil or real butter. Brown for 8 to 10 minutes on stove over medium heat, stirring constantly. Then add fresh tomatoes, tomato sauce and a can of Italian style stewed tomatoes. Stir to blend. While simmering on low heat add tomato soup, stir and add beans, mustard, bread crumbs and fresh mushrooms. Stir well. Cover and simmer on low heat at least 1 hour but not more than 1½ hours. Serve into large bowls for family, friends, or hunters at camp to enjoy.

A Tasty Venison Corn Chowder

1	pound or 2 large baking potatoes, cubed small	1	tablespoon Italian seasoning
¼	cup butter or olive oil	1	cup milk
1	pound venison steak, cubed small	1	cup sliced mushrooms
⅓	cup diced onion	2	teaspoons chili powder
2	garlic cloves, diced	¼-½	teaspoon cayenne pepper, or to taste
2	(14½ ounce) cans cream style sweet corn		

Peel potatoes and cut into small cubes. Put potatoes into a Dutch oven; add water to cover and salt and pepper to taste. Bring to a boil. Meanwhile, heat butter or olive oil in a frying pan and brown cubed venison, onion, and garlic about 10 minutes. Drain any remaining oil or butter; then add the venison mixture in frying pan to boiling potatoes. Turn heat to simmer. Add cans of creamed corn, Italian seasoning, milk, sliced mushrooms, chili powder, and cayenne pepper to Dutch oven. Cover and simmer 1 hour or so. So good with your favorite bread.

Note: 1 pound of venisonburger or sausage can be substituted for venison steak if you use only about 2 tablespoons butter or olive oil and drain it before adding to Dutch oven.

Spicy Barbecue Venison

1	oven cooking bag, regular size	1	teaspoon chili powder
1	tablespoon flour	1	teaspoon garlic powder
1½	cups barbecue sauce	1½	pounds venison stew meat
1	tablespoon prepared mustard		

Preheat oven to 350 degrees. Shake flour in oven bag; place in 13x9x2-inch baking pan. Add barbecue sauce, mustard, chili powder and garlic powder to bag. Squeeze bag to blend ingredients. Place venison in bag. Turn bag to coat venison with sauce. Close bag with nylon tie provided; cut 6 (½-inch) slits in top of bag. Bake 1½ hours. Enjoy!

*"Secret ingredient" sour cream changes a homemade chili com-
pletely and compliments come from all around the table whether at
lunch at home or anytime at your hunting camp! You will want to
double this recipe next time.*

Our Masterpiece Venison Chili

¾-1   pound venison steak or stew
      meat, cubed small

3   ounces sliced pepperoni, diced
    (about 1 cup)

2   tablespoons butter or olive oil

½   medium green pepper, chopped
    small

½   cup chopped green onions

1   (4-ounce) can sliced mushrooms

1   cup prepared instant beef broth

1   (14½-ounce) can diced tomatoes

1   (15-ounce) can chili style beans,
    undrained

1½   teaspoons chili powder

½   teaspoon garlic powder

¼   teaspoon black pepper

¼   teaspoon cayenne pepper

½   cup sour cream or barbecue sauce

Cook venison and pepperoni in olive oil or butter in a large frying pan or saucepan for 10 minutes or so, stirring occasionally. Add green pepper, chopped green
onions and can of sliced mushrooms. Stir and add 1 cup prepared beef broth, and the
can each of diced tomatoes and chili style beans in sauce. Add your chili and garlic
powder. Stir and add black and cayenne pepper. Turn up your stove to have the chili
boil briefly. Then turn down to simmer for 1 hour or more. Then add the "secret
ingredient," sour cream or barbecue sauce and simmer 30 to 60 minutes. Enjoy!
Guaranteed delicious!!

Our recipe for chili soup will delight most anyone's taste buds. This spicy soup is just filled with nutritious venison and beans. It will help you warm up on a cold winter night after putting up a fresh supply of this next year's venison.

Steve's Venison Chili Soup

1	pound ground venisonburger
½	cup finely chopped onion
½	teaspoon garlic powder
1	(6-ounce) can tomato paste
2	(15-ounce) cans diced tomatoes

2	cups water or 1 cup water and 1 cup catsup
1	(15-ounce) can chili beans in sauce
½	teaspoon each salt and black pepper

In a large saucepan brown venisonburger over medium heat. When it begins to change color, add onion and garlic powder and cook until meat is browned and onion is wilted. Add remaining ingredients to pan, combine well and bring to a boil. Reduce heat to simmer, stir and cook 60 minutes. Let set for a few minutes before serving.

Lone Brave Venison

1	pound venisonburger
2	large cloves garlic, minced
1	(14½-ounce) can stewed tomatoes
1	(15 to 16-ounce) can tomato sauce
1	(15 to 16-ounce) can whole kernel sweet corn, drained

1	(16-ounce) can kidney beans, drained
2	tablespoons chili powder
1	tablespoon onion flakes
	Hot pepper sauce or cayenne pepper to taste

In Dutch oven, brown venison and garlic. Add remaining ingredients. Simmer, uncovered, 20 minutes, stirring occasionally. Add hot sauce or cayenne pepper to taste. Serve in bowls with hot bread or rice. Enjoy!

Make this dish to eat right away, or freeze it for a special occasion. Serve with sweet potato and a vegetable or by itself with a side of pasta or rice. It is guaranteed to please even the fussiest eater.

Gale's Wined and Dined Venison Meatballs

1	pound venisonburger	4	green onions and greens, sliced thin
¾	cup Italian-style bread crumbs		
¾	cup milk	1	teaspoon salt
1	egg	1	teaspoon garlic powder
½	small onion, chopped	¼	teaspoon black pepper
		1	tablespoon Worcestershire sauce

Sauce Ingredients:

2	tablespoons salad oil	1	beef bouillon cube
2	tablespoons flour	¾	teaspoon sugar
1	cup water	1	teaspoon salt
1	cup Burgundy wine	⅛	teaspoon black pepper

Preheat your oven to 350 degrees. In a large bowl mix the first 10 ingredients thoroughly. Shape the mixture into 1½-inch balls. Bake the meatballs on a 9x13x2-inch baking dish sprayed with non-stick cooking spray at 350 degrees for 30 minutes or until browned on all sides. While meatballs are browning, heat salad oil in large skillet. Stir the flour into the oil until well blended. Gradually stir in the water, wine, bouillon cube, sugar and salt and black pepper, stirring constantly until sauce is thickened. Add the browned meatballs and heat to boiling. Reduce the heat and simmer, covered for 15 minutes. Serve with one of our side dishes in this book; "Easy Does It Veggie Rice Pilaf" would go nicely with this dish, or serve with one of your favorite side dishes, baked potato, or wild rice. The combinations are endless...

Just one taste of this one dish tasty meal will want you to ask for seconds. It will serve 3 to 4 hungry hunters or a family.

Uncle Dom's Tasty Meatloaf

1½ pounds ground venison or
    venisonburger

2   slices bacon, minced

1   teaspoon salt

1   cup minced carrots

1   cup minced raw potatoes

1   small onion, minced

½   cup finely chopped celery

1   small (3 or 4-ounce) can
    mushrooms and liquid

½   cup Italian-style bread crumbs

1   teaspoon chili powder, optional,
    but delicious

2   eggs beaten lightly with ½ cup
    water

⅓   cup Parmesan or Romano shaker
    cheese

In a large bowl combine all ingredients, except shaker cheese; mix well and place in loaf pan. Top with shaker cheese. Bake at 325 degrees until done (1½ to 2 hours.) Delicious!

Tip: Make ahead of time, storing it in the refrigerator, and pop into the oven 2 to 2½ hours before eating. (It will take longer to bake right out of the refrigerator than if you just prepared it.) Be assured you will want to make this dish again.

While cooking with my dad at our restaurant I heard him say more than once to the staff, "if we are always thinking before, during, and after cooking a meal that we would love to eat this ourselves, then our customers will enjoy it too!"

Our Aunt Marge is a very special woman in our family, so we dedicated this recipe to her. We know they will enjoy it as much as we did even if they have to use ground round or lean sausage and not venison.

Aunt Marge's Cheesy Venison and Veggie Bake

1	pound lean venison steak, cut in thin strips, 1x2-inches	1	(10¾-ounce) can Cheddar cheese soup
2	tablespoons olive oil or real butter	½	cup sour cream
1	(10-ounce) package frozen vegetable of choice	½	cup soft torn bread pieces or bread crumbs
2	cups cooked rice, after being cooked to package directions	1	teaspoon basil
		1	teaspoon parsley flakes

In a skillet or large frying pan brown your venison steak strips for 5 to 8 minutes in oil or butter. Set aside in a covered dish. Heat your oven to 350 degrees. Cook your vegetables as directed; drain and set aside. In a 9x13x2-inch baking dish sprayed with non-stick cooking spray, combine rice, soup and sour cream, and stir. Stir in cooked vegetables and browned venison steak strips. In a small bowl combine bread or bread crumbs, basil and parsley flakes; add to the baking dish and stir. Bake for 30 to 35 minutes or until thoroughly heated. Enjoy! So - so - good and good for you too!!

A hunter's venison from the whitetail deer is to be appreciated and never wasted because the deer is a gift from God. It is a "myth" that venison has a gamy taste. It is the spoiled fat when left on venison and frozen, that gives venison a gamy flavor. Any cut of venison from the whitetail deer, whether from the treasured tenderloin, the hindquarter, or front shoulder, when it has been quality cared for after a clean one shot kill, carefully aged and boned, all fat trimmed and removed before freezing, and double freezer wrapped, is as delicious as it is nutritious. Steve has been carefully doing it this way for over twenty-five years and our family has never had a "gamy" venison meal. — Gale Loder

"You Just Have To Try It"
Venison Sausage Casserole

1	pound hot or mild venison sausage	1	teaspoon crushed basil leaves
1	tablespoon butter	1	teaspoon oregano
6	ounces (3 cups) uncooked egg noodles	½-1	teaspoon salt
½	cup chopped celery	2	medium tomatoes, cored and chopped small, divided
½	cup sliced green onions	1	small yellow summer squash, scrubbed and sliced thin, divided
1	cup dairy sour cream		
2	teaspoons prepared mustard	2	cups shredded or cubed Monterey Jack or Cheddar cheese, divided
½	cup mayonnaise-type salad dressing		
1	teaspoon ground thyme		

Preheat your oven to 350 degrees. In a large skillet or frying pan brown venison sausage in butter 10 minutes or so turning occasionally. Set aside. Cook noodles according to package directions. Drain and rinse in hot water. In a large bowl combine noodles with the venison sausage, celery and green onions. Blend in the sour cream, mustard, mayonnaise, thyme, basil, oregano, and salt. Spoon ½ the mixture into a 3-quart casserole dish sprayed with cooking spray to prevent sticking. Top with ½ the tomatoes, ½ the squash and ½ of the cheese. Repeat layers, topping with the cheese. Bake uncovered at 350 degrees for 30 to 45 minutes or until hot and bubbly. Um! Um! Gooood! Leftovers will never hit the freezer!

Years ago I came across a recipe for venison ragoût. It sounded good so I gave the recipe to my dad. Some time later I recall him serving my hunting companions and me this savory venison dish. Dad modified the recipe some according to his creative tastes. Give this special recipe a try on some of your venison soon. Good choice indeed!

Loder's Restaurant Venison Ragoût

3	tablespoons olive oil	3	carrots, peeled and cut into ½-inch slices
2	pounds venison shoulder or stew meat, cubed	2	tablespoons parsley flakes
2	tablespoons butter	1	(16-ounce) jar chili or picante sauce, (chili sauce is sweeter)
1	cup chopped onion		
2	garlic cloves, diced	2	tablespoons cornstarch
1	cup chopped green pepper	1	cup red wine
1	teaspoon Italian seasoning	1	(14½-ounce) can beef broth
	Salt and pepper to taste	1	cup Parmesan cheese
3	large tomatoes, chopped		

Preheat your oven to 350 degrees. In a large frying pan use olive oil to brown venison over medium-high heat until browned on all sides, stirring frequently. Remove to a bowl. To your pan add 2 tablespoons butter and brown onions, garlic, green pepper, Italian seasoning, and salt and pepper to taste 10 minutes or so. Stir occasionally. Then add chopped tomatoes, carrots, parsley flakes, and chili or picante sauce. Let it cook 10 minutes and then blend cornstarch into red wine until smooth. Add it and beef broth to skillet, stir. Cook over medium heat 10 minutes. Spoon ½ the venison into a 2-quart baking dish and add ½ of the skillet vegetables and seasonings. Repeat. Top casserole with Parmesan cheese. Cover and bake 30 to 40 minutes.

Serving suggestions: Serve over rice or egg noodles cooked to package directions or serve as is with baked Idaho or sweet potatoes as a side. Either way it will be a memorable meal for sure. Enjoy!

Jim Trotta's Venison Steak in the Bag

1	large size oven cooking bag	1	teaspoon sugar
3	tablespoons flour	1½	teaspoons powdered mustard
1	teaspoon chili powder	½	teaspoon salt
2	(14½-ounce) cans Italian style stewed tomatoes	½	teaspoon black pepper
2	cloves garlic, diced	1½	pounds venison hindquarter steak

Preheat your oven to 350 degrees. Shake flour in the cooking bag; place it in a 13x9x2-inch baking dish. Add chili powder, tomatoes, garlic, sugar, mustard, salt and black pepper to cooking bag. Blend with flour by squeezing the bag. Add venison steak and an optional spice of your choice, if desired. Turn the bag to coat venison with sauce. Close the oven bag with nylon tie provided; cut 6 (½-inch) slits in the bag top, or according to package directions. Bake for 50 to 60 minutes depending on the age of the deer. Let stand 5 to 10 minutes before serving. Serve with baked sweet or Idaho potatoes and a glass of your favorite red wine. Leftovers are great too! Enjoy! Thanks, Jim and Linda for giving me your recipe - it has easily become a family favorite.

Ways to "Share The Harvest:"

Over the years Steve has had the habit of sharing his wild game dishes with neighbors, relatives, friends, and the priests at our church's parish. He will often make a big Dutch oven or crockpot of wild game stew, chili, soup, or pasta sauce and freeze it in give-away plastic containers. When the opportunity arises for him to share his tasty wild game dish, he does, and it is always much appreciated. He has even "hooked" a few people on wild game who had never had wild game dishes before, too! Many of our recipes in this book have been taste tested on these people, all with positive encouraging responses. —Gale Loder

Clyde's Venison Roast

1	regular size oven cooking bag	1	medium onion, sliced
1	tablespoon flour	2-3	pounds venison roast
1	(⅞-ounce) package brown gravy	1	teaspoon Italian seasoning
	mix	½	teaspoon each salt and black
¾	cup water		pepper
12	ounces fresh mushrooms, halved		

Preheat oven to 325 degrees. Shake flour in oven bag; place in 13x9x2-inch baking pan. Add gravy mix and water to bag. Squeeze bag to blend ingredients. Place mushrooms and onion in bag. Turn bag to coat ingredients with gravy. Rub roast with Italian seasoning, salt and black pepper; place venison roast in bag. Close bag with nylon tie provided; cut 6 (½-inch) slits in top of bag, or to package directions. Bake 1 to 1½ hours. Let stand in bag 5 minutes. Serve with sweet potatoes or side of choice and enjoy!

Ella's Farm Raised Venison Roast

1	oven cooking bag, large size (14 inches x 20 inches)	4-5	medium potatoes, cut in quarters (about 1½ pounds)
¼	cup flour	1	fresh green pepper, cut into strips or 1 (12-ounce) jar of fried peppers
1	(16-ounce) jar medium picante sauce or salsa		
2	fresh garlic cloves, diced	1	bunch of green onions, including greens, sliced, (about 1½ cups)
3-3½	pounds boneless venison hindquarter roast		
6-7	fresh carrots, chopped	¼	cup soy or Worcestershire sauce

Preheat your oven to 325 degrees. Shake flour in cooking bag; place in a 13x9x2-inch baking pan. Add picante sauce or salsa and garlic to cooking bag. Squeeze oven bag to blend with flour. Now place roast in the oven bag and turn to coat roast with salsa or picante sauce. Arrange carrots, potatoes, peppers, and green onions in the bag. Add soy or Worcestershire sauce to bag. Close bag with plastic tie; cut 6 (½-inch) slits in top of bag, or to package directions, and bake 2 to 2½ hours so your roast is "fork" tender. Enjoy!!

We named this recipe after our daughter, Kelly, because this is one of her favorite recipes to prepare. Try it and you will see why. It's not only "quick" to prepare, but it will please your taste buds, too.

Kelly's Quick Venison Stroganoff

8	ounces uncooked egg noodles, any width, cooked to package directions	1	(4-ounce) can sliced mushrooms, drained
1	pound venison round steak, thinly sliced	1	teaspoon garlic powder
2	tablespoons butter or olive oil	1	(10¾-ounce) can condensed onion soup
1	cup water	1	cup sour cream
		2	tablespoons flour
		1	tablespoon chili powder

Prepare noodles to package directions. Lightly butter noodles and set aside in a covered bowl to keep warm while preparing remaining dish. While the noodles are cooking, cut venison in small pieces and brown in a large skillet or frying pan in 2 tablespoons butter or olive oil for 10 minutes or so. Add water, mushrooms, and garlic powder; stir in soup and heat to boiling. In a small dish blend sour cream, flour and chili powder; add to skillet mixture. Cook, stirring until skillet venison mixture thickens. Add your hot buttered noodles to venison mixture and stir. Serve with a fresh green salad or a vegetable side of choice.

This easy to prepare and so tasty venison meal will certainly have your "better half" hugging your neck if you make time to prepare it. As a suggestion you will want to double it when prepared so you will have possible leftovers for your next "from the freezer meal" or use 2 pounds of venison steak so as to be able to treat another special couple for dinner.

Our Country Kitchen's Specialty of "The House"

3	tablespoons olive oil or real butter	½	of a (6-ounce) can of black olives, drained and sliced
	A small seasoning bag of any kind	1	cup beef both
½	cup Italian-style bread crumbs	¼	cup barbecue or steak sauce
1	pound venison hindquarter round steaks or loin, cut 1 to 1½ inches thick	¼	teaspoon black or cayenne pepper (spicy)
⅓	cup sliced green onions	1	cup sliced fresh mushrooms
½	teaspoon garlic powder	¼-⅓	cup shaker or shredded cheese of choice
½	cup of your favorite salsa or even catsup		

Heat butter or olive oil in a large frying pan. To a bag add bread crumbs and venison round or loin steak; shake well to coat. To your large frying pan add venison, green onions, and garlic powder. Over medium heat fry venison steak, turning occasionally to brown nicely for 8 to 10 minutes. While browning, preheat your oven to 325 degrees. Spray a 1½-quart casserole dish with non-stick cooking spray for easy clean-up. Add salsa or catsup, sliced black olives, and beef broth to casserole dish; stir. Before adding venison steak from frying pan, use the same stirring utensil to remove all bread crumbs and green onion from the pan and add to casserole dish with the venison. Lastly add barbecue or steak sauce, black or cayenne pepper, and fresh mushrooms to casserole dish; stir well to coat. Top with your favorite shaker or shredded cheese of choice. Bake uncovered for 25 to 30 minutes. Stir and serve with a favorite vegetable or two to enjoy a deliciously, nutritious dinner for you and yours. Enjoy!

LET'S COOK THE "OTHER" WILD GAME

As you will see after reading some of our "other" wild game recipes, you can use whatever "other" game you have on hand that you have been fortunate enough to have harvested, using comparable serving amounts. We always encourage you to experiment by adding or substituting spices or other ingredients. Remember, cooking isn't an exact science. And if you need to substitute chicken parts, Rock Cornish game hens, or other domestic meats in similar amounts, our recipes will still be great.

Our tender and tasty small game, with any one of our delicious sauces from *Quality Venison II,* is delicious! Simmer over medium heat, quartered squirrels or rabbits in enough water to cover, 45 minutes or until tender, then drain. On your broiler or grill rack arrange your small game over medium coals. Grill uncovered just 10 minutes a side or so, turning often to not overcook while brushing generously with one of our special sauces. Serve small game with additional sauce that was kept heated on your stove while grilling. You can also use your stove broiler pan with this small game recipe. Spray your broiler pan with non-stick cooking spray and coat small game with our sauce or (even store bought, if in a hurry.) Broil at 400 to 450 degrees basting frequently with sauce and be careful not to overcook.

If you don't feel so adventuresome, try some of our recipes in this section. Whether it is a duck stroganoff, waterfowl stew, Italian style, or even a Mexican style wild game recipe we guarantee you will be glad you did!

Venison is a dark, red meat and is delicious with sour cream in a stroganoff meal. It took only one meal for us to realize substituting a pieced large puddle duck for venison will also provide a very special meal for 2 or 3 people!

Believe It! Wild Duck Stroganoff

8	ounces any egg noodles, cooked to package directions
¼	cup olive oil or butter
1	large, skinned wild duck, each breast and legs removed from the carcass, each breast cut into strips
8	ounces fresh mushrooms, sliced
½	cup chopped green onions
1	tablespoon flour
1	cup water or ½ cup each water and a good dry red wine
2	teaspoons instant beef bouillon crystals or 2 cubes
1	cup sour cream

Cook noodles to package directions. Meanwhile, in a large frying pan, heat olive oil or butter over medium heat; add your sliced duck, duck legs, mushrooms and green onions; stir. Cook until browned and vegetables are tender. Add flour, water and wine if using, and beef bouillon; stirring constantly, cook 1 minute or until your gravy gets thick and bubbly. Cover and simmer on low heat 45 to 60 minutes or until the duck legs are tender. Then stir in sour cream. Heat well but try not to boil it. Serve deliciously over noodles.

Dan's Southern Style Wild Duck

1	large puddle duck, breasts and legs removed and parboiled in water 35 to 40 minutes or until tender	½	teaspoon Italian seasoning
		½	cup flour
		½	cup red wine, water, or beer
8	tablespoons spicy prepared mustard	½	teaspoon cayenne "hot" pepper or black pepper
⅓	cup olive oil	1	(4-ounce) can green chili peppers (mild) or 2 "hot" jalapeño peppers from a jar, diced (This "secret choice" ingredient makes this recipe special.)
½	teaspoon minced fresh garlic		
½	cup chopped green onions		
½	teaspoon basil		

In a large bowl or plastic bag add cooked duck and remaining ingredients. Shake well to coat. Place your duck and remaining ingredients in a 9x9x2-inch baking dish and bake at 325 degrees for 25 to 30 minutes. Be careful not to over cook since all ovens are not created equal. Add a side dish of wild or dirty rice, a vegetable side dish and a beverage of choice for a delicious meal.

Delicious Wild Duck and Wild Rice Stew

2	cups sliced fresh mushrooms	2	cups milk
¾	cup chopped onion	1	large wild puddle duck, deboned into bite-size pieces except for legs
¾	cup chopped celery		
2	garlic cloves, diced	½	cup parsley flakes
2	(14½-ounce) cans beef broth	¼	cup dry red wine (not cooking wine)
1	(6-ounce) package long grain and wild rice	3	tablespoons Worcestershire sauce
1	(10¾-ounce) can cream of (your choice) soup		

Spray your crockpot to prevent sticking. Slice and chop mushrooms, onion, celery, garlic, and add to crockpot. Next, add broth, rice, soup, and milk. Remove meat from the duck, add it, parsley flakes, wine and Worcestershire sauce to crockpot. Stir well to blend. Cook on high 4 hours or low for 5 to 6 hours. Add a green salad and your favorite bread to enjoy this hearty meal.

If you carefully field dressed, and protected fowl from freezer burn, then this recipe will satisfy the taste buds of family and friends alike. So if you want to serve more than 2 just double or triple it. If you share this dinner with him or her you will see that it is easy to prepare and even easier to enjoy.

Our Duck Eleganté for Two

1	cup of your favorite rice
2	skinned duck breasts from 1 large wild puddle duck, thinly sliced
½	teaspoon garlic powder
½	teaspoon Italian seasoning
¼	teaspoon ground black pepper
2	tablespoons cider or red wine vinegar

2	tablespoons olive oil or real butter
½	cup sliced green onions
½	cup strips of green pepper
1	(4-ounce) can mushrooms, drained
1	(10 to 14½-ounce) can beef broth, divided
¼	cup good red wine or catsup
1½	tablespoons flour

Cook your rice to package directions and then set aside when tender. While the rice is cooking, in a bowl, season sliced duck breasts with garlic powder, Italian seasoning, black pepper, and vinegar. Coat a heated large frying pan with olive oil or butter and brown duck 2 minutes. Add green onions and pepper strips; sauté 2 minutes or so. Add mushrooms, beef broth, (reserving ¼ cup), and wine or catsup. Simmer for 10 to 12 minutes. Meanwhile mix flour with the ¼ cup reserved beef broth; blend and add to frying pan. Stir until meal thickens. Now serve over prepared rice of choice.

We are proud to say that our homemade wild game recipes are not just restaurant quality, but even better. Our book buyers and recipe samplers at book signing events for years have told us this.

Good red wine, fresh mushrooms, and a crockpot make the heartiness of this meal special on waterfowl. Double or triple the ingredients if using a 6-quart crockpot on a Canadian goose that you are fortunate enough to have. A marvelous waterfowl dish for sure, so just add your favorite rice, noodles, or pasta cooked to package directions. Guaranteed, everyone comes back for seconds if the fowl has been properly handled from field to freezer.

Our Italian Duck with Mushrooms

8	ounces fresh mushrooms, sliced	1	teaspoon dried basil
1	cup finely chopped onion	1	teaspoon dried oregano or Italian seasoning
1	large garlic clove, diced		
1	large puddle duck, dressed and skinned and deboned or meat removed from the carcass	½	teaspoon sugar
		½	teaspoon each salt and black pepper
1	cup beef broth	2	tablespoons shaker type Romano or Parmesan cheese
1	(6-ounce) can tomato paste		
⅓-½	cup good dry red wine, optional or water if preferred		

Spray the crockpot with non-stick cooking spray. Place your mushrooms, onion, and garlic in the crockpot. Place your pieced waterfowl over the vegetables. In a bowl combine broth, tomato paste, wine or water and stir well. Add basil, oregano or Italian seasoning, sugar, salt and black pepper. Stir well. Add to your crockpot of waterfowl and vegetables and stir well. Cover and slow cook on low 7 to 8 hours or on high for 4 to 5 hours or until your favorite fowl is deliciously tender. Serve over cooked rice or noodles cooked to package directions, and top with Romano or Parmesan cheese. Enjoy!!

This recipe is in remembrance of my friend, Billy S. Arliss who lost his life in 2001. Billy, you are in our prayers.

Billy Arliss' Duck Breasts in Tomato Cream Sauce
It's Quick and Delicious, Too...

1	whole large puddle duck's breast, skin removed and each ½ removed from the breast bone, (about 1½ pounds)
½	teaspoon each salt and black pepper
1½	tablespoons real butter or olive oil
½	teaspoon garlic powder
½	teaspoon onion powder
½	teaspoon Italian seasoning flakes

1	(4-ounce) can mushrooms, undrained
½	cup dried parsley flakes
½	teaspoon dried basil
⅓	cup dry red wine (optional) or ⅓ cup steak sauce
1	teaspoon prepared mustard
1	fresh medium tomato, diced small, (about 1 cup)
½	cup whipping cream

First, sprinkle duck breasts with salt and black pepper and brown lightly 5 minutes or so in a medium size frying pan in butter or olive oil. As you turn your duck breast to brown the other side add garlic and onion powder, Italian seasoning and mushrooms with liquid. Simmer for 5 minutes or so. Add parsley flakes, basil and red wine or steak sauce, stir. Add prepared mustard, diced fresh tomato and whipping cream. Turn down heat to low and simmer covered 30 to 35 minutes so your duck is delicious and tender. Place your duck breasts in a baking dish and serve with a favorite rice or baked potato and a buttered vegetable for you and yours. Been there and done that!!

While we lived in the deep south we were exposed to Cajun and Creole cooking. We like it but Cajun can be too hot in some dishes. Like chili, wild duck gumbo is made very hot to mild depending on the hunter's preference. This savory stew makes enough for an "army." Freeze leftovers to enjoy gumbo all winter long.

New Orleans Style Wild Duck Gumbo

1	pound smoked sausage, sliced thin	1	(4-ounce) can (mild) green chili peppers or (hot) jalapeño peppers
1	large wild duck, skinned and deboned, cut in bite-size pieces	1	(14½-ounce) can beef broth
1	(6-ounce) can shrimp or oysters	1	cup gravy, any kind (optional)
1	cup diced onions	¼	cup cocktail sauce or chili sauce
1	cup chopped green onions	½	cup bottled clam juice
2	stalks celery, chopped	1	teaspoon Italian seasoning
2-3	garlic cloves, diced	1	teaspoon chives
2	cups frozen okra, thawed	1	teaspoon basil
1	(14½-ounce) can tomatoes, crushed (save can for measuring water)	1	teaspoon powdered mustard
		¼	cup parsley flakes
2	tomato cans of water	2	teaspoons chili powder

Brown smoked sausage in a frying pan; drain before adding to your crockpot. In a 5 to 6-quart crockpot add sliced smoked sausage, duck, shrimp or oysters, and all remaining ingredients. Cook on high 6 to 7 hours. Enjoy this Cajun stew over hot rice of your choice. Add cayenne pepper or hot sauce if desired.

Be on guard when this stroganoff meal is cooking in your crockpot. Family members or friends will be tempted to uncover the crockpot to get a better sniff or even sneak a taste. Have snacks ready to feed them just in case - but don't feed them too much because they will want to have an appetite when the duck is finally ready.

Steve's Wild Duck Stroganoff

1	deboned and pieced large black or mallard duck	2	(4-ounce) cans mushrooms, undrained	
1	package dry onion soup mix	2	(10-ounce) cans mushroom soup	
½	cup good Burgundy wine or water	1	teaspoon garlic powder	
		1	teaspoon black pepper	

Place in crockpot in above order and mix well. Cook 6 to 8 hours on low heat or on high heat for 4 to 6 hours, or until duck is very tender. Cook 1 pound package egg noodles, drain, and mix with duck mixture. Great that day; better a day or two later.

As you will see after reading some of our "Other" wild game recipes, you can use whatever "other" game you have in your freezer that you have been fortunate enough to have harvested, using comparable amounts. We always encourage you to experiment by adding or substituting spices or other ingredients because cooking should be fun and certainly is not meant to be an exact science.

Our artist friend and his family have joined us in a publishing partnership for years now. Jack and Marian Paluh have allowed us to use their wildlife art prints on our first two venison cookbooks. There is yet another one of Jack's prints on the front of this book. (At the time this recipe was created a print had not been picked for the cover yet.) This recipe is written and dedicated to Jack Paluh and his family with many thanks.

Jack's Cajun Spiced and Pieced Canadian Goose

1	Canadian goose, breast and leg meat	1½	teaspoons black pepper
		1½	teaspoons cayenne pepper
1½	cups Caesar-style salad dressing	1	teaspoon chili powder
½	cup Worcestershire sauce	2	cups Burgundy wine or water
1	teaspoon chives or parsley flakes	1	(12-ounce) jar of fried peppers or pepper sauce of choice
½	cup chopped onion of choice		
3	fresh garlic cloves, diced	1	fresh green bell pepper, chopped

Let's take 1 field dressed Canadian goose and remove and debone the breast and leg meat. Put goose in a 5-quart crockpot after spraying your cooker bowl with a non-stick cooking spray for easier clean-up. Add your remaining ingredients and stir well to blend. Slow cook on low for 8 to 10 hours or on high for 7 to 8 hours, so the goose legs are tender. Add a side dish of your favorite potatoes and a fresh vegetable for a delicious waterfowl meal.

Yes, wild duck over pasta, just like venison, is delicious. Even those duck legs are tender and very tasty. This will be a special meal for anyone who joins you whether at home or duck camp. Pass the Italian bread, please!

Our Italian Style Waterfowl

2	puddle ducks (woodies, teal, mallards), breast meat removed and cubed small, legs removed whole	1	teaspoon salt or to taste
½	cup water	½	teaspoon black or red pepper flakes
½	cup of a good red wine	½	teaspoon basil
¼	cup prepared mustard	½	teaspoon oregano
¼	cup grated Parmesan cheese	1	(8-ounce) can tomato sauce
1	(4-ounce) can sliced mushrooms	2	(14½-ounce) cans Italian style or stewed tomatoes of choice
2	tablespoons Worcestershire sauce	8	ounces of pasta or 1 cup of a favorite rice, cooked to package directions

Remove and cube your duck breasts into small pieces. Remove legs and leave whole. Add duck pieces to your crockpot along with the remaining seasonings and ingredients, stirring well. Cook on high for 5 to 6 hours or on low from 7 to 8 hours. Thirty minutes or so before duck is ready, prepare a favorite pasta or rice according to package directions.

You will enjoy this duck over pasta or rice, we can guarantee it.

We aim to please! If you are looking for that always "special recipe" for wild goose or two puddle ducks, for that matter, look no further. You've got to prepare this easy recipe. Serve with hot buttered bread or garlic bread and your favorite red wine for a memorable meal.

Steve's Italian Style Goose/Duck Stew

½   of a Canadian goose - 1 side of breast pieced small and 1 leg (whole) or you can use 1 to 2 puddle ducks pieced like goose (2½ pounds fowl)

2   carrots, sliced

3   stalks celery, sliced

1   cup tomatoes, crushed or stewed

1   cup chopped onions

3   garlic cloves, diced

1   teaspoon red pepper flakes, optional

1   bay leaf

1   teaspoon each salt and black pepper

1   teaspoon Italian seasoning

1   teaspoon parsley flakes

1   cup red wine, (not cooking wine)

1   (10-ounce) can golden or cream of mushroom soup

1   (14½-ounce) can beef broth

1   (12-ounce) jar roasted peppers, drained and chopped

1   (15-ounce) can Italian cannellini beans or garbanzo beans

Spray 4 to 5-quart crockpot bowl with non-stick spray for easy clean-up. Add small cubes of goose breast or duck breasts and whole goose leg/duck legs to your pot. Add carrots, celery, tomatoes, onions, garlic and red pepper flakes if using. Add remaining seasonings and stir in wine, soup and beef broth. Cover and slow cook on high for 6 hours. After 6 hours add chopped roasted peppers and can of cannellini or garbanzo beans. Add water if needed; stir well and slow cook 1 to 2 more hours or until your fowl is cooked. Tender!

We know you loved "Jocelyne's Marinated Swiss Steak" if you were lucky enough to prepare it. Now we want to use her very recipe on wild ducks from our game bag. Once again a delicious meal for sure at home or duck camp.

Jocelyne's Marinated Waterfowl Supreme

4-6 single duck breasts from black, mallard, or wood ducks and legs removed, also or the breasts and legs of 1 pieced Canadian goose. Flexible ingredient amounts depending on the amount of waterfowl you are preparing.

¼-½ cup soy sauce

¼-⅓ cup butter, melted or olive oil

2-3 tablespoons lemon juice

1-1½ teaspoons diced fresh garlic

¼-⅓ cup good red wine or red wine vinegar

2-3 tablespoons Worcestershire sauce

½-1 teaspoon cayenne or black pepper

1 teaspoon onion powder

½-1 cup chopped fresh green onions

1 (12-ounce) can beer, (optional)

½ of a (6-ounce) can black olives, drained and sliced

As much water as needed to cover in crockpot by 2 inches

Combine the ingredients above with waterfowl in a large bowl or marinade container and turn it several times to coat thoroughly and marinate 3 or 4 hours, turning a couple of times. Spray your bowl of the crockpot with non-stick cooking spray for easy clean-up and add your waterfowl pieces and marinade. Then add the following ingredients to your crockpot:

2-3 tablespoons butter

½ cup diced fresh onions

1 teaspoon oregano

1 teaspoon powdered mustard

1 teaspoon Italian seasoning

2 cups of your favorite medium or mild salsa

Cook in your crockpot on high for 5 to 6 hours or until fowl legs are tender or on low 8 to 10 hours; adding more water if needed. Serve over rice or noodles with a favorite bread. Enjoy, you will!!

This is an easy but delicious meal for 2 when it is served over your favorite rice or noodles. Pass the Parmesan cheese, please, would you, honey? The problem is "what, no leftovers?"

Steve's Pheasant/Grouse/Rabbit Parmesan

⅓   cup sliced green onions

1   garlic clove, diced, or ½ teaspoon garlic powder

2   (8-ounce) cans tomato sauce

2   medium tomatoes, diced

1   (4-ounce) can mushrooms, drained

1   teaspoon salt

½   teaspoon black pepper

1   teaspoon Italian seasoning

¼   cup white wine

1   dressed and skinned pheasant/grouse/rabbit, cut in serving pieces, (quartered)

⅓   cup Parmesan cheese

Preheat your oven to 350 degrees. Spray your 11x7-inch baking dish with a non-stick product (easy clean-up). To a small bowl add all your ingredients except wild game and Parmesan cheese. Stir well. Pour ½ in the baking dish. Add your wild game and pour the remaining vegetables and spices from bowl over the top of the meat. Top with Parmesan cheese. Bake for 1 hour or until tender.

Here is a guaranteed cooking tip worth trying...

Over the years of our marriage, due to missed shots or job relocations, we learned that despite our preference for wild game or fish on our family's dinner table, it was not always possible. An alternative to our enjoying wild game was to use some of our tasty wild game recipes using comparable amounts of similar domestic meats. The recipes also turned out very good, so don't hesitate to substitute your favorite domestic meats in our recipes if you don't have wild game.

After only 30 minutes our crockpot aroma was sending signals that this recipe was going to be something special. The taste test that we did after 4 hours was exceptional. The mozzarella cheese topping is just the "icing on the cake." This dish put over one of our favorite pasta, ziti, had all of us looking at each other and smiling with delight. We agreed that small game and bird hunting is well worth the time, dollars and effort when you can share a tasty nutritious meal like this...

Crockery Cooked Small Game Mozzarella
"That's Italian"

3-4	squirrels, dressed, skinned, quartered and backs cut in ½ or 2 cottontail rabbits, dressed, quartered and backs cut in ½ (If you have 1 ring neck pheasant or 2 ruffed grouse, they can also be used, dressed and skinned; breasts and legs removed.) (If you are out of small game, resort to 2 pounds chicken, skinned.)	1	(15-ounce) can or 2 (8-ounce) cans tomato sauce
		1	cup water
		½	teaspoon oregano
		½	teaspoon parsley flakes
		½	teaspoon onion powder
		½	teaspoon garlic powder
		½	teaspoon each salt and black pepper
1	(12-ounce) jar roasted peppers, drained, or pepper sauce	8	ounces your favorite pasta, cooked to package directions
1	(10¾-ounce) can tomato soup of choice		Top with 1 cup mozzarella cheese

Spray your crockpot bowl with non-stick cooking spray for easy clean-up. Add small game or upland birds, pieced. Add roasted peppers or pepper sauce of choice from your grocer. Add tomato soup, tomato sauce and water, then stir. Add remaining seasonings and stir. Cook in your crockpot on high for 4 to 6 hours or on low for 7 to 8 hours. About 45 to 60 minutes before serving this tasty dish, prepare your favorite or on-hand pasta according to package directions. Top your "crocked" small game specialty with 1 cup mozzarella cheese and continue cooking until cheese is melted and bubbly. When your crockpot meal is done serve over your cooked pasta. Enjoy!!

We suggest deboning game pieces before serving.

Pass the cheese please, ah!! Now, this is an Italian entrée. Italian restaurants, you are jealous... We shared and enjoyed this meal together to celebrate Father's Day. Kelly, our daughter, and her boyfriend came to visit later but had to be disappointed when there was not much "Pheasant Italiano" left for them to take home. Maybe next time, Kelly! This is tasty even using 2½ pounds of chicken.

Steve's Pheasant or Grouse Italiano

1	pheasant or grouse, dressed and skinned
2	fresh tomatoes, thinly sliced
1	clove garlic, diced
1	teaspoon oregano
1	teaspoon Italian seasoning
½-1	cup Italian or Caesar-style salad dressing
3-4	fresh mushrooms, sliced
3	whole green onions, chopped
¼	cup white wine (not cooking wine)
2	(8-ounce) cans tomato sauce
1	(12-ounce) jar roasted peppers, drained and chopped small
¼	teaspoon red pepper flakes (optional)
½	teaspoon salt
¼	teaspoon black pepper
2	tablespoons Parmesan or Romano cheese
	Rice, noodles, or baked potatoes (your choice)

Preheat oven to 350 degrees. Place the pheasant or grouse in an 11x7x2-inch casserole dish, sprayed with a non-stick cooking spray, breast side up. In a medium bowl add tomatoes, garlic, oregano, Italian seasoning, and your dressing. Stir. Add mushrooms, green onions, white wine, tomato sauce, and roasted peppers. Stir well and pour over the meat to cover. Add red pepper flakes, if using, along with the salt and black pepper. Top with your favorite shaker cheese. Bake for 1 hour or until the meat is tender. (Prepare the rice, noodles or baked potatoes while the pheasant or grouse is baking.) This dish will feed 2 to 3 but do not plan on leftovers. Serve over your choice of rice, noodles or even baked potatoes.

Mike and Sharon Fletcher, our neighbors, had again given us some of their home grown tomatoes and we were delighted to enjoy a nice taste difference when their tomatoes were used in this recipe. When you have a couple of prized pheasants or even more rare, three or four chucker or ruffed grouse, for a special dinner, this is the one for you. A crockpot never goes wrong. If you want to serve pheasant to kids in your family get-together, see "option" at the end of this recipe.

Italian Style Slow Cooker Pheasant Stuffed with Pepperoni and Black Olives
A truly special dinner for "4" or "6"

1	(26 to 28-ounce) jar of a favorite pasta sauce, divided	2	whole dressed, washed, and skinned "prized" pheasants
3	garlic cloves, diced small	1	cup thinly sliced pepperoni, diced in small cubes
2	tablespoons dried minced onion		
2	tablespoons olive oil	1	cup pitted and sliced in ½ black olives
1	(14½-ounce) can chicken broth		
1	tablespoon parsley flakes	2	cups fresh diced tomatoes or a (14-ounce) can if fresh is not available
1	tablespoon oregano leaves		
1	teaspoon Italian seasoning	1-2	cups shredded mozzarella or Parmesan cheese
½	teaspoon chili powder		
½	teaspoon sugar	1	pound linguine or your favorite pasta, cooked to package directions
2	tablespoons apple cider vinegar, (optional), or white wine		

To a large size bowl add pasta sauce, garlic cloves, minced onions, olive oil, chicken broth, parsley flakes, oregano, dried Italian seasoning, chili powder, sugar and either apple cider vinegar or white wine, (not cooking wine). Stir to blend. Spray your 5 to 6-quart crockpot with non-stick cooking spray to help with easy clean-up and add ½ of your sauce and then your 2 pheasants. Stuff each bird with pepperoni and pitted olives; then to birds, top with the remaining ½ of your pasta sauce. If olives and pepperoni remain after stuffing birds add to sauce, along with the diced tomatoes. Slow cook on low for 6 to 7 hours or on high for 4 to 5 hours. ½ hour before serving top with cheese. Serve ½ of a pheasant with sauce per person over

Italian Style Slow Cooker Pheasant continued

linguine or other favorite pasta, and be sure to top each memorable dish with the black olives and pepperoni dressing. Homemade buttered garlic/cheese bread goes well with this special Italian meal!! Oh, before serving let anyone top their meal with more shredded cheese. The saying goes, "what a sight for sore eyes." Well this special dinner is one of them, guaranteed. Leftovers will not make it into your freezer!

Option: If you want to serve this nutritiously delicious meal to a family of little ones, just debone pheasants and add to your crockpot and stir. Follow same preparation directions as above, but before serving cut pheasant into small pieces.

Here's a Handy Tip:

Before even lighting your barbecue grill, spray your grill with any non-stick cooking spray to help keep your lean game from sticking to it. This way both game and vegetables will come off the grill or skewers that were also sprayed before threading, easily. Also, spray your barbecue spatula with non-stick spray for easy clean up. If you are frying any kind of wild game indoors or even baking it, too, spray your pan or baking dish with non-stick spray of choice and enjoy easier clean-up.

Please prepare this easy meal and share it with that special person in your life after bagging a ring neck pheasant or two ruffed grouse. You will be glad you did!!

Quick Pheasant Cacciatore

6	ounces of any favorite pasta	½	teaspoon onion powder
2	skinned and deboned pheasant breasts	½	teaspoon black pepper
2-3	tablespoons olive oil or butter	1	(14½-ounce) can of diced or stewed tomatoes
1	cup sliced mushrooms	1	(8 to 15-ounce) can tomato sauce or 1 to 2 cups salsa
1½	cups sliced yellow (summer) or zucchini squash		
½	teaspoon garlic powder	1½	teaspoons Italian seasoning

Prepare your pasta according to package directions. In the meantime in a Dutch oven, large pot, or large frying pan, fry pheasant breasts in olive oil or butter over medium heat 3 to 4 minutes a side or until lightly browned. Remove from cooking pan and keep warm in a covered baking dish. To your Dutch oven or frying pan add a little olive oil or butter and sauté or cook mushrooms and squash with garlic and onion powder and black pepper for 3 to 4 minutes, stirring occasionally. Add tomatoes, tomato sauce or salsa, and Italian seasoning. Stir and add back pheasant breasts. Now simmer only 15 to 20 minutes covered on low heat. Serve over your favorite pasta.

Steve's Rabbit/Squirrel Italiano

1	wild rabbit, quartered or 2 gray squirrels with the backs cut in ½	½	teaspoon garlic powder or 1 garlic clove, diced
1	cup mild or medium (spicy) salsa	1	teaspoon dried minced onions
½	teaspoon Italian seasoning	1	teaspoon chicken bouillon granules
½	teaspoon poultry seasoning		
½	teaspoon black pepper	¼	cup shaker style Parmesan or Romano cheese

Preheat your oven to 325 degrees. Spray a 7x11-inch baking dish with non-stick cooking spray for easy clean-up. Add rabbit or squirrel pieces and remaining ingredients, except shaker cheese. Turn meat pieces to coat Add enough water, ½ cup or so, to just cover your meat if needed. Top with shaker cheese. Bake at 325 degrees for 50 to 60 minutes or until tender. Now that's tasty Italian. Serve with garlic bread and a vegetable of your choice or serve rabbit/squirrel over rice or noodles. Enjoy!

Steve's Rabbit Cacciatore

4	tablespoons olive oil for browning	1	bunch green onions, chopped
2	rabbits, deboned and in small pieces	2	garlic cloves, diced
		1	tablespoon Italian seasoning
1	(14½-ounce) can chicken broth	1	(6-ounce) can tomato paste
1	cup good Chablis wine	½	teaspoon oregano
1	pound fresh mushrooms, sliced	½	cup your favorite salsa or picante sauce

In a Dutch oven add olive oil, and over medium heat brown rabbit for approximately 5 minutes. Then add remaining ingredients. Bring to a boil, cover and simmer 35 to 45 minutes, or until rabbit is tender. Serve over your favorite type of spaghetti. Great with garlic bread.

Can serve 4 to 6.

Even in Pennsylvania, without a good hunting dog, you do not have much success with taking grouse. I was blessed with the taking of a rare grouse in Lycoming County on a November Saturday. We made a special recipe to celebrate my first grouse in years and saved it especially for you.

Steve's Pheasant/Grouse Ranchero

1	skinned pheasant or grouse	½-1	cup ranch-style dressing, amount depending on using pheasant or grouse
2-3	large fresh mushrooms, sliced		
2	medium red potatoes, sliced	½	teaspoon each salt and black pepper
1	carrot, chopped		
1	stalk celery, chopped	1	teaspoon Italian seasoning
1	clove garlic, diced	1	teaspoon parsley flakes
⅓	cup diced onions		
¼	cup white wine (not cooking wine)		

Preheat oven to 350 degrees. Place 1 pheasant or grouse in a 2 to 3-quart casserole dish, sprayed with non-stick cooking spray, breast side up. In a medium bowl add sliced mushrooms, sliced potatoes, chopped carrot, chopped celery, diced garlic and onions, wine, and ranch-style dressing. Stir well and add salt, pepper, Italian seasoning, and parsley flakes. Mix well and pour over meat. Bake for 1¼ hours or until the meat is tender and potatoes are done, also. Enjoy!

It takes precious time to make anything right, so the next time you prepare a wild game sauce, make enough so you can freeze some for a future meal. It's almost like having bottled sauce on hand in the refrigerator, but much tastier! We suggest storing it in a plastic food container that is microwave safe so you can thaw it in a flash if you don't have the time to thaw it slowly in the refrigerator.

This is a tasty one, guaranteed. When having non-wild game eaters over for dinner, serve this dish. Your whole house smells delicious. Dinner time is flexible based on cooking steps. Oh, and your upland game dinner is certainly worth the effort. So Good...

Steve's Upland and Sausage Stroganoff

1	pheasant or 2 grouse, skinned, legs and each breast removed
3-4	tablespoons olive oil or butter
½	cup finely diced onion
½	pound smoked sausage, cubed small
¾	cup sliced fresh mushrooms
¾	cup finely diced fresh green pepper
1	fresh tomato, diced small
1	teaspoon garlic powder
1	teaspoon chili powder
1	teaspoon each of salt and black or red pepper flakes
½	teaspoon Italian seasoning
½	teaspoon basil
1	(8-ounce) can tomato sauce, (saving can to measure water, wine and catsup)
½	can of water
½	of a can of white wine
½	of a can of catsup or salsa
½	cup sour cream
	Rice or noodles, cooked to package directions

In your large Dutch oven brown your pheasant or 2 deboned grouse in olive oil with onions and smoked sausage for 10 minutes or so. Stir in fresh mushrooms, green pepper and tomato. Add your next 6 seasonings and tomato sauce and water, stir well. Add white wine and catsup or salsa, stir. Cover Dutch oven, bringing mixture to a boil. Once the mixture comes to a boil, lower to simmer your game for 1 hour or until tender. When your game is fork tender add sour cream and blend well. Heat on medium heat for 10 minutes to get it all tasty hot for your dinner table. While your game is cooking, cook rice or noodles for 4 to 6.

*Please try this recipe and if it is not one of your favorite Mexican recipes with family or at camp, fall, winter or spring, we will certainly be surprised. It is well worth your preparation time and effort but it is a lot of food, so ask guests to come <u>hungry</u>!! *Leftovers are exceptional too.*

Mexican Style Small Game with Venison Sausage and Fresh Tomatoes

2	cups of any favorite rice, cooked to package directions and set aside in a covered dish
1	cup finely chopped whole green onions
3-4	cloves fresh garlic, diced small
1	pound venison bulk sausage or <u>good lean</u> store brand sausage
1-3	tablespoons olive oil or real butter
1	cottontail rabbit or 2 gray squirrels, dressed, skinned, quartered and back(s) cut in ½
1-1½	cups cored and diced fresh tomatoes

1	(16-ounce) jar of a favorite salsa and 1 jar of water
1	(8-ounce) jar taco sauce, mild or medium
½	cup large (canned) black olives, drained and cut in ½
1	(4-ounce) can (mild) green chili peppers or 4 ounces of (hot) jalapeño peppers, (your choice), chopped
1	(16-ounce) can refried beans
1	cup shredded Mexican or Monterey Jack cheese

Now let's cook. In a medium size 10-inch frying pan add green onions, garlic, sausage, and olive oil or butter. Brown sausage over medium heat 10 minutes or so.

*Cooking tip: spray your crockpot enamel bowl with a non-stick cooking spray to help with easy clean-up. Add frying pan fixings plus remaining ingredients except for the shredded cheese of choice. Now slow cook on low heat for 6 to 7 hours or on high heat for 4 to 5 hours. Just before serving over bowls of rice with tasty bread, top your crockpot Mexican dish with shredded cheese. Extra spicy cayenne pepper can be added with hot pepper sauce if people prefer "their" meal a bit more spicy. Enjoy!

This is easily a tasty recipe for even young hunters to prepare. Try it out on your first of the season rabbit or squirrels and you will be glad you did.

Our Easy Small Game Soup

2 squirrels or 1 rabbit, cut in pieces	1 (10¾-ounce) can of your favorite cream of soup and 1 soup can water
2 fresh tomatoes, diced	
2 small zucchinis, cut in ½ lengthwise and diced	1 teaspoon Italian seasoning
2-3 green onions, thinly sliced	1 teaspoon basil or oregano
2 cups or 1 (14½-ounce) can chicken broth	4 ounces uncooked small pasta

In a large covered pot or covered Dutch oven parboil your small game 45 to 60 minutes, or until tender. Remove it from the pan and place on a plate to cool. Empty your Dutch oven and add tomatoes, zucchini, onions, and broth. Stir well. Add the can of soup, 1 can of water and seasonings. Stir well. Now bring it to a boil. Remove rabbit or squirrel from the bones adding it and pasta to the Dutch oven. Stir well. Simmer covered 15 minutes until pasta is soft.

Young hunters will want to ask for help to prepare this tasty dish from the fall squirrel bounty they earned.

Peppery Squirrel Jambalaya

1	(14½-ounce) can chicken broth	5-6	ounces roasted red peppers, diced or pepper sauce, your choice
1	squirrel, cut into 6 pieces and parboiled	½	cup rice, uncooked
8	ounces smoked sausage or kielbasa, chopped	3	teaspoons hot pepper sauce
½	cup chopped onion	½	of a (14½-ounce) can diced tomatoes of choice
1	garlic clove, diced small		
2	tablespoons butter or olive oil		Cayenne pepper, black pepper and salt to taste

Pour chicken broth in a medium saucepan and parboil squirrel pieces on low heat 45 minutes or until squirrel is tender. Remove squirrel from the pan and debone pieces, setting the pan with the chicken broth aside to use later in the recipe. Place deboned squirrel pieces in a large pot or Dutch oven with sausage, onion, garlic, butter or olive oil and stir well. Brown over medium heat 5 to 10 minutes, stirring 2 times. Add peppers or pepper sauce, rice, reserved chicken broth, hot sauce, and diced tomatoes; stir and bring to a boil. Then reduce heat, cover and simmer 30 minutes until your rice is tender. Lastly, add cayenne pepper, black pepper, and salt to taste. Enjoy!

Our Upland Stew

This is a meal worth waiting for any time of the year!

2	squirrels or 1 rabbit, each cut up into 5 pieces	¼	teaspoon garlic powder
		¼	teaspoon black pepper
2	small white potatoes, quartered and sliced	1	cup canned whole kernel corn, undrained
1	stalk celery, chopped	1	(10-ounce) can of your favorite cream of soup
1	carrot, sliced		
1	cup sliced fresh mushrooms	1	cup chicken broth

Preheat your oven to 350 degrees. Cut up your squirrel or a rabbit you were "lucky" to get. Chop your potatoes, celery, and slice a carrot and fresh mushrooms, and add garlic powder and black pepper. Place the squirrels or rabbit and vegetable mixture in an 8x8 or 9x13x2-inch casserole dish sprayed with non-stick cooking spray for easy clean-up. Add corn over the top and spoon top again with the can of your favorite cream of soup. Pour the broth over the top and stir. Bake until your game is tender, possibly 90 minutes.

A Hunter's Small Game Stew

1	rabbit or 3 squirrels, pieced for parboiling	1	teaspoon Italian seasoning
		1	teaspoon parsley flakes
1½	cups chopped celery	1	teaspoon chili powder
1	cup chopped carrots	½	teaspoon each black pepper and salt
1	cup broccoli florets		
1	large red or white baking potato, diced	2	(14¾-ounce) cans chicken broth
		1	(10¾-ounce) can cream of chicken soup and 1 soup can water
½	cup chopped onion		
2	garlic cloves, diced	1	cup sour cream
1	teaspoon poultry seasoning	½	cup shredded cheese, your favorite

In a small saucepan cover rabbit or squirrel with water; bring to a boil and simmer for 30 minutes. Meanwhile chop your fresh vegetables and place in your crockpot. Add seasonings, chicken broth, soup and water, and squirrel or rabbit to crockpot; stir. Cook on high 4 hours. Add sour cream and cheese and stir. Enjoy this stew as is or serve over rice or noodles. So so good!

This stew is certainly yummy as is, but if your family or hunting camp guests want to add some "heat" then add 2 to 3 diced jalapeño peppers from a jar or more black or red pepper flakes to taste. Hotter is not always better!

Our Autumn Squirrel Stew

2	gray or 1 large fox squirrel, cleaned and skinned	1	onion, chopped (about 1 cup)
4	cups chicken broth	2	garlic cloves, diced
3	celery stalks, chopped	¼	cup white wine
3	large fresh mushrooms, sliced	2	tablespoons flour
3	carrots, chopped	½	cup shredded Cheddar cheese
1	pound potatoes, peeled and chopped small	1	(14½-ounce) can your favorite "cream of" soup
			Salt and black pepper to taste

In a Dutch oven parboil squirrel in broth for 1 hour or until tender. Reserving chicken broth in Dutch oven, remove meat from the broth and remove bone after allowing it to cool, and set aside. To broth add celery, mushrooms, carrots and potatoes; stir. Add onion and garlic. Use a small cup to blend wine and flour; add to broth mixture and stir well. Cover and simmer stew 45 to 60 minutes. Add squirrel, cheese, and cream of soup; stir well, cover and simmer 15 to 30 minutes. Salt and pepper to taste.

If you are ever unfortunate enough to be out of your supply of venison or other wild game, you can prepare one of our easy recipes by substituting a similar amount of meat; understanding that there are fat content differences to drain when necessary. Although the meal will not taste as good as if it were made with your wild game, it will still be tasty for your family and friends.

It may take 20 to 30 minutes to prepare this, what will be a deliciously hot and spicy crockpot meal, for one and all, at dinner time, but we are sure you will not be disappointed at the results. This Cajun spiced winter time warmer stew may not be for everyone the first time, but if given a second chance your guests will develop a taste for spicy versus same old!! The rest of us, after a tasty first serving, will be back for second helpings with hot buttered French or Italian bread. You have to try this hearty wild game stew...

Easy Cajun Spiced Wild Game Gumbo

2	squirrels or 1 rabbit, quartered and with the back(s) cut in ½	2	(12-ounce) cans beer or an equal amount of water
2	more squirrels or 1 rabbit, quartered with the back(s) cut in ½ or 1 pound of venison shoulder or stew meat trimmings, cubed small	1	(4 to 6-ounce) can green chili peppers, mild or ½ cup diced jalapeño peppers, (hot), diced
		1	cup sliced celery
		1	cup bottled clam juice
½	pound venison or good pork sausage of your choice; even turkey sausage, for those of you who are very health conscious and do not have venison sausage	½-1	teaspoon cayenne red pepper, or to taste
		1	(3½-ounce) can shrimp
		1	(3½-ounce) can minced clams or oysters
2-4	tablespoons olive oil or butter	1	teaspoon onion powder
1	(16-ounce) package of frozen okra or broccoli, thawed out!	1	teaspoon garlic powder
2	(15-ounce) cans crushed or diced tomatoes	1½	teaspoons salt

In a large frying pan or Dutch oven brown your squirrel, rabbit, or cubed venison and sausage in olive oil or butter 15 minutes or so. Spray your 5 to 6-quart crockpot with non-stick cooking spray to make for easy clean-up and add your browned game meat. Add thawed out okra or broccoli, tomatoes, beer or water, and stir well. Add peppers, celery, clam juice, cayenne pepper to taste, stir well. Last add shrimp, clams or oysters, onion and garlic powder, and salt. Stir well to blend and cover crockpot. Cook on low heat for 6 to 7 hours or on high heat 4 to 5 hours. You will enjoy!

You young hunters out there, after a successful small game hunt in the beautiful outdoors will want to prepare this easy and delicious recipe for your family or friends.

Troy's Upland Surprise

1	rabbit or 2 squirrels cut in pieces, parboiled for 30 to 40 minutes or until tender
6	tablespoons spicy prepared mustard
4	tablespoons olive oil

½	teaspoon onion powder
½	teaspoon garlic powder
½	teaspoon oregano
½	teaspoon basil
½	cup bread crumbs

Preheat your oven to 350 degrees. In a large bowl or plastic bag add cooked rabbit or squirrel and remaining ingredients. Stir or shake well to coat your game, depending on whether using a bowl or plastic bag. Place game in a 9x9x2-inch baking dish, sprayed with a non-stick cooking spray for easy clean-up. Bake at 350 degrees for 25 minutes and be careful not to over cook. Add side dishes of rice or pasta salad and a favorite vegetable and enjoy.

An Upland Game Special

1	rabbit or large fox squirrel, thawed and quartered
½	cup chopped onions, your choice
½	cup chicken bouillon
1	tablespoon soy sauce
½	teaspoon thyme

½	teaspoon chives or Italian seasoning
½	teaspoon basil
	A sprinkle of cayenne and black pepper, to taste
¼	cup ranch-style salad dressing
½	of a (4-ounce) can mushrooms, drained

In a small pan, parboil the squirrel or rabbit 30 to 45 minutes so it is tender. Preheat oven to 350 degrees. Drain and add meat to an 8x8x2-inch casserole dish, sprayed with a non-stick cooking spray for easy clean-up. Add your remaining ingredients and mix well. Now bake for 40 minutes. Serve over your favorite rice or with potatoes or vegetables of your choice for a light nutritious meal.

This is an easily prepared game dish for even young hunters to prepare. This tasty dish will feed 2 to 4 people based on appetite and the amount of wild game supplied. We guarantee if there are leftovers for any reason, that the next day they are gone.

Loder's Upland Game Special

1   pound upland game of any kind; 1 cleaned and quartered fox or 2 gray squirrels, 1 cottontail rabbit, or 1 lucky grouse. (1 pheasant will be delicious prepared this way, too, but we suggest you double all the ingredients below since 1 deboned pheasant will be about 2 pounds of meat.)

¼   cup chopped fresh onion

½   teaspoon minced garlic or garlic powder

1   cup instant turkey or chicken gravy mix, fixed to package directions

¼   teaspoon each salt and black pepper

1   (4-ounce) can mushrooms

¼   teaspoon poultry seasoning

¼   teaspoon Italian seasoning

2   teaspoons prepared mustard

1   teaspoon horseradish sauce

1   teaspoon Parmesan cheese

½   cup good white wine or water to cover your game dish while baking

Preheat your oven to 350 degrees. Depending on the amount of your chosen game, spray a 1½ to 2-quart casserole dish with non-stick cooking spray to make for easy clean-up. Add your wild game and all the remaining ingredients to the casserole dish. Stir well to blend. Bake uncovered for 1 hour and then stir again. Bake 30 to 60 minutes more so your game is fork tender and very tasty. Add a favorite side dish of potato, rice, or a fresh vegetable for a light and nutritious meal.

Upland Game with
Fresh Celery and Mushrooms

1	grouse or rabbit, skinned and quartered	1	cup instant chicken or turkey gravy, fixed to package directions
2	teaspoons fresh or 1 teaspoon dried parsley flakes	1	cup sliced fresh celery
½	cup chopped onions	½	cup sliced fresh mushrooms
2	teaspoons fresh or 1 teaspoon dried basil	1	cup cooked rice of your choice, cooked to package directions, (optional)
1	clove garlic, minced or ½ teaspoon garlic powder		

Mix all ingredients, except rice, in a large bowl and stir well to evenly distribute seasonings. Add to a 9x13x2-inch baking dish and bake uncovered for 45 minutes and then turn your game and bake 45 minutes more. Serve over your rice or on the side, or serve with a baked Idaho or sweet potato. Salt and pepper to taste. Guaranteed Yummy!

Our friend, Dave Elluinger of Zelienople, Pennsylvania, who has run his own butcher shop for over fifteen years now, spent some time with us talking about his whitetail deer processing experiences. He encourages all hunters to carefully field dress their deer before taking their deer to his shop because that is when the quality of the venison begins. He wants Elluinger's custom cut venison to be done just right so it is never gamy for his customers' families' dinner tables. Dave is also an advocate of outdoorsmen taking our youth hunting or fishing.

APPETIZERS
AND SIDE DISHES

You will find a variety of recipes in this section, from fish fillets, that can be served as an appetizer or main course, to chowders to salads; some made with game and others created to accompany one of our wild game dishes, or perhaps one of your own recipes. We had fun creating these recipes and we hope you have fun preparing them.

Denny's Venison Salami

If you like salami, you'll love this recipe. It is well worth the effort!

4½	pounds ground venison	6	teaspoons salt
½	pound ground beef	2½	teaspoons liquid smoke
3½	teaspoons whole mustard seeds	1½	teaspoons red pepper flakes,
2½	teaspoons black pepper		(optional for spicy)
2	teaspoons garlic powder	1½	teaspoons onion powder

Thoroughly mix all ingredients in bowl (nonmetal), cover, and refrigerate. Daily, using your hands, thoroughly knead the mixture. Do this for 3 days. On fourth day, divide mixture into 5 parts, knead, and form into long, thin logs about 12 inches long. Place the logs on cookie sheet and bake for 10 hours at about 155 degrees. Use oven thermometer to monitor oven. We suggest setting your oven at 200 degrees and check it now and again to see if you get an average of about 155 degrees. Adjust it accordingly. Halfway through baking time (5 hours), turn logs over. Remove salami from oven after baking and roll in paper toweling to remove excess grease. Cool, place in plastic food storage bags and refrigerate. The salami will keep in refrigerator for about 3 weeks. To freeze, double-wrap, first in plastic wrap and then in plastic freezer bags. May be kept up to a year in a good freezer.

Makes 5 (12-inch) salamis.

Our friend, Bob Mitchell, Editor of Pennsylvania Game News *magazine, spent some time recently with us on the phone and said he enjoyed our first* Quality Venison *cookbook, where it devoted a section on "Quality Venison From Field To Freezer." This is where there is so much valuable information on the hand processing of your deer, so it is carefully trimmed of all fat, bone and tallow before it is frozen and later used in so many easy, tasty and nutritious meals. Bob said, "from my carefully cared for burgers to steaks or venison roasts, it does not get any better at meal time than this."*

Lockpit Venison Sausage

3	garlic cloves, crushed	3	tablespoons fennel seeds
½	cup dry red wine	2	tablespoons onion salt or powder
5	pounds ground venison	½	teaspoon chili powder
5	pounds ground port butt	½	teaspoon poultry seasoning
6	tablespoons salt	½	teaspoon hot pepper flakes,
1	tablespoon black pepper or cayenne pepper		(optional)
3	teaspoons powdered allspice	2	teaspoons liquid smoke

Soak crushed garlic cloves in wine for 4 hours, then toss away garlic. Mix all ingredients together well. Use your hands to mix so it is thoroughly blended. *Tip: You can check seasonings by frying a small patty. Allow it to cook thoroughly and then taste. When seasonings are to your liking, form your sausage mixture into patties. If sausage is too dry add a little more red wine. Freeze patties by double-wrapping in plastic wrap and then in freezer bags.

Makes 10 pounds so you can enjoy it in recipes or on the grill all year round.

Gerry's Venison Jerky

4-5	pounds venison, cut into ¼x½-inch strips, (from stew meat trimmings and/or front shoulder meat)	½	teaspoon each black and red pepper
1	tablespoon salt	⅓	cup Worcestershire sauce
1	teaspoon onion powder	¼	cup soy sauce
1	teaspoon garlic powder	1	tablespoon prepared mustard
		4	tablespoons liquid smoke, unless using smoke house

Cut venison in ¼x½-inch strips, and place in a marinator or large bowl. Combine remaining ingredients, and mix well. Pour sauce mixture over venison, tossing to coat all the venison. Cover and refrigerate overnight. Pat dry on paper towels before drying in oven. Dry in oven at lowest heat possible until meat is firm and dry, 4 to 5 hours. Put jerky in a plastic bag and let it stay in your refrigerator 1 or 2 days, then sample it. Add more seasoning to your taste and shake bag well. Everyone will want some of your tasty, nutritious jerky, guaranteed!

Gerry Smerka, Hamburg, NY

Jack Paluh, our artist friend from Waterford, Pennsylvania, near Lake Erie, suggested that we sample and write some new "wild game" <u>red meat</u> jerky recipes in our third cookbook. So Jack, this new one is named after you. The next time we are traveling your way we will have to bring you a jerky sample of this.

Jack's Marinade For Big Game Jerky

2-3	pounds wild game red meat, sliced in 2x¼-inch strips	2-3	garlic cloves, minced small
1	cup soy sauce	1	tablespoon onion powder
2	tablespoons Worcestershire sauce	2	tablespoons hot pepper sauce of choice
1	teaspoon black pepper	⅓	cup brown sugar
		2	teaspoons salt

We suggest you marinate your wild game 2 or 3 days, turning it daily… This is enough marinade for 2½ to 3 pounds of wild game red meat. Many people love their jerky that is slow cooked in a dehydrator and that is great. But over the years when we wanted game jerky for an appetizer we just used a large baking tray and our oven; door cracked on a low 180 to 200 degree heat for 4 to 6 hours. The time depends on the venison cuts that you use and do not forget to turn your jerky once or twice during cooking, also. After cooking, allow it to cool and refrigerate in an air tight freezer bag. We share small bagged samples with special friends!!

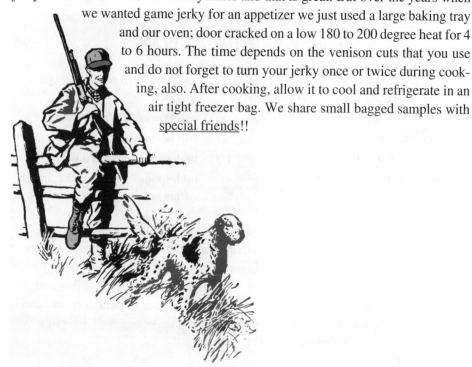

Cranberry's Cheesy
Venison and Potato Chowder

8	ounces venison steak, cubed small	½	cup light cream
1-2	cloves of fresh garlic, minced very small	½	cup finely diced green onions
1	tablespoon olive oil or butter	1	(10-ounce) can cream of potato soup, (saving can to measure water)
1	pound fresh potatoes, peeled and diced		
2	cups water, enough to cover potatoes	1	soup can water
		1	cup fresh sliced mushrooms
½	cup sour cream	1	cup any favorite shredded cheese

Brown venison steak with garlic in olive oil or butter 2 minutes or so, stirring occasionally over medium heat. We suggest you brown venison in a small Dutch oven or soup pan with a lid that will be used in the remainder of this recipe. After browning, remove venison to a dish and set aside. To your Dutch oven or soup pan add potatoes and cover with about 2 cups of water. Then turn stove to medium heat to heat your potatoes for 10 minutes to near boiling and then cover and simmer potatoes for 30 minutes. Add your sour and light cream and remaining ingredients, including the browned venison, <u>except</u> the cheese. Cover and simmer another 30 minutes. Add cheese and stir well to blend and simmer for 15 minutes. Serve as an appetizer before dinner or as a wild game side dish. It will surely please family and guests time after time, yes sir!

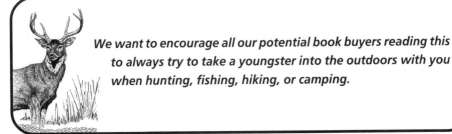

We want to encourage all our potential book buyers reading this to always try to take a youngster into the outdoors with you when hunting, fishing, hiking, or camping.

After sampling this chowder the very first time that I made it, I decided it was to be one of our family favorites. When winter sets in, or you just want to impress family or friends when enjoying dinner together, serving this chowder with any wild game dish or alone as a winter warming meal, will bring smiles and compliments for sure!

Our Cheesy Venison Chowder with Green Onions and Roasted Peppers

1	pound venisonburger or venison sausage, (hot or mild)	1	cup fresh sliced mushrooms
1	bunch green onions, (about 1 cup), chopped	½	teaspoon thyme leaves
		½	teaspoon parsley flakes
1-2	fresh garlic cloves, diced	½	teaspoon black pepper
¼	cup butter or olive oil	½	teaspoon chili powder
1	(10¼-ounce) can cheese soup	½	cup clam juice
½	of a (12-ounce) jar roasted red peppers, drained and chopped	1	(4-ounce) can tiny shrimp
		1	(6½-ounce) can chopped clams, (undrained) and 1 can water
8	ounces chicken or beef broth		
2	fresh tomatoes, chopped, (about 1½ cups)	2	tablespoons Italian-style bread crumbs

Let's cook: In a large saucepan with a lid or a standard 4 to 6-quart Dutch oven, brown your venison with green onions and garlic in butter or olive oil for 10 minutes, stirring occasionally. Then add a can of cheese soup, chopped roasted peppers, 1 cup of broth, tomatoes, and sliced mushrooms; stir pan well to blend. Now add thyme, parsley flakes, black pepper and chili powder seasonings, and stir. Add clam juice, shrimp, clams with 1 can of water, and seasoned bread crumbs; stir well. Heat your pot to nearly boiling, then turn down to low or simmer and time your covered pot for 1 hour or more. Before serving, can top individual serving bowls with shredded or shaker cheese of choice as a delicious side dish or appetizer with favorite crackers or bread, and then serve your wild game dinner. Enjoy!

This colorful and tasty salad will be a treat at any patio or picnic meal. It goes especially well with barbecued meats. We prepared it to go with our "Easy and Cheesy Venisonburgers," which is also in this book. We barbecued grilled chicken at the same time, and enjoyed the salad with the grilled chicken the next day. Delicious!

Delightfully Different Summertime Salad

2	(15½-ounce) cans red kidney beans	2	teaspoons prepared mustard
2	(15-ounce) cans French or regular green beans	1	teaspoon salt
		½	teaspoon black pepper
1	(15-ounce) can whole kernel corn	1	teaspoon Italian seasoning
⅔	cup olive oil	1	teaspoon onion powder
2	tablespoons Worcestershire sauce	1	(12-ounce) jar roasted red peppers, drained and diced small
2	tablespoons soy sauce		
2	tablespoons vinegar (any flavor; we used red wine vinegar)		

Drain canned beans and corn and mix together in a large bowl. Set aside. In a medium bowl make dressing by combining oil, Worcestershire and soy sauces, vinegar, mustard, salt, and black pepper. Stir well to blend. Add Italian seasoning, onion powder, and diced roasted peppers. Stir and pour over beans and corn, mixing well. Cover and chill salad in refrigerator at least 1 hour before serving, but overnight is best. Stir again just before serving. Leftover salad can be stored in a covered container in the refrigerator up to 3 days, if there is any left after your meal. We halved the ingredients for the 2 of us, and had leftover salad, but it did not last 3 more days. Enjoy!

Serves 6 to 8. To serve 2 to 4, halve all the ingredients.

Tip before fixing this recipe: Save the liquid drained from the beans and the corn, and refrigerate or freeze for use in another recipe. It would make a great "beginning" for a homemade soup, or mix a can of condensed soup of your choice with the vegetable liquid to liven it up instead of using water.

Louise's Just Right Potato Salad

1	cup mayonnaise-type salad dressing of your choice	1	(6-ounce) can tuna packed in water, drained
1	clove garlic, minced or ½ teaspoon garlic powder	1	(9 to 10-ounce) package frozen cut green beans or peas, thawed
1	teaspoon salt	1	cup halved cherry tomatoes
¼	teaspoon black pepper	¼	cup minced red or Vidalia onion
1	pound small red potatoes, quartered, cooked and cooled		

In a large bowl combine dressing, garlic, salt and black pepper. Add potatoes, tuna, beans or peas, tomatoes and onion; toss to coat. Cover; chill to blend flavors. Delicious!

Steve's Fish Fillet Appetizer

¼	cup white wine, (not cooking wine)	2	tablespoons soy sauce
¼	cup ranch-style dressing	1	tablespoon powdered mustard
¼	cup prepared salad dressing of choice, (Italian, Caesar, or other)	1	pound any favorite fish fillets, skinned

Preheat oven to 325 degrees. Spray your baking dish with non-stick spray for easy clean-up. In a small bowl mix all ingredients, except fish. Stir well and pour ½ of your seasonings into your baking dish. Add your fillets and top with the other ½ of seasonings. Bake for 30 minutes. Now you only need to use a fork to cut fillets into small pieces. Use a spoon to put on small plates as a very tasty appetizer for 4 to 6 of family or friends.

When Steve tasted this vegetable dish cold after I made it for the first time, he could not stop raving about it. His exact words were, "I really like your salad cold. It can go with anything, hot or cold, or even barbecue, too. It has a different taste!" Although this recipe is meant to be eaten as a hot side dish, I have to admit it was tastier eaten cold than when I reheated it to go with my meat dish. This vegetable side will go great with any wild game dish; turkey, rabbit, venison, or even chicken if you don't have any wild game on hand. Try it and you will find out why "surprise" is in the name...Gale

Gale's Green Bean and Potato Surprise

8	ounces frozen cut green beans, cooked and drained	¼	cup <u>apple</u> cider vinegar
2	medium red potatoes, cooked and sliced	1	teaspoon sugar
		½	teaspoon powdered mustard
6	medium fresh mushrooms, sliced	2	tablespoons water
1	tablespoon olive oil	1	tablespoon parsley flakes
	Butter as need for cooking potatoes and mushrooms		Salt, black pepper, and Parmesan shaker cheese to taste, (all optional)

In a medium saucepan cook green beans to package directions. While the beans are cooking, in a large frying pan cook potatoes and mushrooms in oil over medium to high heat until potatoes are thoroughly cooked, adding butter as needed if olive oil is not sufficient. When beans are done, drain and add to the cooked potatoes and mushroom in the frying pan. In a cup combine vinegar, sugar, mustard and 2 tablespoons water, and mix well. Pour over bean, potato, and mushroom mixture in the frying pan and add parsley flakes. Cook until moisture is almost gone, stirring occasionally. Season with salt and pepper to taste if desired, or even 1 shake or 2 of Parmesan shaker cheese. (I did not use pepper, and only a few shakes of salt).

Serves 4, but don't expect any leftovers. It can be easily doubled to serve more or to have leftovers to go with another meal.

Tip: If you don't have apple cider vinegar on hand, it will be worth your while to buy some for this recipe. We are convinced that the apple cider vinegar "makes" this recipe special. We guarantee it will be a big hit!

Serve with your favorite vegetable or rice for a delicious low fat meal or serve alone as an appetizer. Hey, if you have more guests or family, double or triple the fish and ingredients. Tasty for sure - none the less!

Gale's Tasty Italian Fish Fillets

1	teaspoon Italian seasoning	¼	cup white wine or water
2	teaspoons soy sauce		Dash of salt and black pepper to taste
2	teaspoons prepared mustard		
2	tablespoons of an on-hand prepared salad dressing	1	pound of your favorite fish fillets (walleye, bass, trout, crappie, or other) (even store bought will do if necessary.)
1	tablespoon Parmesan shaker cheese		

Spray a baking dish with non-stick spray for easy clean-up. Preheat your oven to 350 degrees. Add Italian seasoning, soy sauce, mustard, salad dressing, and Parmesan cheese to a cup and stir. Add wine, salt and black pepper to taste. Add your fish fillets to baking dish and add your cup of seasoning. Turn to coat well. Bake for 30 minutes.

Chuck Mac Quaid, a friend of ours in western Pennsylvania, shared a fresh fish fillet cooking tip with us. He had experienced the most tasty fish of his life when at an Amish fish fry. When asked why this freshly caught walleye was so delicious they explained, "we take fresh fish of any kind, soak it in milk 18 to 24 hours. Then in a dish of bread crumbs we bread each side and pan fry each side in oil or butter of choice." It is that simple, but so - so good fish. Try it!

In restaurants, generally not enough time is taken to create very tasty side dishes that equal the quality and delight enjoyed with the main dishes or entrées on the menu. We have again taste tested this delicious side dish and want to share it with you and your friends. Please stay away from cooking possible "fishy" tasting fish fillets and you will find this fish side dish a "keeper" when served with any wild game main dish.

Our Easily 'Bodacious' Fish Fillets

¼-½   cup any bottled prepared salad
       dressing

¼   cup of either white wine or
       bottled clam sauce

2   tablespoons soy sauce

2   tablespoons barbecue or
       Worcestershire sauce

1-2   tablespoons prepared spicy
       mustard

½   teaspoon chili powder

½   teaspoon black pepper

½   teaspoon parsley flakes

½   teaspoon Italian seasoning

6   ounces roasted peppers, drained
    and diced

1-1½   pounds fish fillets of choice,
       thawed and set aside in a dish

¼-½   cup any shredded cheese of
       choice

In a small bowl add salad dressing, white wine, (not cooking wine) or clam sauce, soy sauce, barbecue or Worcestershire sauce and stir to blend. Add mustard, chili powder, black pepper, parsley flakes, Italian seasoning and diced peppers and stir. To a 7x9-inch glass baking dish add ½ of your bowl ingredients. (You may want to spray your baking dish with non-sticking cooking spray to aid in easy clean-up.) Add ½ your fillets to ½ your bowl of seasonings in the dish and toss to coat well. Add remaining fish fillets and bowl ingredients, then toss to coat all fish. Refrigerate baking dish of fish fillets for 30 to 60 minutes to marinate the fish or if you prefer, cook right away. Preheat your oven to 350 degrees and when ready, bake your "Bodacious Fish" for 15 to 20 minutes, depending on species and thickness of fish fillets, and whether you marinated your fish in the refrigerator or not. A cold baking dish will take longer to heat up. (Also, keep in mind that all ovens are not created equal. It is better to check your fish after 10 or 15 minutes to see how quickly it is cooking than to wait and perhaps end up with mushy fish.) Remove from oven and top fish fillets with cheese. Let your "Easily Bodacious Fish" set for 1 or 2 minutes to allow the cheese to melt and serve it along with any wild game or other entrée.

Side dish for 4.

My mother, Doris Flack, did not care to cook much, but the dishes she did prepare were good, and especially this one. I lost my mother to cancer in February of 2001, but I know she would love sharing it. It makes plenty, so try it and see if you do not agree...Gale. This could be a delicious main meal with a favorite bread or crackers or a wonderful cup of soup appetizer before any wild game main meal for family, friends or at deer camp.

My Mom's New England Clam Chowder

2-4	slices bacon	2	teaspoons parsley flakes
1	cup finely chopped onions	1	(4-ounce) can sliced mushrooms, (undrained)
3	cups diced potatoes of choice		
1	cup finely chopped celery	1	teaspoon salt
2	cups store bought clam juice	1	teaspoon black pepper
2	(6½-ounce) cans minced clams, (undrained)	1	teaspoon butter or margarine
		½	cup sherry, white wine or water, (add more water after cooking to get the desired chowder consistency you like)
2	bay leaves		
1	cup flour		

In a 3-quart pot or Dutch oven cook bacon until browned and crispy. Remove it from pan and save on a plate. When cooled, crumble the bacon into small bits. To your pan with the bacon grease add onions, potatoes, celery and clam juice and stir to blend. Cover and cook 10 minutes or so, stirring occasionally. Add cans of clams and bay leaves and slowly add flour while stirring to thicken. Add parsley flakes, mushrooms, bacon bits, salt, pepper, butter or margarine, and sherry, wine or water and stir. Cover and simmer 25 to 30 minutes over low heat, making sure the potatoes are done, and add more water to get the desired consistency you like for chowder. Discard bay leaves before serving.

Kathy and Mike from our church agreed that this was the very best homemade clam chowder they had ever had. Thanks Mom Flack and God bless you.

Marie's Marinated Mushrooms

⅔	cup vegetable oil	½	teaspoon salt
1	clove garlic	½	teaspoon black pepper
1	teaspoon lemon juice	½	teaspoon sugar
⅓	cup wine vinegar	2	pounds whole fresh mushrooms, cleaned and left whole
1	teaspoon parsley flakes		

In a bowl large enough for the mushrooms mix all the ingredients except the mushrooms. Add the mushrooms to the marinade mixture and toss to coat thoroughly. Cover, and leave for 2 or 3 days in the refrigerator, turning often. A delicious appetizer or anytime snack.

Ron Wilson from New York State, called to thank us for receiving our Quality Venison *cookbooks in time to give them as Christmas gifts to his lifelong hunting partner, Rick. He read our recipe for "New Orleans Style Venison Gumbo" in our second book, and said, with the Super Bowl coming Sunday, and it being played in New Orleans, he wanted to use this venison recipe to feed family and friends when they came over for the game. We told him if you use quality cared for venison from the field to freezer this recipe will delight everyone, for sure!*

Just before my birthday in 2002, two weeks after the big game, Ron called to give us permission to use his deer photo, tale, and recipe for this book. He also mentioned how much all of his Super Bowl guests enjoyed our "New Orleans Style Venison Gumbo." It was ironic that a business trip took Ron to New Orleans the week before and he tried one of the restaurant's seafood gumbo while there and was disappointed after just having enjoyed our "New Orleans Style Venison Gumbo," page 116 in Quality Venison II. *Enjoy!*

Ok, you are having some family, friends, or those hunting buddies over for a wild game meal. After some good experience, most will be polite, but come in hungry. Before your delicious wild game dinner is served because you smartly use one of our book's wild game recipes, serve either one or both of these very tasty game appetizers...

Our Herby Venison and Cheese Spread

1	(8-ounce) package cream cheese of choice, softened	1	tablespoon oregano
4	tablespoons sour cream	½	teaspoon onion powder
1½	tablespoons lemon juice	½	teaspoon garlic powder
1	tablespoon parsley flakes	1	cup fried venisonburger or venison sausage, (8 ounces)

In a medium size bowl add all above ingredients except venison, and stir well. In a small frying pan fry venison in 1 teaspoon butter or olive oil for 8 to 10 minutes over medium heat, stirring frequently. Transfer it to the bowl of cheese spread and mix well. Spread over crackers or fresh bread or it can be eaten as a dip, too, with fresh raw veggies.

Perhaps you are going to watch a new hunting video or special sporting event on your television set. Before your wild game entrée try serving this hot and spicy dip that is easy to make and sure to satisfy most everyone!

Our Venison in Mexi-Cheese Dip:

1	cup fried venisonburger or venison sausage, (8 ounces)	1	pound package processed cheese spread, cut into cubes
1	(16-ounce) jar mild or medium salsa	½	teaspoon chili powder
		½	teaspoon garlic powder
		½	teaspoon onion powder

In a medium saucepan add 1 teaspoon olive oil or butter and venisonburger or sausage and brown 8 to 10 minutes, stirring constantly. Then stir in your favorite salsa, cubed processed cheese, and seasonings; stir and simmer 5 minutes or so, stirring frequently. Pour into a serving bowl; serve with crackers and dip chips.

There is no need to look any further for easier and more tasty appetizers than these two. Try them and you will see...

These are 2 very special and yummy appetizers that, once tried, will be before picnic lunch or dinner favorites for you and your guests for years to come.

Our Cranberry Twp. Pepperoni Dip

8	ounces sour cream	½	teaspoon chives or Italian seasoning
1	(10½-ounce) can cream of onion or broccoli soup, undiluted		
		3-4	ounces pepperoni, sliced thin and diced small
1	teaspoon parsley flakes		
½	teaspoon paprika		

Put all the above ingredients in a medium size pan and simmer over medium heat for 10 to 15 minutes, stirring occasionally. Pour into a serving bowl for all to enjoy with favorite tortilla or dip chips or crackers.

Steelers Bacon and Cheese Dip or Spread:

8-10	slices bacon, diced, fried, drained and set aside in a dish	½	teaspoon garlic powder
		½	cup your favorite prepared salad dressing
8	ounces cream cheese, soft style or regular at room temperature		
		½	cup Romano or Parmesan cheese, shredded or shaker style
8	ounces sour cream		
⅓	cup diced green onion	6-8	drops hot pepper sauce, (optional)
½	teaspoon onion powder		

In a medium size bowl combine cream cheese, sour cream, diced green onions, and stir to blend well with a serving size spoon. Add onion and garlic powder, salad dressing and cheese and stir well again. Stir in bacon bits, and if you like dips even more spicy add hot sauce as recommended or to taste. Refrigerate dip 1 hour or so and serve cold on a variety of good crackers or heat in a microwave and serve this as a tasty hot dip with chips of choice.

When family or friends are coming for dinner you will want to serve this nutritious and <u>delicious</u> vegetable casserole. Do not be surprised to even hear the "<u>kids</u>" asking for seconds.

<u>Easy</u> Cheesy Onion and Zucchini Bake

1	tablespoon olive oil	½	cup shredded Cheddar cheese
1	cup sliced fresh mushrooms	½	teaspoon garlic powder
2	cups diced onions	2	cups thinly sliced zucchini; cut in ½ lengthwise, then slice crosswise
5	eggs		
1½	cups milk		
2	cups chicken flavored stuffing mix in canister or box	¼	cup grated Parmesan cheese

Heat your oven to 350 degrees. Heat oil in large skillet on medium heat. Add mushrooms and onions and cook until tender, stirring occasionally. To a 2-quart casserole dish break and add eggs and milk; stir to blend. Add stuffing mix, Cheddar cheese, garlic powder, zucchini, and mushrooms and onions from skillet to casserole dish; blend well. Top with Parmesan cheese. Now bake 30 minutes until top is lightly browned. Let stand 5 minutes to set. Enjoy!!

Our Favorite Potato and Veggie Casserole

1	pound red potatoes, peeled and sliced thin	½	teaspoon powdered mustard
1	medium fresh tomato, chopped	½	teaspoon chicken or beef granulated bouillon
½	green bell pepper, chopped	½	teaspoon oregano
½	cup your favorite prepared salad dressing	½	teaspoon basil
½	bunch green onions (5-6), chopped	½	teaspoon each salt and black pepper
1	small zucchini, sliced	½	cup water
1	clove fresh garlic, diced	2	teaspoons soy sauce
			Top with ¼ cup Parmesan cheese

Preheat our oven to 350 degrees. In a 7x11x2-inch baking dish sprayed with non-stick spray for easy clean-up, add sliced potatoes, tomatoes, green pepper and your favorite salad dressing. Stir well. Add chopped onions, sliced zucchini and diced garlic; stir and add dry spices. Blend in water and soy sauce, then top with Parmesan cheese. Cook uncovered for 30 minutes and turn after 30 minutes. Then bake for another 45 minutes or until potatoes are soft. All potatoes are not created equal in cooking time. Enjoy!! Tasty!

A good hunter knows that you do not "party all night" if you want and plan to hunt all day from your favorite duck blind or deer stand after sunup. The needed preparations and sunup both come early. So...dedication to and respect for hunting wild game in God's great outdoors is necessary. All of us lovers of the outdoors need to remember to help make hunting a family tradition for generations to come.

Gale's Easy Cheesy Potatoes

3	medium potatoes, peeled and diced (2 to 3 cups)	1	tablespoon all-purpose flour
1½	cups water	½	cup undiluted evaporated milk
1	teaspoon salt, divided	1	(9 to 10-ounce) package frozen peas and pearl onions or peas and mushrooms, thawed
2	tablespoons butter		
1	teaspoon Italian seasoning	⅓-½	cup grated sharp Cheddar cheese
¼	teaspoon black pepper		

Combine potatoes, water and ½ teaspoon salt in a medium saucepan. Bring to a boil and cover and simmer 8 to 10 minutes or until potatoes are tender. Drain, reserving cooking liquid. Set potatoes aside, and use the same saucepan to melt the butter. Add the Italian seasoning, ½ teaspoon salt, and black pepper, stirring to blend well. Stir in flour until well blended. Add milk, ½ of the reserved cooking liquid (approximately ½ cup), and peas and onions or mushrooms. Cook, stirring until sauce is thickened. Add potatoes and cook until heated through. Top with cheese and its ready to serve.

Cooking tips: This dish can be made the day before your meal by leaving off the cheese until it is reheated and ready to serve. Also, the remaining cooking liquid can be used in another recipe, or added to your favorite store bought "cream of" condensed soup to zip it up. Just add enough milk or water to finish filling up the soup can.

Respect for the wild game and fish we outdoorsmen and women seek should always be considered, as we honestly and legally challenge ourselves and others with us, each game season. Always ask permission to access the landowner's property you use to enjoy your outdoor hobbies. Also, by offering to help them with their chores a day or two each year will give you an opportunity to get to know each of the families better. Don't forget to take a youngster with you because you may just start a tradition that lasts a lifetime for both of you. This happened to me with the Arliss family in Clyde, New York, and I am glad it did.

This rice pilaf dish is a perfect side for beginners to prepare, or for anyone who likes to prepare a dish with the minimum of fuss. This side will go nicely with any kind of game. We had it with a venison roast prepared in the crockpot the first time, and it was a big hit.

Easy Does It Veggie Rice Pilaf

2	tablespoons butter or olive oil	1	teaspoon salt (½ teaspoon if do not use low sodium chicken broth)
1	cup uncooked rice, your choice		
1	cup water	½	teaspoon onion powder
1	cup (8 ounces) low sodium chicken broth	2	tablespoons parsley flakes
1	(10-ounce) package frozen mixed vegetables		

Melt butter or heat olive oil in a large frying pan. Brown uncooked rice in the butter or oil until lightly browned, stirring constantly. This will only take 1 minute or so depending on the rice you use. Remove from heat and slowly add the water. (You may want to heat the water in the microwave first because the rice and oil or butter will be very hot.) Add the chicken broth and bring the mixture to a boil. Add the frozen vegetables, salt, and onion powder. Stir and bring the mixture to a boil again; turn heat down and simmer, covered for 20 minutes or until liquid is absorbed. Stir in parsley flakes, and enjoy!

This side dish yields 4 generous servings.

Mexican Style Rice Casserole

1 cup uncooked rice, your choice	1 teaspoon hot pepper sauce or to taste
1 cup water	
1 beef bouillon cube	1 (11-ounce) can whole kernel corn, drained
1 (14½-ounce) can Mexican stewed tomatoes	1 (14-ounce) can kidney beans, drained
1 (4-ounce) can green chilies, chopped	1 cup shredded Cheddar and Monterey Jack cheese blend
1 tablespoon parsley flakes	

Preheat your oven to 350 degrees. In a medium saucepan, combine rice, water, bouillon, tomatoes, green chilies, parsley flakes, and hot pepper sauce. Bring to a boil, reduce heat and cover. Cook 20 minutes. Remove from heat; stir in corn and kidney beans. Pour mixture into a 2-quart casserole dish that has been sprayed with a non-stick cooking spray for easy clean-up. Cover and bake at 350 degrees for 15 to 20 minutes or until thoroughly heated. Remove cover; sprinkle on cheese and bake an additional 5 minutes.

Serves 6

Aunt Lucy's Baked Beans

About 4 cups canned chili style beans in sauce	2 tablespoons hot pepper sauce
½ cup brown sugar	2½ tablespoons prepared mustard
⅔ cup diced fresh onion	½ cup bacon or chopped smoked meat to taste
¼ cup salsa or catsup	Salt, black pepper, and garlic powder to taste
1 cup your favorite barbecue sauce, (from our book *Quality Venison II* or even store bought)	

Mix all ingredients together in a 2-quart baking dish sprayed with a non-stick cooking spray for easy clean-up. Cook your beans in the oven uncovered for at least 1 hour at 350 degrees. Beans are deliciously different and freeze well. They are even more tasty cooked and enjoyed the second time.

We created and have without a doubt enjoyed this recipe since 1993 when we lived in Memphis, TN, where everything is barbecue style. We grew up in the northeast where you eat baked beans. Our recipe blends the 2 types of beans, and WOW! It is a little work but makes plenty! ENJOY...

Our Homemade Barbecue Style Baked Beans

4	cans pork and beans, your favorite	¼	cup your favorite bottled hot sauce or to taste
½	large onion, chopped	1	teaspoon minced garlic or garlic powder
⅓	cup brown sugar		
½	cup catsup or salsa	2	tablespoons dry minced onions
2	teaspoons liquid smoke, optional	2	tablespoons prepared mustard
1	cup your favorite homemade or bottled barbecue sauce	½	pound smoked ham, diced; see note below
		1	(28 to 30-ounce) can baked beans

Mix all ingredients together in a 3-quart baking dish that has been sprayed with a non-stick cooking spray for easy clean-up. Bake bean mixture in oven at 350 degrees for at least 1½ hours. Makes plenty so enjoy and freeze leftovers for other picnics.

Note: May substitute 8 ounces smoked venison (excellent) or 8 ounces browned bacon bits (also very tasty).

Option: Grill beans before barbecuing venison or other meats on your grill for at least 1 hour. Gives them an extra lift because of the smoky flavor.

Whether it is a little boy or girl in your family or in a neighbor's family, we all can make a difference in our youth's outdoor hobby enjoyment, perhaps even for their lifetime. For sure my various outdoor loving mentors in my youth made a life long positive impact on my life and it was all for the better. That is how we were able to write our three Quality Venison *cookbooks for you to enjoy, be it for cooking or reading our "folksy been there and done that" hunting tales.*

If you want to make a tasty "picnic" side dish with little or no fuss or muss, this is the one for you. You can make it ahead of time and reheat it, or make it just before an outing or meal. It's sure to please even the fussiest eaters. We have had it with marinated grilled venison steaks and with barbecued chicken. Add a potato or macaroni salad and you have a fantastic meal.

Mom's Barbecue Baked Beans

1	(15-ounce) can pork and beans	½	teaspoon garlic powder
1	(28-ounce) can of your favorite baked beans	1	teaspoon powdered mustard
¼-⅓	cup any smoked meat, diced small	½	cup of any barbecue sauce
		5-6	drops of hot pepper sauce
2	teaspoons dried minced onions	5-6	drops or ½ teaspoon hickory seasoning liquid smoke

Preheat your oven to 325 degrees. To your 2-quart casserole dish (that has been sprayed with a non-stick cooking spray for easy clean-up) add all the above ingredients and with a large spoon, mix well to blend. Bake for at least 1½ hours. It doesn't get any easier or tastier than this!

It is important for all of us to remember the importance of our outdoor experiences. It's in the being there in the chase with family, friends, or others who also share a passion for outdoor wildlife sports, that creates memories for a lifetime.

HUNTING TALES ~ "IT'S TRADITION"

SORRY I MISSED U
"GONE HUNTIN"

When It Is Time To
Hunt In God's Great Outdoors

My husband, Steve, over the years has habitually let me know when the fall hunting season was approaching with his replacing worn hunting clothing and buying the annual hunting licenses for various states. In the morning in early fall we will wake up together and he will have to tell me about a hunting dream that he had, whether successful or not, he is honest. For years I have always been patient to listen to his tales, whether they are imagined or real life.

Then there are the times that he just tells me of his plans to check his hunting gear and do a little outdoors' magazine reading. When he talks guns it means he and a friend or two are headed back to the shooting range, so they do not make any shooting mistakes on wild game or whitetail deer. After all this time and often seeing his shooting targets, even I believe in his shooting skill and hunting tales, too…Gale!!

After nearly forty years of hunting most wildlife it was a pleasure to recall my outdoor memories and to especially recall being a part of hunts with friends that will not be forgotten by any of us. We are sure you will like our photographs, tales, and favorite wild game recipes in this "Hunting Tales" section of our book… Instead of

a "Loder Family Favorite" section of wild game recipes as we wrote for our first two Quality Venison cookbooks, we thought to make a delightful cooking change for you. So after many of our hunting tales in this section we have thought to sample and include special wild game recipes that we and others have created and cooked after the excitement of the hunt. We know that you will enjoy these tasty wild game favorite dishes with family or friends, too! Steve!!

After Having Been There, Let's "Hear" Some
"Hunting Tales"…From Those Of Us Who
"Have Been There And Done That…"

The Family That Hunts Together

Reprinted with permission from the
National Rifle Association of America, from the May, 2001 issue of *American Hunter.*

As long as there have been Americans, American families have hunted together. Way back when, extended-family tribes hunted for everyday survival using primitive tools like the atlatl and chert-tipped arrows. A succeeding wave of immigrants brought with them wheel-lock and flintlock muskets to confront the wild beasts of their new home. More recently, American families have collected their game with centerfire rifles and repeating shotguns.

Regardless of the when or how, there is an unbroken lineage from prehistoric hunting families to yours and mine. We have employed our God-given intelligence to immerse ourselves in the natural world, not to insulate ourselves from it. We have walked the earth and made ourselves part of it; have watched our food walk the earth and made it part of us. We have been the supreme predator, but have done so with conscience. Our families share a bond built on ingeniousness, resilience, humility, and gratitude.

Way back when, all families hunted out of necessity. Until recently most families hunted out of necessity. Now, relatively few American families hunt. We do, and herein salute all the dads and moms, kids and grandparents, uncles and cousins who continue to bear the torch. —*John Zent, Editor*

The Quality Hunter

By Gordon L. Krause

Let's face it hunters, things have really changed. Back when I was in grade school, it wasn't uncommon to have a classmate stand up during 'show and tell' and describe a hunt they went on with their dad. Everyone, including the teachers seemed interested. Recently, my son was told he wasn't able to use bugs in a school science project because it would be cruel to the animals. Yes, times have changed and we hunters are definitely becoming more and more a minority.

The bad news is, the numbers don't lie. Back in 1970, the state of Maryland had about 180,000 licensed hunters. As of 1998, that number has dropped to about 135,000. But that's not the worst of it. Keep in mind that during this decline in hunter numbers, the population of Maryland has increased. This means that the ratio of hunters to non-hunters has really plummeted over the last 30 years. Unfortunately, the trend is unlikely to reverse. With fewer parents hunting and busier family lifestyles, the number of youth hunters (under the age of 16) has dropped 70% since the early '70's. Add to that the constant media assault on hunting and firearms ownership and you can see that fewer and fewer citizens will be raised in an atmosphere that is positive toward hunting.

That brings me to the point of this article. Since we will never have the numbers politically to insure hunting into the future, the only option we have is to show the general non-hunting public that our sport is somehow worthwhile. And I feel the only way to do that is to become *Quality Hunters*. Perception is the key. A *"Quality Hunter"* has always respected the game laws, landowner property rights and the wildlife resources we have all inherited. But now, we have a new tool to further this perception, "Farmers and Hunters Feeding the Hungry." One very dramatic thing I have noticed since becoming involved with FHFH has been the transformation in a person's face once they find out what the program is all about. Their faces simply light up, showing the real power of this ministry. Hunters can make positive use of this power. By supporting the program both financially and through venison donations, we can make a real difference in the way we are perceived, now and in the future. So, with God's help and hunters' continued support, we can finally show the public what we have known all along, *that we really do care.*

Dad Flack's Treasured A.H. Fox Double Barrel 12-Gauge

It's Now A Part Of Our Family Hunting Tradition

It's true what they say that family and outdoors memories cannot be taken from you, just ask Steve. They may be temporarily forgotten, but if they are important enough to you they can be recalled with a little thought down memory lane. And that is just what I have had to do with this antique gun memory. I took my trip and finally recalled some very fond memories of my dad and of when Steve and I were dating over twenty-five years ago.

It all started when we told my dad about Steve's passion for hunting, fishing, and the outdoors. My dad, also, had been an outdoorsman. One of his passions was target shooting at the gun club he belonged to when still living in Auburn, New York. I even got interested in target shooting with him until Steve and I married and we moved to Binghamton, New York, where Steve had chosen a job after completing his college degree in Business Administration.

When Steve and I had been dating for a while, knowing that Steve had a passion for hunting, my dad let us borrow the A.H. Fox double barrel 12-gauge shotgun, that his mother had given him years before, on several occasions. This gun was the only item that she had that had belonged to her husband, who had passed on many years before. She had no need for it, but wanting to keep it in the family, she gave it to my father to use and hopefully one day pass it down to one of his children. At this particular time he wasn't ready to relinquish ownership of the Fox, but he willingly let us use it for target shooting, and Steve also used it for hunting now and again.

I can't remember just when my dad decided to give the Fox to us to use on a full time basis. Perhaps it was when my grandmother, Nana Flack, was struck with Alzheimer's Disease, that he decided that he would give us the Fox to keep so it wouldn't be sold along with all her belongings when she passed away. At different times when he and my mom would visit us I asked him if he wanted it back but he always said to keep it for now. Then when Nana Flack passed on he officially relinquished the Fox to us, saying that it was Nana's gift to us, and we have been safe guarding it under lock and key ever since.

Steve has hunted with the Fox for small game and waterfowl only on special occasions, depending on the circumstances. If he felt the shorter barreled, lighter weight, and tighter shooting shotgun was in order for the hunting trip, he chose the A.H. Fox. He once described a shot the Fox made on a flying cottontail rabbit through

Dad Flack's Treasured A.H. Fox Double Barrel 12-Gauge continued

weeds at 25 to 30 yards. One shot and the rabbit rolled for several feet. Tennessee Dan was his hunting partner that day and yelled, "hey Steve, great shot!" Then there was that other Fox duck hunt when Steve flock shot "by mistake" and fortunately took four mallards with only one shot. That duck tale is in our book, too.

In time, one day we will hand down the antique A.H. Fox double barrel to our artist daughter, Kelly, so that after years of fond hunting memories we can pass on our family symbol and our wild game hunting tradition to our next generation.

This Teenager's First Cottontail Rabbit - 1964

A love of the outdoors and exercise, too, had me outdoors, hunting, fishing, and camping enthusiastically as often as I could. The cub and boy scouts organizations helped for sure. Bagging my first cottontail rabbit at a young age led to a hobby that continued thirty plus years later. This photo was taken after a successful morning cottontail hunt in Yazoo City, Mississippi with Lane and the boys, and rabbit hunting, especially with beagles, was still great fun. Rabbit is so good to eat, and nutritious for you. God rest her soul, my mother-in-law, Doris, was not a wild game eater until she bravely sampled our wild game dishes. Later it was "surprise me, Steve, and fix me anything because I know it will be delicious!"

OK, it was more years than I can count, but like all hunting experiences, they never get forgotten. Maybe God and our "Mother Nature" are responsible for me having captured this outdoor hunting experience and years and years later the memory is in my mind like it happened this month.

After completing my New York hunter safety course at age fourteen, my Uncle Nick, a barber in my hometown of Clyde, New York, let me borrow his 12-gauge double barrel shotgun and a box of paper wrapped low brass shells so I could do some small game hunting. My dad did not hunt, so I took Uncle Nick up on it. I can vividly recall that first brief fall rabbit hunt that has led me to a lifetime outdoors' hobby.

Once I purchased my New York small game hunting license I could not wait to hunt rabbits and squirrels. After all, I had been target shooting and taking woodchucks, too, and I was confident in my shooting expertise. On an October fall afternoon after school was out, it was time to take that man's shotgun and see if I could not get some small game for our family's dinner table. I thought to myself, "I am growing up and I can be a provider like dad!"

I remember telling my mom where I was going to hunt. I then proudly hiked to a familiar hillside where we neighborhood boys would hike, camp out, and spend time with mother nature. It was a beautiful day to be "hiking with a shotgun." I remember thinking 'I would be happy to just catch a glimpse of a gray squirrel or a cottontail

This Teenager's First Cottontail Rabbit continued

rabbit, even if I wasn't able to harvest it and bring it home for dinner.' Moments later I nearly stepped on a cottontail. It bolted, and after gathering my wits, I aimed that 12-gauge double barrel ahead of it on the "fly" and to my amazement it tumbled and never moved. After the gun recoil I was shocked to see the rabbit rolled up against a bush. "Wow," what a thrill for me. I would have carried that one cottontail over forty miles back home to present my "trophy" to my family.

After arriving home, Mom congratulated me and asked me to field dress and skin it. She gave me some field dressing and skinning tips along with a sharp knife. She said, "Here is some newspaper and a pan of fresh water for your rabbit and come see me if you have any questions."

Now, I don't know how long it took me to get that rabbit field dressed and almost ready for the "family pot," but somehow I did it. Little did I know how advantageous that experience would be to the start of a good thing for my life long hunting hobby, and providing for our family's dinner table.

Mom helped me by quartering my rabbit and putting it in a pan of salt water to help drain the blood from the meat. She said that she would buy some chicken and fix a recipe where it would be baked altogether. Well, this young hunter could not wait for this up-coming meal.

Several days later, after changing the salt water in the rabbit pan a time or two, Mom baked the rabbit and chicken after putting it in milk, then bread crumbs, and lightly seasoning it, just like her chicken. There were smiles from all our family after our meal because my "trophy" rabbit was every bit as tender and tasty as "just" baked chicken.

Please take a kid hunting!

Here's a recipe you will definitely want to prepare after a success-ful rabbit hunt. It'll be a delicious, can't-miss hit with everyone who joins you for lunch or dinner.

Sherry Baked Wild Rabbit

1	rabbit cut into service pieces
	Seasoned flour to taste (salt, pepper, Italian seasoning, etcetera)
¼	cup butter or olive oil
1	cup catsup
½	cup sherry
⅓	cup water
2	tablespoons lemon juice

1	medium onion, minced
1	tablespoon Worcestershire sauce
1	tablespoon soy sauce
1	teaspoon parsley flakes
1	teaspoon thyme
1	cup sliced fresh mushrooms
½	teaspoon chili powder (optional)

Using a bag, coat rabbit with seasoned flour. Heat oven to 325 degrees. Meanwhile, use your butter or olive oil to fry your rabbit. When evenly browned, remove and place in a 2-quart casserole dish. Combine your remaining ingredients in a saucepan; bring to a boil and pour over your rabbit. Bake covered for 1½ hours or until tender. Serve with your favorite rice and biscuits or fresh bread.

The future of hunting depends on introducing youngsters to the outdoors. If you don't get involved, who will?

Take a Kid Hunting

By Dennis Russell

Hunter-Trapper Education Instructor

By permission of the Pennsylvania Game Commission @ 2000 by the Pennsylvania Game Commission from *Pennsylvania Game News,* June, 2000 issue.

Outdoor TV shows often impress upon viewers to take a youngster hunting or fishing. The hosts are fully aware that continuing our hunting and fishing heritage depends upon getting today's youngsters involved in the outdoors.

Three HTE instructors from northern Westmoreland County have put this idea into practice. Wayne Weitzel and Leo Kantorski got the idea to take some youngsters who otherwise would not have had the chance to go hunting out during the special youth squirrel hunt last season.

The instructors asked students at an HTE class to sign a form if they were interested in going on a squirrel hunt with an instructor. Ultimately selected were Jason Proctor from Irwin and Darryl Rosenbauer from New Kensington. Jason, age 13, would hunt with Wayne and carry a 20-gauge shotgun. Darryl, also 13, would use a .22/.410 combo and hunt with Leo.

As we teach in HTE classes, hunting season doesn't begin on the morning of the hunt. It starts long before, by asking landowners for permission to hunt. In this case, the landowner was happy to allow the boys to hunt on his land, and both hunters were anxious to go when the morning of the hunt arrived. In fact, Darryl told me that he hadn't slept much the night before. I explained that that was the fire that burns inside a true hunter, the desire to get into the woods and be close to nature, whether or not any game is taken.

Soon after daylight the hunters were posted at promising spots, waiting for squirrels to start moving. A short time later Jason heard a squirrel cutting acorns and soon saw his first target of the day. He waited for the right shot, made sure he had a safe background, then shot and missed. Wayne explained that missing is part of hunting. After all, they call it hunting not getting. Jason saw one other squirrel, but didn't get a shot.

Take a Kid Hunting continued

Darryl didn't see any squirrels, but had a great time with
Leo. He told me that it was such
a great feeling to see and hear the
woods come alive with sounds
from songbirds to the yelping of
turkeys. Darryl was full of questions and asked Leo where the
topsoil and peat moss came
from. Leo explained that the
fallen leaves and trees decay and
convert to nutrient rich soil that
helps the trees grow and produce

mast crops such as acorns and hickory nuts for wildlife. These are the kinds of questions young hunters need answered, so they can understand the ways of the woods.

With the action slow in the woodlot, Wayne and Leo decided to take the boys
elsewhere. At the new spot they asked the landowner for permission to hunt. He was
agreeable and showed them where he thought they might get some shooting. Unfortunately, the day was warm and the squirrels weren't active. Both boys had a great
time, even though they didn't get any squirrels. They learned to read tracks and other
sign left by a variety of game animals, and although both boys returned home tired,
they were happy and anxious to go again.

A person doesn't have to wait until a youngster reaches 12 years of age to take
him hunting. HTE instructor Mike Bell takes his daughter Kimberly on deer, squirrel
and bird hunts, but she doesn't carry a gun. You see, Kimberly is only four years old,
but she loves to be in the woods with her dad.

Well aware of passing on the tradition of hunting to our youngsters, Mike often
takes Kimberly along on scouting trips. Four years old is not too young to take a
youngster into the woods, and you can teach them plenty about wildlife. Already
Kimberly can recognize a deer track and tell which direction it is going.

The future of hunting depends on people like these three HTE instructors. The
challenge is for all hunters to take a kid hunting. Do you remember how good it felt
when your dad or uncle took you hunting for the first time? Why not give that same
feeling to a youngster and help pass on our hunting heritage. Don't wait for someone
else to take the initiative. Do it yourself; take a kid hunting.

A Fond Waterfowling Memory - 1966

On The Arliss Farm

Now some thirty-five years later it is hard to describe my lone, successful, teenage duck hunt on the Arliss farm at 16. But as I recalled this hunt I realized how important and meaningful it was to be a part of the Arliss family when growing up and how it seems to have been a part of God's plan for me and my life. Nothing can replace these fond memories that have helped shape my life. Please remember to take our youth into the beautiful outdoors so they can get to know "mother nature" and enjoy her as much as we do.

It was my sophomore year in high school and I was playing football with Rog and Larry Arliss at Clyde High School in upstate New York. When Rog and Larry worked their dad, "Bill's" dairy farm when not in school they saw ducks and Canadian Geese feeding and nesting on the farm all the time. So they invited me out to hunt their waterfowl anytime.

With the waterfowl season opening in early October I went out to get my small game hunting license and my required waterfowl stamp so I could test my shooting skills on ducks and maybe even the very challenging Canadian geese that occasionally landed on their property. Hey, right place and right time and who knows, I may experience a memory for a lifetime. I thought to myself, "we have never had wild duck or goose on our family's dinner table, so now could be the time."

On the Saturday morning opening of the New York waterfowl season, even after a Friday night football game, the alarm went off at 5:30 in the morning and I was up to experience my first waterfowl hunt. Talk about excited! I had no interest in anything but going to the bathroom, brushing my teeth, getting dressed, grabbing my Uncle Nick's borrowed double barrel shotgun and shells and driving to the Arliss farmhouse. Taking waterfowl was on this teenager's mind.

A Fond Waterfowling Memory continued

My other mom, Ella, Rog and Larry's mother, met me at the farmhouse door at about 6:00 that morning and Rog and Larry were up soon after. They had to milk the dairy cows, of course, but they encouraged me to hunt near the field where we had bailed hay earlier that summer. The cattail swale at daylight should have wood ducks and black and mallard ducks coming up out of it and flying into it from any direction. What a challenging hunt was in store for me.

As people usually are who live off the land; they were right. Little did I know that while walking down this tractor road with only a flashlight and some verbal instructions from Rog, Larry, and "mom," that a memorable waterfowl experience would be coming up at daylight. Fortunately I remembered to take my camera with me to capture any memorable moments.

With my light and shotgun in hand I waded into the cattails that were over my head while it was still dark until the water went over my boots. *Key point; then I turned around so any duck that I took would fall in the reeds or cattails in front of me and if I <u>could</u> locate it, it would be in low water where I <u>would</u> not get cold and wet before driving my dad's new car home.

Just after daylight the blackbirds were starting to fly everywhere and were a distraction to my aiming at ducks flying at blazing speeds into and out of this cattail marsh. Over enthusiastic, I missed the first couple of ducks, but even young hunters can "settle" down and <u>concentrate</u> on their waterfowl or challenging upland birds that they hunt. So I did.

After taking my first duck that was a mallard hen, I then missed several shots at ducks in range. After instructing myself to calm down and be patient, over the next hour or so I was able to take a mallard drake and a mallard hen. Despite the high cattails I was able to find all three of the mallards.

You talk about a teenager starting out the day on the right foot, this was it. Take a youngster hunting someday and both of you will be glad that you did!

This Teenager's "First Ruffed Grouse" - 1967

Why are these "woodland pheasants" called "ruffed grouse?" In my opinion it is because of the male's annual ruffling of their feathers and strutting to attract attention and favor of the female grouse during her mating period.

As a teenager growing up in central New York State (Finger Lakes), when we ventured out into the snowy winter woods we would often "jump" ruffed grouse in our travels by accident. Even without a shotgun or small game hunting license it was usually an unexpected and exciting experience for me and a friend or two who happened to be with me.

After our usual Friday night high school basketball game, Rick, Paul and I decided to hunt for rabbits and maybe the sneaky ruffed grouse in the fields and woods across the road from Paul's house. This December hunt, as all of them over thirty years ago, was to be a cold and snowy one, but that is life in the New York winter time.

Paul and his mother greeted us warmly when we arrived just before daylight. Paul assured his mom that we would bring her home some rabbits, at least, for the dinner table. Paul's pet beagle was itching to hunt, too, when he let it out of the barn.

If memory serves me right, that morning we did manage to take two or maybe three cottontail rabbits. But our hunting highlight came while we were pursuing a cottontail hopping out of a field into the woods. Rick and Paul went to the far end of the woods to spread us out so Paul's beagle could push and circle that cottontail by one of us. The beagle-rabbit chase was a good one, as usual, and during the excitement of Paul's howling beagle, a grouse came soaring through the hardwood trees within my shotgun range. As luck would have it, this teenager did it right. Following the grouse between the trees when it flew through an opening, my Uncle Nick's 12-gauge double barrel went off and that grouse folded!

Shock and pride are the first two words that come to mind when I remember picking up that grouse. Rick and Paul congratulated me on taking my "prize game bird." That rabbit finally holed up and slipped away from our beagle supported hunting effort. By noon we were happy and hungry so we called it quits and returned to Paul's house.

Paul's mom was in the kitchen to greet us. She gave us a big pan of water and a stack of newspaper and asked us to clean or field dress the rabbits out back on the edge of the field. Both Rick and I donated each of our hard hunted rabbits to Paul's

This Teenager's "First Ruffed Grouse" continued

mom. But you can bet that my sneaky and challenging ruffed grouse came home with me in my game bag for our dinner table.

This memorable hunt took place about thirty-five years ago and it is still recalled so easily that it is incredible. But then, safe and successful hunts are fond memories for all of us who enjoy the outdoors and hunting of all kinds.

We want to encourage all of our hunters out there to make a difference for our youngsters by introducing and encouraging them to the safe sport of hunting all kinds of wild game and the personal satisfaction that comes with it...

Firsts and Fond Memories

By Jerry Zeidler Jr.

It's the firsts we remember most. What hunter cannot remember his first squirrel, first grouse or first deer? Shining moments like those in which we confirm our capabilities as hunters of wild game are precious, and seem even sweeter when we can share those accomplishments with family or friends. One of those firsts that will always stand out in my storehouse of fond memories was the first whitetail I ever bagged with a flintlock. In fact, it was the same hunting season in which I bagged my first buck with a modern rifle, but that's another story for another time.

I was sixteen at the time. My father and I had been hunting in eastern Lycoming County, Pennsylvania, for the first few days of the muzzleloader season that year, on a fairly large tract of private land. We were the only two hunters utilizing the property during the flintlock season. But despite extensive scouting, there were simply too many trails being used by the deer as they traveled from feeding areas at the top of one hill to bedding areas in some thick cover on an adjacent hillside. We split up to watch two trails instead of one, but whichever travel lanes we set up to observe, the deer inevitably chose another one to use. To double the number of trails we could watch and thereby increase our chances of connecting, we invited another father and son hunting team, our friends Bob and Robbie Gresko of South Williamsport, Pennsylvania, to join us afield. The day we chose for the hunt was, of course, the coldest day of the winter.

A light snow had fallen the night before, but the sky was clear as we drove to the woods long before dawn. When we reached the parking spot, we bundled up, readied our gear, and planned our hunt. We decided that I would guide Bob and Robbie to a spot overlooking a major deer trail which crossed a small stream, then backtrack several hundred yards to take up a stand watching a secondary trail. My dad would only walk in about half of the distance before stopping along an old logging road, well uphill from the stream, to cover a third travel lane. The plan called for my father to leave his stand and to put on a one-man drive through a 100 x 50 yard thicket where deer commonly bedded, in an effort to move deer to Bob, Robbie and me down by the stream. Once we were all in place, I leaned up against a dead tree and made myself as comfortable as one can be in six layers of heavy clothing. We had allowed ourselves over an hour to reach our stands before legal shooting time, and the walk in consumed just over fifteen minutes.

Moonlight glowed over the snowy landscape, and marveling at the beauty of the setting, I silently thanked the Lord for this wonderful world and for special moments like this in which to enjoy it. As daylight banished the velvet blue night, I enjoyed

Firsts and Fond Memories continued

the rarest sort of silence that only occurs after a long snow, and even then, only for a few moments. Had the forest not been so utterly silent, I might not have even heard it, but the soft swishing of an animal walking through snow was suddenly the only perceptible sound. For what seemed like an eternity, the feet-through-snow noise drew closer and closer, but a screen of thick branches in that direction blocked my view. I readied my smoke pole with a charge of priming powder and rested my thumb on the lock.

The deer stepped into a small clearing directly in front of me, not twenty yards away. By some miracle, I was able raise my muzzleloader and cock the hammer without alerting the deer. Flint met steel and the black powder rifle spoke. An enormous, billowing cloud of smoke filled the clearing between me and the spot where the deer had been, lingering in a tantalizingly thick veil. Did I hit it well? Did it run far? With so many questions in my mind, I almost forgot to reload. By the time I seated a new pumpkin ball atop a fresh powder charge, the smoke had cleared before me, and I peered into the clearing for some sign of the deer. To my delight, my shot had cleanly and instantaneously felled the magnificent animal in its tracks. With no one else immediately at hand, I tagged the deer, then set about the task of field dressing it. By the time my dad found me, I had already tied a rope on and begun the long uphill drag.

Dad seemed to be pretty proud of me. It was only my second deer ever, and my first with a flintlock, but I had managed to harvest it, dress it and drag it out all on my own. And though nobody else took a deer that day, we all were very excited that the plan had worked and one of us had filled a tag. We celebrated that successful hunt not too many days later with my mom's spectacular venison sauerbraten, complete with gravy and dumplings. The recipe has been in our family for a number of generations, and to this day, whenever I sit down to a plateful of this traditional German meal, it takes me back to that cold, beautiful moonlit morning when I recorded one of my first and fond hunting memories. You know with my love for the outdoors there are more hunting memories to be told.

Mom's Spectacular Venison Sauerbraten

½	cup vinegar		Black pepper to taste
1	bay leaf	1	clove garlic, minced
½	cup water	1	(2 to 3-pound) venison roast
2	onions, sliced, (about 1½ cups), divided	2	tablespoons shortening
1	teaspoon salt	1	(14½-ounce) can crushed tomato

Boil vinegar, bay leaf, water, one onion and seasonings in enamel or glass pan for 10 minutes. Pour over roast in glass bowl. Marinate in the refrigerator for 3 days, turning twice each day. Remove meat from marinade, reserving liquid. Brown meat in hot shortening in a heavy pan. Add remaining sliced onion, tomato, and ½ cup marinade. Cover pan and simmer 1½ to 2 hours until tender. Remove roast from pan. Allow to cool on serving plate for about 15 minutes while making gravy. Slice just before serving.

Gravy:

1	tablespoon flour	1	tablespoon butter
½-1	teaspoon vinegar/lemon juice or to taste, (start with ½ teaspoon and add more if needed)	1	tablespoon cream
		⅛-¼	cup red wine, (start with ⅛ cup and add more if needed if gravy
½	teaspoon sugar		is too thick or for more flavor)
	Salt to taste		

Mix flour with liquid in pan and the rest of the marinade, (about ½ cup). Stir and boil until smooth and thickened. Add (to taste) the vinegar or lemon juice, sugar, salt, butter, cream and wine. (After adding cream, do not boil again.) Pour over meat and dumplings.

Potato Dumplings:

2	pounds potatoes		Nutmeg to taste
2	cups flour	2	slices bread
2	eggs, beaten	1	tablespoon butter
	Salt to taste		

Cook potatoes in skins. Allow to cool and "rest" overnight. Peel and mash potatoes. Combine with flour, eggs and seasonings. Knead into a firm dough. Cut bread into small cubes and sauté lightly in butter. Roll dumplings into portions about 2 inches in size, making a hole in the center of each. Place some of the sautéed bread cubes into each hole, then seal by pinching dough back together. Cook dumplings in large amount of boiling water, about 10 minutes or until tender.

My Duck Hunt with Tennessee Dan

Here are Steve and Tennessee Dan when we lived in Bristol, Tennessee back in 1983 after one of their rare successful duck hunts. Fortunately their hunting success that afternoon led to one delicious duck recipe and a beautifully mounted male mallard for our home...

While we were living in Bristol, Tennessee, Dan Moore, an avid hunter, and I managed to meet while shopping at a local gun show. Since we were both looking for new hunting partners at the time we easily became friends and agreed to do some target shooting and hunting, too, in the fall of 1983. We did target shoot and small game hunt, also, and since we got along so well and were the same age with young families, it looked like we would be Tennessee hunting partners for a long time.

My hunting passions were primarily for whitetail deer and wild ducks, but hunting all wild game was on both of our hunting resumes over the years. Despite our work and family responsibilities, waterfowl season was here and with several good locations that I had heard about, Dan was eager to go with me.

One creek, as told to me from a friend, was a magnet for roosting mallards daily just before dark. Jack, the landowner, said to be careful shooting because his house and vehicles were nearby. "No problem, Jack," was my assurance to him. The weekend before the Tennessee waterfowl opening day I called Dan with my plan and we agreed to hunt that farm stream on the Saturday afternoon of opening day. After purchasing our licenses and duck stamps neither of us could wait for Saturday.

After finishing my usual Saturday morning chores, it was duck hunting time, so with my family owned A.H. Fox 12-gauge double barrel and all hunting gear loaded up we met at Dan's house. We loaded his gear and some sandwiches up and were off on our anticipated duck hunting afternoon.

My Duck Hunt with Tennessee Dan continued

It took us an hour on the interstate to get where we would begin to hunt this farm stream of ducks. We knew their evening retreat or "honey hole" of this local mallard flock was the pool at the end of the stream nearest the farmhouse. We wanted to slowly jump shoot the ducks who may be feeding along the other end and hunt toward the pool at the end. Then at dusk, if we did not take our limit of ducks on the way up to the pool we would each try to limit out on the pool before dark.

As we gathered our guns, calls and gear for our hunt, I happened to mention that I had promised my wife, Gale, that if she would take out my last duck in the freezer from last year, I'd be home in time from this waterfowling opening day hunt to fix her a nice duck dinner and hopefully add some fresh ducks to our freezer for our healthy and unique enjoyment. Wrong!! Always plan for the unexpected, hunters, because it happens almost every time over the years. You'll see.

As Dan and I approached the shallow creek we split up with me on one side and Dan wading across the stream to the other. We still hunted each side of the half mile or so stream more like deer hunters than duck hunters so we would get the best shots at any unsuspecting ducks feeding in the creek. We kept abreast of each others' location by occasionally seeing each others' brush movement or a whistle or two. We did managed to jump a few ducks and Dan dropped and found what looked like a female mallard in the middle of the creek. "The hunt was well worth our trip," I thought. As we approached Jack's farmhouse we knew the "honey hole pool" was near. It was not really "ducks' roosting time," but we would not have to wait too long for sundown and possibly some challenging waterfowl shooting.

Despite being careful and quiet we spooked ducks off the creek and they flared toward me. I was so excited I made the mistake of flock shooting instead of picking out individual ducks to target. It is not often that a flock shot pays off, but this one sure did! Four big mallards dropped from the sky and into the middle of the creek and <u>never moved</u>...

A few minutes later, as I was out in the stream collecting my ducks, Dan waded up to me and said, "if I did not see <u>that shot</u> from your <u>old Fox double barrel</u> I would not have believed it. One shot and four ducks!" After throwing Dan one of my mallards I said, "this one is yours because we are 'hunting partners.'" "Yes sir, it will be years before you will ever see one shot and four ducks dropping again, from your shotgun or anyone else's," Dan said. I could only agree.

After field dressing all our ducks, Dan's two and my three, we were late getting home after our hunt, to say the least. After taking Dan home I was looking forward to telling Gale this water fowling tale and showing her three field dressed mallards for our dinner table. I had forgotten all about my promising Gale to fix that last season's duck for us. The whole house smelled great when I got home to tell my duck tale, because Gale prepared what ended up becoming "Whitetop Wild Duck," true story, so please try our delicious duck recipe that follows this tale soon. You will be glad you did.

Recipe: Whitetop Wild Duck
The Whole Story

In 1983 Dan, a duck hunting buddy of mine and I were to go duck hunting on Saturday. I had taken a duck out of our freezer and told my wife, Gale that I would cook it when I returned from hunting that Saturday evening. I said, " we plan to get home early so I'll get a rest and cook the duck when I get up. But just in case I am late, it would be nice if you would fix it, Gale." I made some suggestions as to how she could bake it, never dreaming that she would actually take me up on it.

Well, "as luck would have it," we got into the ducks and were much later arriving home than we had planned. The house smelled good when I walked in, but Gale wasn't speaking to me because I was over two hours late. Later I said, "the house smells good, what did you cook?" She said, "I roasted your duck! It is still in the oven." 'Oh no,' I thought, 'she has never cooked duck before.' I went to the stove and took out the roasting pan with the duck in a cooking bag. Then I opened the bag, removed the duck from the carcass, and put it in a pan and added the liquid and vegetables. While it was heating I made some of our favorite rice. It was not long before we were sitting down to a delicious mallard meal. When I raved about how good her duck was, she thought I was exaggerating so she wouldn't be mad.

The next day Gale gave me all the ingredients she "found" in the kitchen to cook our special wild duck. I wrote down the recipe and when we used the recipe again I was hooked on it and sent it to all my waterfowl hunting friends.

Two years later our local area newspaper, the *Meridian Star*, was having its annual cooking contest. I told Gale I was entering her duck recipe and we had to name it because it was going to win the contest. To our surprise, two months later someone from the *Meridian Star* called to tell us that her "Whitetop Wild Duck" recipe was the game and fish category winner.

My Duck Hunt with Tennessee Dan continued

Fortunately we had a duck in the freezer because to be eligible for the grand prize she and the other five category winners would have to prepare their recipes for the newspaper's panel of judges. Gale asked me to prepare the recipe the evening before the contest judging since she only made it once by accident two years earlier.

The taste judging was fun for all and Gale's "Whitetop Wild Duck," (named after the road we lived on in Bristol, Tennessee when she first cooked it) was chosen runner up to the grand prize. Her runner up prize was nice, but personally I have more fun cooking the meal and telling the whole two year story to friends and family alike. Since this wild game cooking event, our recipes have been newspaper cooking contest winners, have appeared in nationally sold wild game cookbooks, and have been in state and nationally sold hunting magazines, too…

Whitetop Wild Duck

1	tablespoon flour	½	teaspoon salt
1	large oven cooking bag	3-4	fresh carrots, peeled and sliced
1	small onion, peeled, (for duck cavity)	1	medium onion sliced, (about 1 cup), (for around the duck)
1	large wild duck	1	can cream of celery soup, (saving can to measure water)
½	teaspoon onion salt		
½	teaspoon garlic powder	1	soup can water
½	teaspoon black pepper	½	cup rose wine (not cooking wine)

Preheat oven to 350 degrees; coat cooking bag with 1 tablespoon flour. Put the small onion in the duck cavity and place duck in cooking bag. Combine remaining seasonings and ingredients in a medium bowl and pour over and around the duck in the bag. Close bag with nylon tie provided and make 6 (½-inch) slits in top of bag. Bake for 2 hours. Turn oven off and leave duck cooking in oven for 1 hour. Then remove duck and piece from carcass. Add pieced duck and entire bag contents into a saucepan and simmer on stove until heated through. Serve over your favorite rice or noodles. This recipe is time consuming, but well worth the wait!

Cooking tip: Be sure to use fresh sweet carrots. It will make a world of difference in the taste, for sure…

Our Daughter's First Wild Turkey Hunt

Kelly Age Seven

After our first ever day break wild turkey hunt together I emptied my Ithaca double barrel shotgun and asked Kelly if she wanted to hold my shotgun. You can see that she took me up on it, turkey or not! Kelly at age seven...she is now twenty-four and counting.

This photo from over seventeen years later shows you my Ithaca Model 100 we used the first time we turkey hunted together, as well as the first "all important turtle shell" that Kelly found along that very special creek in Mississippi. Please introduce any kid to God's beautiful outdoors!!

In the fall of 1985 I was fortunate enough to meet Jesse in Meridian, Mississippi. We swapped a few hunting tales in a sports shop and we exchanged business cards. A couple of weeks passed, when at work, Jesse called to invite me to deer hunt on his property anytime before the end of the long deer season.

One Saturday morning, after phoning Jesse for directions, I took him up on some whitetail buck hunting. Before daylight with flashlight in hand, sun up was not far off as I walked the thirty minutes on a logging trail from my vehicle to one of Jesse's favorite permanent deer stands. Since Jesse would not be hunting today he wanted me to use it. There were three does that came within range that morning but not a buck to be seen. That morning gray squirrels were everywhere. I thought to myself, "make a note, I will be back!"

At about noon my stomach was grumbling so I said to myself, "it's time to call it a day. Thank you Lord, it was a beautiful day to be outdoors in your woods just the same." On the walk back to my vehicle I thought to wander the woods parallel to the

Our Daughter's First Wild Turkey Hunt continued

logging road in order to get a better understanding of other wildlife sign. Wild turkey scratching and their droppings was the dominant sign. Since fall turkey season was over maybe Jesse will give me permission to hunt his woods come spring gobbler season. Okay, it sounds like a plan.

Before we knew it we had celebrated the birth of Jesus our savior and we had just paid our income taxes. Now was the time to check back with my friend, Jesse to get his okay to hunt turkeys on the opening of spring gobbler season. It was only weeks away! When I reached Jesse by phone our then seven year old daughter, Kelly overheard our conversation. After my call Kelly excitedly asked if she could come and hunt with me. This was a hunting first, so I said sure, sure, let's go turkey hunting early in the morning. I told Kelly, "you can count on me to wake you up but are you sure you want to go now?" Kelly replied, "yes, I want to go, okay?" "Okay," I said, "we will have a great time, Kelly. God Bless you." And then I gave her a kiss on the cheek...

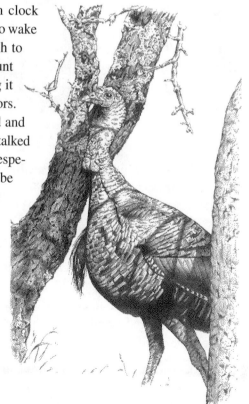

At 4:30 in the morning my alarm clock blasted me out of bed and when I went to wake Kelly she was game and moving, much to my surprise. This would be our first hunt together so I was excited about making it a good experience in our Lord's outdoors. After a little breakfast we were packed and down the road to Jesse's. On the way we talked about how important it was for Kelly, especially with a blaze orange vest on, to be still and quiet when I would be calling in those big tom turkeys with "that big beard feather," coming out of its chest. "Whisper to let me know when you see the beard on the turkey, Kelly," I told her.

We arrived at Jesse's mobile home and parked. It was a good thing that I had hunted deer here before, because it was still very dark. It was going to

Our Daughter's First Wild Turkey Hunt continued

be a comfortable and beautiful sunrise in half an hour. We had some walking to do to be in call set up position by daylight, so with flashlights in hand we left the car and ventured down the logging trail that I had deer hunted from four months earlier.

After checking my watch, we would walk the trail for twenty to thirty minutes and then come off it by fifty yards for our first set up or calling location.

Personally, I will never forget what I felt like at sunup with my daughter on our first wild turkey hunt. That beautiful sunrise is memorable, even today, over fifteen years later. Although we took Jesse's instructions and set up beyond the railroad tracks and near the stream bed, we did not hear any "turkey talking" of any kind from our daylight position. Calling and calling on a box and slate call did not help. Kelly was surprisingly patient for her age.

Eventually we had to move to see if we could locate our would be gobbler. We relocated along the stream and between the logging road two more times. But my calling was not effective and we never saw or heard a turkey. Hey, that is why they call it "hunting" instead of killing, even on opening day. By noon we called it quits.

The highlight of our hunt came as we were walking the stream bank. Kelly saw something unusual, picked it up and said, "dad, what is this?" I was surprised to see my very first turtle shell. They shed their shells like deer do their antlers, but after years of being in the outdoors hunting and fishing I had never found one.

Kelly carried her prized turtle shell home with her - it was her trophy. We would tell her mom after we stopped for a lunch of a hot dog and ice cream. That shell was cleaned up and placed on a book case in Kelly's room. So we did not call in our gobbler on opening day, but we did make an outdoor memory together that will last a lifetime. And we have Kelly's prized turtle shell as a keepsake of that memory. Thank you, Lord, for your great outdoors.

Please take any kid hunting or fishing in God's great outdoors. You can pass on the memory and experience that will not be forgotten for either of you.

 *As Steve so often does, he prepared this newly created turkey recipe and shared some with a neighbor in order to get an unbiased taste opinion. The neighbors had family over at the time and it was thoroughly enjoyed by all, so much so that days later our neighbor asked if we would mind giving them a copy of the recipe. Their relatives had raved about it and wanted to prepare it for a get-together they were planning. We were later told that they did prepare it and it was enjoyed, once again, by one and all. They said it was nothing like they had ever eaten before! Don't just take our word for it, try it for yourself, and we promise you will not be disappointed.*

Kelly's Marinated Wild Turkey
<u>So Good!</u>

1   **small wild turkey, plucked and skinned, (8 to 12 pounds)**

This is also delicious with a <u>skinned</u> domestic bird. If you are preparing a turkey larger than 12 pounds, you will need to buy a package of turkey size roasting bags. You will also need to double the ingredients in this recipe for a larger than 12 pound turkey. The cooking instructions will be the same. <u>Please note that you will need 1 bag for marinating the turkey and 1 bag for baking the turkey.</u>

1½	**cups any favorite prepared salad dressing**	**1**	**tablespoon Italian seasoning**
½	**cup soy sauce**	**1**	**tablespoon parsley flakes**
½	**cup Worcestershire sauce**	**½**	**cup chopped green onions and greens or regular white onions**

To marinate your turkey, place your thoroughly cleaned and rinsed wild or domestic turkey in a large or turkey size cooking bag. To a medium to large bowl add all the above remaining ingredients and stir to blend well and add to the cooking bag. Close bag with tie provided and move marinade in bag around the turkey to coat well and place in your roaster or aluminum turkey size cooking pan. Place in your refrigerator. Over the next 18 to 24 hours toss your bird 4 to 6 times or when convenient, to help marinate it thoroughly.

When ready to cook turkey, preheat your oven to 350 degrees. Please refer to the cooking guide in the box of oven cooking bags. The directions will most likely suggest you coat your oven cooking bag with flour before adding your turkey. After marinating your turkey for 18 to 24 hours, place in a new large or turkey size oven

Kelly's Marinated Wild Turkey continued

cooking bag, (make sure you have a partner to help with this transfer or you may end up with "turkey on the floor" instead of "in the bag") and add ¼ to ½ cup of water and 1 to 2 tablespoons of flour; then toss to coat bird. Place back in metal or aluminum roasting pan. Tie off the end of cooking bag with twist tie provided and with a knife cut 6 to 8 (½-inch) slits in the top of the cooking bag as instructed. Now follow the cooking bag instructions for cooking time. Small bird 8 to 12 pounds not stuffed 1½ to 2 hours or large turkey not stuffed 3 to 3½ hours is a good estimate, but check your bird several times so as not to overcook and dry it out. Make some store bought turkey gravy to go along with your meal.

Cooking Bag Cooking Tips

We have used this tasty recipe on both small wild and domestic turkeys as well, with tasty and tender success because the cooking bag holds the moisture in while your turkey bakes after being in a delicious marinade. That helps tenderize your bird before and while baking. However, wild turkey, depending on their forge/diet in their habitat and their age, can sometimes, regardless of a marinade or a cooking bag, still be tough and dry according to a couple of my turkey hunting friends. This is the best recipe we have used and it should most always work for your family, too. It makes for a delicious store bought turkey, for sure!

First Gun

IVER JOHNSON
Champion

By Tom Mitchell

By permission of the Pennsylvania Game Commission @ 2000 by the
Pennsylvania Game Commission from *Pennsylvania Game News,* June, 2000 issue.

When learning to shoot, most kids start with a BB gun or a .22 rimfire then graduate to a small bore shotgun. I was an exception, though. My first gun was an old Iver Johnson Champion 16-gauge single-shot. Oh, I had borrowed a single-shot .22, and had fired a friend's BB gun hundreds of times, so for a young man I felt that I was adequately acquainted with firearms to make my first gun "a man's gun."

Part-time jobs in those days paid rather well, and I managed to earn as much as 50 cents an hour. After a summer of bailing hay and cutting a neighbor's lawn, I had managed to put aside the staggering sum of $12. With this small but hard-earned fortune, I was able to purchase my shotgun. Actually, a 16-gauge would not have been my first choice; a 12-gauge would have been more to my liking. But at the pawnshop where Grandpa and I made my purchase, only two shotguns were in my price range, a 20-gauge and a 16-gauge single-shot. Naturally, I opted for the larger "more powerful" gauge.

Upon learning of my new acquisition, a relative donated a box of shells. I can still remember the brand, Remington-Peters, "high brass" in number 7½ shot. Of course, I was now not only the proud owner of a "big bore" shotgun, I also considered myself somewhat of an expert on guns. After all, I had been reading about them for nearly three years before I owned my own. I knew that the first thing to do with my new shotgun was to pattern it, so I tacked up a few sheets of newspaper on an old fence. I learned a lot from that first shooting session, mainly that my new gun kicked like the proverbial mule. After the first two or three shots my shoulder was bruised

First Gun continued

and battered, but I would never admit it to anyone, not even to myself. Forcing a grin and holding back a grimace, I turned to my grandfather who was overseeing the operation. "That wasn't too bad," I said, "but I'd better not shoot too many shells, gotta save some for hunting, you know."

"Yeah, right," and a wry smile was his only reply.

Hunting season was two months off — a virtual eternity — but at last, opening day arrived. Our party of three flushed four or five pheasants, and I got shooting at two, missing both. I blamed it on the small shot size. "Should have had 6s" I said. Several weeks and about 20 or so shells later, I connected on not one, but two birds in the same day. Now I was an expert.

November was progressing rapidly and the opening day of deer season was quickly approaching. I couldn't afford to buy a deer rifle, and I tried, in vain, to borrow one. "Use your old shotgun and 'punkin' balls'" a relative suggested. So, with the last of my savings I bought a box of slugs. Drawing on my deep expertise and vast experience, I knew that a shotgun shooting slugs could be an effective, although a short range firearm. I also reasoned that the lack of a rear sight would make aiming difficult, but I was determined to get a deer with my all-around, "game-getter" shotgun.

After punishing my shoulder by firing 10 or so slugs at a makeshift target, I managed to get a few of the slugs to actually print on the cardboard; two were even close to the bullseye. A few more "make sure" shots left me with five shells, more than enough to bag one deer I reasoned. I was ready.

When a few school chums and a relative or two heard that I would be hunting with a full choke, single-shot 16-gauge shotgun — one without a rear sight, no less, I received plenty of guffaws and outright laughter. Perhaps that was good, because the ridicule made me more determined than ever to bag my first deer.

My plan was simple. I would hunt in an old swamp near my grandparents' farm. I had trapped the swamp for the past two seasons and knew that the nearly impenetrable 4-acre tract was loaded with deer. An older relative assured me that deer don't live in such places, but if I wanted to waste my time by going there, I was welcome to do so. He added insult to injury by suggesting that if I had a "regular" deer rifle, he might consider letting me accompany him on his annual deer hunting pilgrimage to Potter County. I mumbled an insincere "thank you," and excused myself.

At 5 a.m. the old alarm clock jangled for no more than a second, and I rocketed from my warm bed, pulling on my socks and jeans, oblivious to the room's chill.

First Gun continued

After wolfing down a quick breakfast, I headed out over frosty, snow covered fields to my deer laden swamp.

First light, I shrugged and shivered inside my canvas hunting coat, a treasured hand-me-down that only a true "deer hunting expert" would wear, and tried to ward off the bone-chilling cold.

It was well past daybreak, but no sun appeared in the overcast sky to warm my shivering body. Then I heard it. The soft crunching of what had to be deer hooves. Suddenly, out of a stand of thick brush, three, perhaps four doe moved ghost-like over patches of snow covered land and delicately clicked-clacked their way across a narrow channel covered with ice.

I held my breath for fear they would see my frosty exhaling, then they disappeared as quickly as they had appeared. Was this an apparition? A dream? Then I heard more crunching coming my way, but from only one deer. A buck? Yes, there he was in all his glory, sporting a magnificent set of spikes.

Despite shaking so bad that I nearly dropped my gun, I eased it up to my shoulder and cocked the hammer. At the click, the buck stopped and cast a suspicious look that bore a hole right through me. He was a scant 20 feet away. I think I fired. At least I remember a dull roar and being momentarily blinded by an orange flame that blazed out of the muzzle. When I recovered from unfelt recoil, the buck was nowhere to be seen. How could he vanish so quickly? Then I saw a faint movement in the spot where he had stood. A leg flailed in the air, then another. Reload! I thought. Shoot him again! But there was no need. My prize lay still on a sheet of ice. The "expert" hunter had connected with his first buck.

In the days that followed, I delighted in recounting my adventure — and in giving my best deer hunting advice to my older but "deerless" relative who had gone north. For some reason he never invited me on a Potter County deer hunt, even when I did have my first "regular" deer rifle. And with all the hindsight of a young man, I reasoned that this deer hunting was easy — but only if you're an expert.

Now that I'm a wee bit older (wiser, too), I no longer consider deer hunting to be easy. And with each passing season I come to the realization that perhaps I'm somewhat less of an expert than I was back then. However, each hunt, successful or not, is just as exciting and memorable as that first hunt in 1956 — well, almost.

In Memory of Sherman

Welcome to Dick's Mississippi Duck Camp
This was my first and it turned out unfortunately to be my last opportunity to hunt waterfowl with Dick Lind and his favorite hunting partner, a Labrador retriever named Sherman. Upon arriving at the state park cabin in Hollendale, Mississippi I could easily see Dick's sign on the side of the door of cabin number three. It read, "Welcome to Dick's Duck Camp. So This Isn't Home Sweet Home, You Will Have to Adjust." Our chosen camp cook expects all of us to be enjoying fresh duck gumbo by tomorrow night. Need we say more? Don't miss a shot because good shootin' always means a welcome back to our duck camp.

Thank goodness Sherman was a good dog this night in 1986, and despite his coming to visit me in my bed during the night I still got a good night's sleep. Walking in a Mississippi mud rice field the next morning I would need all my energy. Been there, Steve.

Photo of Sherman's last hunt: December 1994 Sherman and Dick's young lab they were starting to train to follow Sherman's hunting lead on the Mississippi delta. Even good to great dogs don't live forever. Mary Lind, Dick's wife, said that Sherman died of heart failure, but he is a very special animal memory in their life and always will be! Sherman died September 9, 1996 at the age of twelve and Dick and Mary agree that he was one of their best friends!!

In Memory of Sherman continued

Because of God's guiding hand, it is funny how life's circumstances happen. After lunch on a Friday in December, 1986, together Dick and I would be packing our waterfowl gear and guns to hunt ducks on Dick's leased flooded field in Hollandale, Mississippi. While gearing up, Sherman, Dick's Labrador retriever was the most eager first one in the car.

As we drove from Vicksburg, Mississippi north to Hollendale where we would spend the night in the Department of Parks and Recreation cabin, I noticed the endless miles of flat highway almost without other traffic of any kind. Sherman was a good dog, lying patiently on his doggie blanket in the back seat. It was a blue sky afternoon but we both talked about our hopes to "get into the wild ducks" some that afternoon before dark and especially early Saturday morning when other duck hunters would be out to keep the ducks moving in the Mississippi River delta. This was my first Mississippi flyway duck hunt. I was a born and raised east coast Atlantic flyway waterfowl hunter for over thirty years. Waterfowl hunting has always been an early morning thrill for me - especially seeing the sun rise as mother nature wakes up above and around me.

When we finally got checked into our cabin we unloaded our hunting gear in a hurry because the sooner you are in any duck blind the better. Sherman was the first one of us to climb into Dick's 1965 International Scout with bus seats in the back where Sherman could ride until we would nearly reach our duck blind. You could easily tell from Sherman's excited behavior that he knew it was soon time "to duck hunt."

As usual, even in the Mississippi delta on a blue sky day the duck hunting was very slow despite all of our expectations and heavenly pleading. Finally, just before dark, we had a lone duck coming in to Dick's calling and Dick said, "I want you to take'm and I will say when to stand and take it." Time stood still until Dick said "take'm" and then I fired three duck loads and missed the first and only male pintail duck that I had ever seen. At closing time we walked back to the Scout without a duck for Sherman or for us. We hopefully talked about tomorrow morning, certainly giving us a better duck hunt. We knew that "Sherman" was certainly all for more ducks coming to his "retrieving" way.

After a hot shower we went to a local restaurant in Greenwood, Mississippi that served the largest beef steaks that I had ever seen and it tasted great, too. We met up with Dick's personal friend, Chuck Cage, so we had a visit. Knowing we planned to duck hunt in the morning and Chuck owed Dick a couple of favors, Chuck offered to take us to one of his guided blinds and do the expert duck calling needed for us on Saturday morning. Dick said, "sure thing and we will pick you up at your house at 5:00 A.M."

In Memory of Sherman continued

By 10:00 Friday night Dick and I were talking about getting some "shut eye" and Dick said, it's OK if you want to set an alarm, but I have a clock in my head and I will wake you around 4:00 A.M., give or take a couple of minutes." "OK with me but how is "Sherman" overnight?" "He is quiet and he will curl up on the bed with me, I'm sure." Sometime before hunting time Sherman wanted to try my bed out and curled up with me. That was OK since I knew we were hunting buddies.

Sure enough, Dick's mental clock went off and he got up just before my alarm went off. He and Sherman walking around the "cold cabin" easily woke me. After jumping into my hunting clothes for fear of frost bite (only kidding) I turned my alarm off and was gathering up my hunting gear. It was easy to see that Dick and faithful Sherman had been through hunt preparations before and I was not keeping up. Dick went out to <u>cold start</u> the Scout which proved to be difficult. Before I knew it we were all in this frosted over rugged hunting vehicle that finally started. "I sure hope I have everything for this hunt," I thought, as we hit the smooth hard top road. You could not see lights anywhere.

Chuck was ready and waiting, in fact, when we pulled into his driveway. He spoke very confidently about being able to call ducks into one of his more successful guided blinds for us that morning. This Atlantic flyway, "Yankee" was really excited about this "good waterfowl news."

Even in Dick's Scout we arrived at Chuck's blind location off a dike surrounding the flooded rice field well before daylight. Chuck already had his duck decoys out, so following Sherman's enthusiasm we all settled into the duck blind. Although it was very cold when daylight came it was another "bluebird" clear sky, windless start of the day. Chuck was a very good and relentless duck caller so between Dick and me we managed to take three or four mallards in a few hours. You could see how Sherman really liked his opportunities to retrieve even those few ducks for us. With blue sky conditions and very few ducks, by mid-morning we were calling it quits and thinking about a big breakfast. Never the less, our morning with mother nature was full of story telling and the country's problem solving, so we made a lasting memory together.

"Let's go get breakfast," we agreed. Now that is when it happened to me. When leaving the blind for the Scout my hip boots got stuck in the "MISSISSIPPI MUD" of this rice field. Before I knew it one hip boot was sucked off and I was about to fall on my face in two feet of cold water. With the air temperature about 30 degrees that was not an acceptable option. Anyway, the other boot got stuck, too, and the only way out was barefoot. When Dick and Chuck saw me arrive at the Scout there were lots of questions, kidding and laughter at this Atlantic flyway duck jump shooter. No harm done, so let's go <u>eat</u>!

In Memory of Sherman continued

That turned out to be all the good news of the day because when we got to the nearest restaurant our faithful retriever, Sherman, was not in the back of the Scout. So after a fast breakfast we all went back to look for him in the delta, but could not find him.

Dick recalls the details of the search for Sherman, even after all these years. And it went like this; "We looked for him for two days without a sign of him. I put my hunting jacket out there for him as the nights were below freezing. In the morning there were dog tracks around the coat, but no Sherman. We went to all the neighbors, but no one had seen him. Fearing that someone had picked him up, I returned home to grieve. Four days later I got a phone call from my buddy, Mitch, who had found him in the field. He had been sleeping in some hay bales, and was very leery about coming to him. Sherman must have tangled with a skunk and got sprayed which made him disoriented, because he stunk real bad and was filthy. It took two gallons of tomato juice rubbed into him to get the smell out. It didn't matter, I was very happy to get him back."

Sherman continued to faithfully waterfowl hunt for Dick, Mitch and other friends from 1986 to December of 1994. In 1996 he passed after heart failure. He was a valued friend to many people and was twelve years old. Out of respect for Sherman he was cremated and his ashes were saved in an urn that is now on Dick and his wife, Mary's fireplace mantle; never to be forgotten.

Dick recently sent me a 1994 photograph of himself, Sherman, and one of a pair of new labs they own named Nickie. Nickie is now a house dog and Dick is waterfowl hunting with a yellow lab named Sam.

After this inspirational story, let's hear it for God blessing us all with a love of the great outdoors, the friends, dogs and the waterfowl that make our outdoor experiences possible. Memories, it does not get any better than this!! Thanks Dick and Sherman...

You will not want this freshly made stew to leave your house. You may be tempted to share it with friends and/or relatives, but we guarantee it probably won't last long enough. We suggest doubling the recipe if you are preparing it for dinner guests.

Dick and Sherman's Duck Camp Stew

1½-2	pounds wild duck breasts, cubed small (2 ducks) and legs removed	1	(15 to 16-ounce) can diced tomatoes
2-3	cloves fresh garlic, diced	2	teaspoons any prepared mustard
½	cup chopped onion	1	teaspoon sugar
½	cup chopped green onion	1	teaspoon parsley flakes
1	teaspoon salt	½	green pepper, thinly sliced
½	teaspoon black pepper	1	(15-ounce) can of your favorite beans
1	cup pepper sauce or salsa	1	(12-ounce) can beer or 1½ cups water
½	teaspoon chili powder		

With a sharp knife remove the back meat, breasts, and legs of two large puddle ducks and add to your 4 to 5-quart crockpot. Add diced garlic, chopped onions, salt, black pepper, and pepper sauce or salsa. Stir well. Now add your remaining ingredients except the beans and beer and water and stir again. Cook your stew on high for 2 hours or so. Add the can of beans and beer or water and stir. Cook another 2 to 3 hours until even the duck legs are tender. Everyone can enjoy this dish in bowls with bread as is or you can stretch it by serving it over rice or noodles cooked to package directions or just add buttered Idaho or sweet potatoes to compliment your meal.

If you do not have 2 wild ducks you can substitute 2 pounds of cubed venison stew meat and still enjoy our recipe.

My long time friend, Dick Lind, grew up hunting in the cold, wintry state of Wisconsin, much like my home state of lake effect, wintry New York. As tradition would have it, Dick's corporate career relocated him south to Mississippi, but his heart is still into going home to deer hunt with family and friends. This is my tradition, too, so this recipe is dedicated to my friend, Dick, because it is so - so good!!

Dick's "Southern Style" Venison Hindquarter

1	large or turkey size plastic cooking bag for roasting
1	hindquarter of deer, (10 to 12 pounds), shank (end of leg) removed
1½	cups creamy or regular Italian salad dressing
½	cup soy sauce
½	cup Worcestershire sauce
1	tablespoon parsley flakes
1½	tablespoons black pepper
4-5	cloves fresh garlic, diced
1	teaspoon cayenne (hot) pepper, (optional)
2	cups of a good Burgundy wine, (not cooking wine)
4	ounces jalapeño (hot) or mild green chili peppers, chopped or sliced
1-1½	cups chopped fresh green onions

Mix all the above marinade ingredients, except the venison hindquarter, in a bowl. Place your venison in a large container or roasting pan and pour marinade mixture over it, turning it several times to thoroughly coat the venison. Cover and marinate for 18 to 24 hours in your refrigerator, turning occasionally. When ready to bake your hindquarter, preheat your oven to 325 degrees. Meanwhile, coat your roasting bag with flour, following instructions on the box, and place the bag in a large turkey size roaster or store bought aluminum turkey size roasting pan. Then place your venison in the bag, pouring the marinade over the venison. Use the twist tie that came with the cooking bag to close the bag up and cut 6 to 8 (½-inch) slits in the bag, or according to the directions on the box. Bake for 2½ to 3 hours or until venison is tender. All deer are not created equal depending on state and diet. Add preferred vegetable side dishes and enjoy! <u>Delicious</u>! So write to tell us how you liked it.

It Was To Be Ella's Last Buck - 1987

I Just Happened to Photograph This Precious Memory...

Ella that evening was still excited and took time to pose with her dandy 10 point buck. Best she had taken in a long time. It was to be her last. Maybe it was "meant" to be that I missed that nice buck!

OK, so I was the only deer hunter that was enthusiastic enough about the outdoors and the deer hunting experience to carry my camera in my hunting coat, or at least in my car. That is why after helping my buddy, Rog, drag his deer and his mom's even bigger 10 point (that I had missed), I photographed Rog in the dry edge of the Arliss triangle with the two "fat" farm fed bucks. We were three very happy deer hunters!

With another job promotion it caused our family to relocate from Meridian, Mississippi to a northern suburb of Philadelphia, Pennsylvania, called Lansdale, in mid-summer 1987. The new sales job would certainly prove to be a challenge, but I had not hunted waterfowl or deer with the Arliss family and crew in nine years, so this relocation would give me a chance to enjoy my hunting hobby with old friends, once again.

With our young daughter, Kelly, with us, after months of preparation, on the week-end before Thanksgiving we made the drive from Lansdale, Pennsylvania to Clyde, New York. We would be staying with Mom and Dad Loder while I tried to tag a deer of either sex for our family's freezer. On Saturday we visited with Mom,

It Was To Be Ella's Last Buck continued

Dad, and my sisters. Sunday after Catholic mass and a quick pasta meal we visited Bill and Ella Arliss at their legendary farmhouse. Then it was off to visit our best of friends, Rog and Polly Arliss.

It was four years since our families last saw each other, so we had plenty to talk about, not to mention Rog's well conceived plan for us to put some fresh corn/ alfalfa fed whitetail venison in our freezers.

All Rog would say about tomorrow's opening day was "dress for our cold and windy weather and mom, (Ella Arliss), will be hunting with us at daylight down at the end of the triangle." Both Rog and I had taken bucks at the end of the triangle shaped woods on their farm years earlier, so all three of us could do it again.

After an, as usual restless night's sleep anticipating the opening day's deer hunting, the alarm blasted me out of bed at 5:30 in the morning. Because all my gear was all checked, rechecked, and packed the night before, with coffee and pizza in hand I was out the door in thirty minutes. Hunters of all kinds know this as "the drill."

At Bill and Ella's farm house just after 6:00 in the morning, Rog, over a second cup of coffee, described his shotgun opening morning's deer hunt for Ella, Rog, and me. With flashlights in hand the three of us would walk the tow path, a dike that separates the old Erie Canal from the swampy Arliss woods they called the triangle. "Hunting pressure from a neighboring farm land owner was sure to push whitetails our way by noon time," Rog claimed. "If we don't get our bucks by noon let's all meet on the tow path and go in for a lunch of Steve's duck gumbo, previously provided by his successful waterfowl hunting on the farm last month. Then we can make a new plan with our crew putting on some drives, as usual before we sit on watch until dark."

Walking the tow path with flashlights in hand, it was cold, windy and ready to snow at anytime. What else is new in the lake effect finger lakes area of New York during the deer season, and before the season is over it is likely to get worse. New York shotgun deer season is not for the fair weather deer hunter, for sure.

Rog dropped me off at the tow path at 6:30 that morning and into the (swampy) triangle first, with positioning instructions. He said because of Ella's health limitations she would be sitting or standing on the tow path 50 to 75 yards between us. Ella had landowner deer tags for either sex so she wanted her Ithaca Model 37 pump to once

It Was To Be Ella's Last Buck continued

again take a deer for her. Ella had always been a good, safe, successful deer hunter. It must "be in the Arliss family genes" to be a good shot when it comes to deer.

Rog went off the tow path and into the triangle (swamp) 75 yards or so below his mother like he put me to the north. The plan was to take our chances and sit until noon before regrouping for lunch. After my being gone for years, all the day break shotgun slug fire from near and far was familiar "music" to my ears. Optimistically I was hunting for a buck only.

As daylight became brighter, the lake effect winds and light snow slowly picked up so you would have to see deer moving because you certainly would not be able to hear them coming. Shotguns were firing near and far constantly until just after 8:30 in the morning. Then here came the deer!!

After hearing Rog fire his Ithaca 37 one time there was a pause before I saw four deer out thirty and forty yards from me, so I aimed at a nice buck with good horns, for the Arliss farm, and waited for him to hit a clearing before firing my 12-gauge Ithaca Deerslayer. There was only time for one shot and it was a miss. Then the four deer turned and ran toward a waiting Ella who had a bird's eye elevated view from the tow path.

Now Ella was in her mid-sixties then, so with years of experience we could only hope she dropped that nice buck. We heard her shotgun go off and after a pause it went off again. After about thirty minutes Rog came walking through the swampy triangle woods to tell me he had a fat six point down and field dressed. I told him I missed a nice buck after he shot, so it was time to check with Ella.

As we made our way through the swampy "triangle woods" toward Ella we talked about it being 10:00 in the morning and that it was finally getting warmer. As we sloshed our way toward Ella on the tow path we could see her waving her arms with relative excitement. It's no wonder.

She motioned to us where to look for her deer. It was not hard to find, considering its size and antlers, even in the swampy cover. I am sure glad I had my camera to photograph Rog's buck and Ella's last whitetail buck, together! It was a deer hunt that we three shared and will never be forgotten. Deer hunting is a tradition that all of us who love being in God's great outdoors should share with people young and old who mean the most to us. Deer Hunting! In other words, making another fond outdoor memory.

I asked Ella Arliss, (my "other" mom), if she would like to contribute a favorite wild game recipe of hers that would appear in our third wild game cookbook. In a joint effort and after a sampling, it is below for all deer camp hunters or family and friends to enjoy year after year. This delicious, taste tested favorite is very hard to beat. Enjoy, to say the very least!!

Ella Arliss' "Farm House" Venison Steak with Gravy and Fresh Mushrooms

1	(16-ounce) package egg noodles, cooked to package directions	2-3	packages instant mushroom gravy, prepared to package directions
2½-3	pounds venison round steak, sliced thin	1½	teaspoons dried minced garlic or garlic powder
1½	cups flour		
2-3	sticks real butter, (1 to 1½ cups)	3	cups sliced fresh mushrooms
1½	teaspoons each salt and black pepper	1	cup water and 3 tablespoons flour, mixed in a cup - blend and add more water if needed
1½	cups chopped fresh onion		

Cook egg noodles to package directions, drain and set aside in your pan. In a brown paper or plastic bread bag add ½ of your venison steak, that is thinly sliced and cut into 2 x 4-inch small cutlets, and ½ of the flour and shake well to coat. Next, in a large saucepan or what is known as the Dutch oven add butter, salt and pepper, and sweet onion. Stir and add venison steak cutlets from bag. While browning for 10 minutes or so, stir occasionally. Add remaining venison steak cutlets and flour to your shaker bag and toss to coat remaining venison well; add to your Dutch oven; stir and brown another 10 minutes stirring occasionally so as not to stick. If sticking, turn down heat and scrape the pan since it will add good gravy flavor to your dinner. Add water if needed. Then add 2 to 3 packages of instant gravy of choice after preparing to package directions, plus dried minced garlic or garlic powder and mushrooms. To 1 cup water add 3 tablespoons of flour in a small bowl, and blend well. Pour into your Dutch oven or large saucepan over venison and vegetables. Then mix and cover; simmer slowly for 20 to 30 minutes and check to stir and see if pan could use more water and flour for gravy. Simmer your venison slowly for 10 to 15 minutes more so it comes out tender and moist with plenty of gravy. Serve very hot over your cooked noodles. It's guaranteed delicious.

Ella Arliss' "Farm House" Venison Steak continued

Ella Arliss tells me her country style cooking tip secret to tasty spicy that makes her tender venison steak so "hunter good" is to add ½ teaspoon of black pepper per each pound of venison steak. It adds zest without the hot red pepper bite. Ella will tell you that if you processed your deer yourself or if you knew a butcher you could trust to do a great processing job on "your deer," this is a truly cannot miss recipe for anyone to enjoy, even without wine or other beverages of influence. The secret is the black pepper spice... I can remember after eating some of her tender venison steak with gravy and mushrooms for the first time over thirty years ago that it was a good thing "Chippy" stopped Ella's deer so we could have her tasty steak again for lunch on the next deer season's opening day!

"Gotta Have It"

We recently spoke with an outdoors writer from the Johnstown, Pennsylvania Tribune Review, Tom Lavis. He and a few of his other deer hunting friends get together weekly for a coffee and story telling social. Tom introduced all his family and friends, including his boys, who are serious deer hunters, to our easy to use <u>Quality Venison</u> cookbooks. During one of these get togethers at an elderly friend's house Tom noticed there were copies of each of the <u>Quality Venison</u> cookbooks, that he had previously given to his friend and his wife a while before, sitting out on the table. Tom asked about the books and he said, "the wife and I have read them from cover to cover and have really enjoyed the deer tales. The recipes are so easy to fix that whenever we have venison, and that is at least once a week, we use those <u>Quality Venison</u> cookbooks." Thanks Tom, for sharing that with us.

It Was Ella's Deer Tale To Tell

"This Proves She's An Honest Woman"

Nearing the completion of our manuscript of recipes and deer hunting tales from years gone by, that would ultimately be published in our third *Quality Venison* cookbook, we thought to contact our life long friend, Ella Arliss. After years and years of deer hunting experience with "the annual crew of deer hunters" on their farm there must be a special tale "she would like to tell," one and all deer hunters. So here is your chance to <u>listen</u> up to it!!

It was to be a memorable first Saturday of a deer season long gone by. We all met in the Arliss farmhouse kitchen for coffee, donuts and tales at 6:00 in the morning. College had me still living in the upstate New York area and since I had not filled my buck tag as yet I was back with our crew to put a fresh supply of nutritious venison in my freezer.

After everyone had listened to Ella's deer tales or events of the past week, we all decided where we would sit on watch until returning for our anticipated morning's deer drives. Ella and her friend "Chippy" chose stands along a hedgerow that traditionally separated two large corn fields on the Arliss farm. Permission was given to me to hunt from the "old deer stand" at the very west end of the field that was always planted with corn or alfalfa. By 6:30 in the morning our crew was heading in all directions for their early morning deer watch, so with both buck and doe tags being plentiful, most of us should have an opportunity, as they say to "put the meat in the freezer," whether for ourselves or for an area food bank to feed the needy.

By first daylight the lake effect winds started blowing snow from the usual cloudy skies, and the Canadian geese and ducks were flying everywhere overhead. I was dressed for these mid-twenty degree windy conditions, so I thought. College kids know everything, don't they? They are expected to, so after years of study they do think "they know everything." After just an hour and a half in that windy tree, even I was cold as could be. My <u>visions</u> of deer hunting success were diminished greatly, to say the least. "Just where is the extra blanket I should have brought? Maybe a wind breaker?" I thought to myself, "it was a cold lesson learned."

From my cold tree perch both Ella and Chippy, even though over a hundred yards away, were visible to me. Shivering, I checked my watch to see if it was time to head to the warmth of my car and the camp woodstove at the farm. It was 8:00 in the morning and suddenly I heard shotgun slugs from Ella and Chippy's end of the hedgerow, so the hair on the back of my neck stood up in excitement. Thinking the deer they might miss could come within range of my stand, I readied for my opportunity to take a whitetail of either sex.

It Was Ella's Deer Tale To Tell continued

Ella, who had years of deer hunting success must have been having a "bad hair day" or maybe was frozen up, because she fired five times at the big doe and huge buck that crossed the cornfield in front of her and eventually, Chippy. Chippy then shot one slug and there was just a moment of silence before the big racked buck that had gotten by them came up over the hilly cornfield that I was watching.

I aimed, but better judgment prevailed and I decided not to take this long shot with a deer slug. This beautiful whitetail buck had slipped by two seasoned deer hunters and was running "full tilt" at over one hundred yards toward the dense swamp hunted by a neighboring hunting club. Despite wishful thinking, all that I could do was watch that wall hanger buck to run off to better days ahead.

A half an hour later I climbed down from my cold, windy deer stand and managed to meet up with Ella and Chippy. Sure, the big buck separated from his mature doe and skillfully managed to run another day, but the large, farm fed and field dressed doe lay in front of Chippy's ground blind near what was known as "the big oak tree."

Their story was, Ella had emptied her Ithaca Model 37, 20-gauge, at both deer as they ran together across the cornfield when they were fifty yards and closing between her and "deadeye" Chippy. Ella's last slug knocked down the big doe, but it was frantically trying to get up just twenty yards away. Ella did not want to lose this deer so she frantically searched her pockets for a slug to finish the deer. Then she found one, put it in the chamber, and pumped the magazine closed. After careful aim at the struggling deer she fired and only heard a firing pin click as "a tube of chap stick lip protector" fell from her shotgun barrel and onto the ground. Then the doe managed to get to her feet and ever so slowly ran off down the hedgerow toward "deadeye" Chippy. *(Can you believe Ella really told us this??) No problem for Chippy to hit it in the vitals one time. Don't know how the other crew hunters did, but we had one nice deer's venison on the meat pole that night. Ella and Chippy were so busy that they never did see the big buck get away, so I had to fill them in on the rest of the story of how the big buck, again, got away.

*God has blessed us because we have hunted safely, ethically and respectfully for the whitetail deer for over thirty years on the Arliss farm.

OK, yes we do pride ourselves in trying to taste test and give the wild game buyers of our cookbooks "the product of choice," based on our years of cooking and hunting experience. This taste-tested recipe is no different and is again <u>exceptional</u>. But our crockpot is a <u>hot one</u> and your cooking time could be different, so judge on experience. This recipe is named after my best friend and the best man in my wedding, Rog Arliss, because I know how much he likes a lot of flavorful wild game food. I made this recipe 12/6/01 and I will bring this to the farm for opening day of deer gun season 2002 for all our hunting crew to enjoy. Mom Arliss, here is looking at you, dear... No need to cook for us after all these years! Now it's our turn to cook for you!

Rog's Favorite "Slow Cooked" Venison Chili Soup

1	pound bacon, diced small	¼	cup brown sugar
1½-2	pounds venison stew meat, cubed small	1	(10 to 15-ounce) can stewed tomatoes, spicy or regular
½	of a (7¾-ounce) can jalapeño peppers, chopped (hot), or 1 cup jalapeño pepper sauce	1	cup red wine, catsup or salsa, or a combination
1½	cups chopped green onions	2	(15 to 16-ounce) cans chili beans in sauce
2-3	garlic cloves, diced	1	cup of "our" barbecue sauce in *Quality Venison II* or even store bought barbecue sauce if pressed for time
1	(10¼-ounce) can mushroom soup with a soup can of water added		
2	teaspoons chili powder	8	ounces fresh mushrooms, sliced

Spray your crockpot bowl with non-stick cooking spray for easy clean-up. Add bacon, venison, jalapeño peppers or pepper sauce, green onions, garlic, and mushroom soup with a can of water and stir crockpot well. Add all remaining ingredients and again stir well. Cover crockpot and cook on high for 4 to 5 hours or on low 6 to 8 hours. Enjoy for sure !! We guarantee not much of the meal makes it to your freezer even though it makes <u>4</u> quarts. Pass the rolls or buttered garlic bread, please...

A Duck Hunt I Remember Very Well

Wow, it was nice getting a corporate transfer back to the northeast so that we could be close enough to waterfowl and deer hunt with the Arliss family and hunting crew after years of being away. This experience of jump shooting puddle ducks for hours was memorable. I wish a youngster was there with me.

As work would have it, a promotion brought our family back from the Mississippi deep south to Philadelphia, Pennsylvania in the spring of 1987. "Settling in" was not easy or cheap for our family and my new account manager position was very challenging. By October of 1987 I was ready for a work break vacation, so when the waterfowl season came in I was headed to the Arliss family farm once again. After years of living in the south and not being able to hunt waterfowl or deer on their familiar territory without excessive traveling, the waterfowl were "calling me back."

I was looking forward to jump shooting the Arliss farm's streams for puddle ducks of all kinds for the first time in four or five years. Larry, Rog Arliss, and I met at our local high school football game on Friday night after my five hour drive up from Philadelphia, Pennsylvania. We all played high school football together as well as other sports, so it was great that Clyde Savannah Golden Eagles won the game. Our plan was to meet at the Arliss family farmhouse at 6:00 in the morning for coffee and tales of every sort and then be sitting, camouflaged around one of their cow ponds for the would be incoming feeding mallards at daylight.

Well, I remember I thought about setting my alarm and reminded my mom to wake me if she happened to be up at 6:00 so I could go get those "long lost ducks." At 6:30 dad had left to open the restaurant and mom called up to me from downstairs, "Steve, are you going duck hunting?" Wow, in dreamland or not I flew out of bed, jumped into my camo clothes and into the car and off I went. When I reached the pond at about 7:00 that morning, it was just daylight and Rog and Larry were already

A Duck Hunt I Remember Very Well continued

taking shots at incoming feeding mallards. In camo I sat and joined them on the west side of the farm pond. A cool morning rain was falling, but who cares? It is time to shoot challenging puddle ducks for the dinner table! You cannot buy wild ducks at the grocery store.

For the next hour or so we all had occasional easy and sometimes challenging duck shots. After the early feeding activity Larry had taken one mallard drake and a hen, Rog took a mallard drake and I took a mallard hen. Larry and Rog took their ducks and mine back to the farm house because they had urgent work to do. They said I was welcome to hunt the Old Erie Canal or other sloughs that I was familiar with on the farm because no one else was supposed to be duck hunting that day. Can you even imagine that? This good of a chance to hunt waterfowl and no one was going to be out hunting with me?

Rog and Larry took my one duck and theirs to the house and I, despite a lightly falling rain with a temperature in the low forties took up my Ithaca Model 51 shotgun and walked off to jump shoot puddle ducks along the Old Erie Canal. Because of the wet grass along the dike against the canal, hunting these ducks would be like "still hunting deer," and my being very quiet would be relatively easy.

Even though I was silent and careful with every step and every look over the dike and into a pool of water, the ducks on two occasions sensed my approach. On one approach while creeping to the edge of the canal a number of wood ducks sensed me coming and flew off before I could even get a shot. "I do not know how I could have been more quiet," I thought "what did I do wrong?" Jump shooting is a duck hunting learning experience, for sure, every time out!

Meanwhile, I continued my jump shooting duck search. The rain continued to drizzle but with my waterproof poncho and camo gloves, too, I was comfortable and in "my element" in God's great outdoors. What a great time to be in the woods. Just me against the ducks…

As I approached yet another pool in the Old Erie Canal I was creeping really carefully to the dike's edge and saw nothing. Then I backed away to the dike's vehicle trail and at that moment two black ducks erupted into flight from a little pool. They were behind me now and in an instant they were flying through the trees and I could not react to make a good shot, so I did not shoot. They beat me and that will happen in hunting all kinds of God's wild game. With good health there will be a next challenging opportunity for me.

A Duck Hunt I Remember Very Well continued

The sun broke through some that morning, but the light rain continued off and on as my hunt along the Old Erie continued. I thought, "darn, I had hoped to mount a beautiful black duck one day and I had missed my rare opportunity. It was not meant to be today." Within a few minutes, despite my slow and quiet stalking, I jumped or startled several whitetail deer off into a thicket before they crossed the dike over the Old Erie. They must "have winded me" before I could see them. It was easy to see an obvious deer crossing trail coming up to the dike from the woods, over the dike and through the shallow marsh of the Old Erie. "That is easy," I thought, "this is a route between their wooded bedding area and alfalfa field feeding area on the other side of the Old Erie. Hey, remember this area for a ground watch for deer season, Steve." This bit of deer scouting proved useful just a <u>few weeks later</u>.

After over an hour of jump shooting the Old Erie Canal I was about nearing the end where it crosses a dirt road. I still had no more duck shooting opportunities since the two back ducks got the better of me. My last waterfowl hunting chance would be a pothole at the very end of the canal. So you talk about being careful. Not only slowly creeping, but I was thinking about even belly crawling up to this last duck "honey hole" in hopes of taking a couple of ducks to fill my limit and put my game in my freezer. We just love wild game around our house and anyone we feed does too.

Slowly I slipped into the reeds or cattails, squatting with my Ithaca shotgun safe off and ready. Before I could spot the ducks a pair of mallards flushed from the "honey hole" and because of some shotgun practice and a lot help from God, both of the mallards fell onto the cornfield on the other side of the deep pond after my two shots of non-lead shot.

As my prayers were answered and luck would be there, too, I stuffed two big mallards in my game bag and another mallard would be mine at the Arliss farm house, too. So, despite the rain, God's mother nature was good to me on this water-fowl adventure. Oh, thanks Rog and Larry Arliss for giving me your ducks to add to my game bag because they said they could duck hunt some more and I could not. That's friends for you!

It is a real shame that a youngster or two could not have been with me on this rainy waterfowling morning. Please take a youngster waterfowling in order to possibly carry on this valuable hunting tradition. Let's always remember to give thanks to God for the wildlife bounty we hunt from the great outdoors because the wildlife is deliciously nutritious for our families and friends, too.

<u>Sometimes</u> "Bird Huntin' Ain't Easy"

Hunting or outdoors' friendships are very easy to maintain. A lifetime memory is made each and every time you spend time with a friend in the outdoors. A perfect example is a pheasant hunt I went on with my friend Jerry Molettiere. After many changes in both of our lives over the ten years since we last spoke, when I called Jerry to tell him Gale and I were writing yet a third book of hunting tales and wild game recipes, he said without hesitation, "congratulations on your previous two books' sales success. Hey, I had the picture of our pheasant hunt together enlarged and it has been hanging on the wall in my barber shop all this time, and by the way, did you ever learn to shoot yet?" Jerry was kind enough to send a copy of that picture so we could include it with this tale. Jerry is on the left, Steve on the right, and "Maggie" is in between. Our pheasant tale will tell you more.

Jerry's and my one and only bird hunt together was ten years ago, so when I was going through my hunters' journal and wanted to write a tale about our pheasant hunt together before I was relocated because of my job, I had to call Jerry Molettiere for some of the hunt's details. Jerry picked up the phone the evening of my call to him. Jerry said he was glad to hear from me. After asking me where I was working now, his next question was, "have you learned how to shoot yet?" That is an inside joke between us. He knows better.

It all started with my winning a door prize of a guided and bird dog supplied pheasant hunt for two at a local game farm. I asked Jerry, my barber and friend in Lansdale, Pennsylvania to come with me, and he gladly accepted. Our date was set and our plans were made. I would be picking him up at seven thirty on the following Saturday morning.

Sometimes "Bird Huntin' Ain't Easy" continued

Our directions were good from our game farm guide, so we did not have any trouble finding the farm on time. So far, so good, and the hard part would lie ahead. Jack, our guide and dog handler met us at the kennel to secure Maggie, a German shorthair who would "hunt" the pheasants for us this morning. If we recall correctly, Jack had released our eight pheasants out into four different fields hours earlier that morning. Jerry made a comment about the beautiful fall morning, as we were leaving the truck to unleash our dog, "Maggie." She should have been named "Maggie May" after the song by singer Rod Stewart because Maggie's mood for "misbehaven" was a constant problem throughout our three hour hunt, despite Jack's constant reprimands.

Jerry had been shooting trap and skeet regularly and was constantly involved in Montgomery County gun club activities because he was born and raised in the Philadelphia area. Jerry would be shooting a semi automatic Remington 12-gauge and my shotgun would be an Ithaca Model 100 12-gauge double barrel. It is a shame that some outdoor TV show was not on site to film the shooting portion of this hunt. The program would have been titled the "Jerry and Steve Pheasant Hunting Show."

The real problem was with Jack and his relentless attempts to handle our dog "Maggie." He was always yelling, begging, pleading with her to do her job. It is a blessing that we were "eventually" able to get each of our eight pheasants to flush. Jerry, not surprisingly, was a great shot and while we always swung our guns to back each other up on each pheasant flush, Jerry did not miss a bird. My trusty Ithaca double barrel with modified and full chokes was right on the birds also, so I took my share despite "Maggie's" misbehaving.

When we were down to taking our last pheasant it was my friend, Jerry's turn to take it and my Ithaca double barrel would have to be there again to back him up. With the work of Jack and Maggie we jumped that cock bird three times, each time out of range. On our fourth try he must have been tired because we flushed it close. By now Jerry and I wanted this "last bird badly." So I fired at the bird and down it went. Minutes later Jerry showed me his spent shotgun shell, too. We both had fired at the rooster at the same time, so it would not have a chance to reproduce another day. Jerry, being the gentleman he is, even gave me our last lucky pheasant. It was worth the effort to take this last bird, and hunting of any kind is always worth the effort for countless reasons. And persistence and patience always pays off whether you are young or old.

*After the game farm hunt with my friend Jerry, I treated my wife,
Gale and myself to a special dinner of pheasant that I took during
this hunt with the help of "Maggie." This meal was delicious so we
recommend you try it soon, even if you do not have a pheasant. Use
a small skinned and boned chicken and it will still be magnificent
for 4 with a vegetable of your choice.*

Jerry's Tasty Upland Birds

Noodles or rice for 4, prepared to package directions

1 pheasant or 2 grouse, skinned, deboned, and thinly sliced

⅓-½ cup olive oil or butter

½ teaspoon garlic powder

½ teaspoon onion powder

½ cup sliced fresh mushrooms

½ teaspoon oregano

½ teaspoon basil

½ cup white or rose wine

1 fresh small tomato, diced

½ cup sour cream

½ teaspoon each salt and black pepper

½ cup shredded Parmesan or mozzarella cheese, optional

Skin and debone a pheasant or 2 grouse by cutting off the legs and removing each breast from the breast bone. Thinly slice the meat. Add olive oil or butter to your large frying pan. Add game bird(s)' meat to your pan and brown over medium heat 10 to 12 minutes or so, stirring constantly. Add garlic powder, onion powder, mushrooms, oregano, and basil seasonings; stir and turn down heat to simmer another 10 minutes. Pour wine over the meat and simmer covered 30 to 45 minutes until game is tender. While game is simmering take a small saucepan and add tomato, sour cream, salt and pepper; stir well and simmer 10 minutes to cook tomatoes. Set aside while game is simmering and add to pan of game when the game is tender; stir well. Add to plates of prepared noodles or rice. Add fresh shredded Parmesan or mozzarella cheese as a delicious topper for this meal, although the cheese is optional. A good Chardonnay is a pleasant wine of choice to compliment this special meal for family or friends.

Finally A Canadian Goose Success - 1988

It Only Took Me 20 Years!!

Yes, after chasing unpredictable ducks and Canadian geese for over twenty years and never having taken a goose, this morning's hunt will always be a special outdoors' memory for me and our family. This skinned and quartered goose was very good eating, also. Delicious! Try our recipe, please. Oh, I am proud to say that I took this first goose with my wife, Gale's grandfather's A.H. Fox double barrel 12-gauge shot gun.

When youngsters grow up in the Atlantic Flyway of the Finger Lakes in upstate New York they know the relentless call, both day and night, of wild ducks and Canadian geese each fall and spring, with their migration from north to south in the fall and again in spring from the south to northern breeding grounds in Canada.

At age sixteen after taking my state hunter safety course two years earlier, I would be able to hunt our state ducks and geese on the Arliss farm and with other hunting friends that my dad knew from his restaurant business. For a maturing outdoorsman it was an exciting time for me. Using my Uncle Nicky's borrowed 12-gauge double barrel that I used to take my first cottontail rabbit two years earlier, I was in the hunt now for any ducks and geese, even if it meant hunting alone before daybreak. Sunrise is pretty, anytime.

Thinking back there was a teenage friend, Steve Bastian, who was inspirational in getting me excited about waterfowl hunting, even the morning after one of our high school football games, home or away from home field, it would not matter. Up at 5:30 in the morning and shooting puddle ducks for our family and friends' dinner table at sunrise was our goal. We had successfully duck hunted numerous times together and those cold, damp or wet, but joyful mornings will never be forgotten. I also have many memories hunting waterfowl with the brothers of the Arliss family in Clyde, New York. There is nothing like being there as a teenager with friends, rain

Finally A Canadian Goose Success continued

or shine, it does not make a difference, as long as you are taking your chances at daylight in a nearby marsh. Believe me the water fowling memories will last a lifetime, so plan to share them with your children or grandchildren.

In life it is said, you seem to learn the most often the "hard way" or by making your share of mistakes rather than taking the experienced advise of those "special people" around you, maybe even your parents. Here is one of the "special people" learning experiences I would like to share with you before I conclude "the successful first goose hunt."

As an accomplished high school academic student and athlete as a teenager, like most young people, I felt I knew it all, but Canadian geese proved me wrong. Wayne Larson, a friend of my dad's who was a frequent customer at my dad's restaurant, in Savannah, New York, gave me permission to pass shoot ducks and giant Canadian geese on his flooded farm one Saturday morning. Wayne said to jump shoot the puddle ducks in the stream directly behind his house just after daylight and lately about 8:30 to 9:00 in the morning several flocks of geese were coming off a nearby flooded marsh and passing over his house. He said to pocket both small duck shells and the heavier #2 magnum high base goose loads if I wanted to possibly take a big goose home for dinner. I thought to myself, "I have plenty of duck shells and no money for goose shells so hey, use the duck loads (high base 12-gauge #4s) and shoot for the goose's neck and head. No problem if they are flying tree top high when coming off that marsh." Yah, right!! Even at age 17 you do not know it all.

By daylight that Saturday morning with flashlight in hand I was crossing Wayne's flooded cornfield to get to that probable "duck honey hole hotspot" he talked about. It was foggy, and with a light rain falling daylight soon came and went and although a couple of woodies and mallards whizzed by me, not a shot was fired. But as the fog lifted it was a beautiful morning to be the only waterfowler on this stream. By 9:00 that morning, without having any duck luck, it was time to head in to work at my dad's restaurant. Then old Wayne was right! Suddenly, to my surprise, as I sloshed my way across the cornfield to the car I heard geese everywhere in the air. With two hunting vest pockets stuffed with 12-gauge duck loads I was in position to take up to my limit of three geese. Wrong. The geese seemed low enough but despite shooting a half a dozen times at three close flocks of geese, none came down. Thinking "I knew better," I was shocked. When I met up with Wayne for breakfast at the restaurant he loved saying, "I told you , you needed goose loads to take down those tough birds," and he could not stop laughing because this teenager had not listen to him. I am sure he enjoyed his breakfast that was on me!

Finally A Canadian Goose Success continued

Each fall thereafter, for whatever reason, duck hunting by pass or jump shooting streams was the best waterfowling opportunity for me. Then I met up with Ed Doan in Lansdale, Pennsylvania in the fall of 1988. Ed was a nurse in my doctor's office and he invited me to goose hunt a local farmer's field and farm pond with him on any Saturday morning because he hunted alone. With him having some previous goose success from an existing goose decoy spread in the field near the pond, he did not have to ask me twice. We agreed to meet in the doctor's parking lot the next Saturday morning at 5:00, rain or shine, of course.

Despite work and family concerns, the possibility of taking a first Canadian goose that week-end almost never left my mind that week. Although it was a mild Saturday morning at least it was not raining and Ed pulled in right after I got there. We loaded my gun, an Ithaca Model 100 12-gauge double barrel, and gear into his small pick up truck and headed to Ed's neighbor's nearby farm.

It was Ed's plan to use our flashlights to reposition the goose decoys that he had set up last week-end to "shoot over." Then the two of us would split up and try to hunt both decoys left in the cleared cornfield and some placed near a good size cattle watering hole. By daylight we had split up and repositioned the goose decoys so we each "watched our own spread," if you will. You waterfowlers realize most ducks are early risers so that is when you usually get your best hunting, while Canadian goose hunting opportunities are best around 9:00 to 10:00 in the morning. This day would prove to be no different.

There was a blue sky sunrise and although beautiful with mild temperatures, it made a great experience to be out in God's great outdoors, but it often is not to a waterfowler's benefit. So far I was not impressed. But at least Wayne Larson's advise from over twenty years earlier stuck in my mind and the 12-gauge #2 magnum goose shells I bought were loaded in my Ithaca shotgun. Oh, my pockets were stuffed with them too!!

There was not much goose flight opportunity between 7:00 daylight and 9:00 in the morning and only a couple of pair of mallards passed even close to our pond. Neither of us had a shot. Then, reminiscent of years gone by when I thought it was time to head in for breakfast at Loder's Restaurant with Wayne Larson, I heard the call of the Canadian geese. Again this flock came from seemingly out of no where. My heart was racing with anticipation as the flock neared. There was actually a chance that both Ed and I would "get shots."

Finally A Canadian Goose Success continued

As the flock of geese cleared the treetops near the pond, with wings fixed to light, Ed fired 1, 2, and on the third shot he dropped a goose. The flock split and five or six geese were flying toward me so I knelt motionless in full camo for my shot. When I could not wait any longer I stood up and shot once, and with the second shot my Ithaca double barrel dropped the second goose in line from thirty-five yards into the cornfield with an unforgettable "thud" that I had never heard before. If I had to describe my feelings I would say the excitement of that first goose success was comparable to my first "whatever" wild game success in God's outdoors. Please take a kid, yours or anyone else's, hunting or fishing, because believe me, the good memories do last a lifetime and they can make a difference in their life and even the life of others.

Oh, a few words from Gale on this first Canadian goose experience...

Our family cat, Zipper, was just a kitten, probably about three months old, when Steve came home from waterfowl hunting with his first goose. Zipper's favorite room was the kitchen because that's where her food was, and where she could smell our food as it was being prepared. She always sat by Steve's feet when he was preparing a game dish, hoping to scarf up any remnant of food that may drop on the floor.

Anyway, our kitchen had a sliding glass door that overlooked our patio and a small woods behind our townhouse. And because Zipper spent much of her time in the kitchen, she happened to be watching as Steve showed me his goose from the patio. Zipper took one look at that large creature and bee lined it for the nearest safe place she could find - under the couch in the living room. And that's where she stayed until she "thought" it was safe to venture back into "her" kitchen. You had to be there to fully appreciate this memorable moment.

The next time you have a wild goose to cook, try this recipe. It'll be "just what the doctor ordered."

Steve's Lansdale Wild Goose

1	medium cooking bag	3-4	fresh carrots, sliced
1	tablespoon flour	2	stalks celery, sliced
½	wild goose, skinned, (½ breast and 1 leg)	½	green pepper, sliced
		½	bunch green onions, sliced
½	teaspoon onion powder	1	can cream of onion soup
½	teaspoon black pepper	1	soup can water
½	teaspoon garlic powder	½	cup rosé wine
½	teaspoon salt		Your favorite rice or noodles

Preheat oven to 350 degrees. Put 1 tablespoon flour in cooking bag and shake to coat; place in 13x9x2-inch baking pan, and put goose parts in cooking bag. Add seasonings and fresh vegetables; pour the soup and water, and wine over the goose. Close bag with nylon tie provided; cut 6 (½-inch) slits in top. Then bake for 2 hours. Remove goose from oven and prepare your favorite rice or noodles. While the rice or noodles are cooking, open cooking bag and remove goose meat from leg bone. Also piece goose breast into bite size pieces. Mix the goose, gravy mixture, and vegetables together, reheating in a saucepan if necessary, and serve over your hot rice or noodles. Enjoy this scrumptious one dish meal!

The Once in a Lifetime Buck

By Ron Wilson

Writer and deer hunter, Ron Wilson, is photographed here with his trophy eleven point, 201-pound field dressed, whitetail buck, no less. The most important part of this deer hunting memory is, as Ron told me, "it was experienced with my young son and now he's a deer hunter, too." Ron also said, "Oh, thanks Rick, for this time, once again pushing my trophy buck by me. Next time it is my turn to try to push a deer or a trophy buck to you! I hope I can make it up to you."

The 1993 deer hunting season would prove to be an especially memorable one for me. It started out as usual on a cold, windy Monday morning like so many others with my life long friend, Rick Eldridge, on some property that I owned in Niagara County located in extreme northwestern New York State. Talk about deer hunting tradition! We had shared the last twenty-five deer hunting seasons together, give or take a few, but who is counting?

My land that we were hunting was flat farm country broken into small woodlots. Rick was watching this cold opening day of the New York gun season from his usual comfortable tree stand about four hundred yards from me and overlooking this huge cornfield. I in turn was sitting on the ground near a well used trail that led from the woodlot to our "deer's cornfield." Despite warm clothing, food of all kinds, and a soda, our opening day was an uneventful long watch despite our "wishful deer think-ing." The winds continued to blow and snow came with it, too, all afternoon off and on. "So it's snow," I thought, "it will help each of us see a brown moving whitetail." We both had buck and doe tags to fill and we both had used up our last year's supply of nutritious venison, "so it's time to put some meat in the freezer." If God gives us the opportunity and we were paying our dues, it is then that good things happen.

The Once in a Lifetime Buck continued

Over the years, Rick's impatience has made him a very valuable deer hunting partner because I don't know how many times he has pushed deer my way simply because he could not sit still. "Still hunting" on the slow move when you are cold sometimes can pay off but eight out of ten deer are taken waiting for deer to come to them when deer hunters are sitting still. It helps to remember the woods we hunt are the whitetails' home and they know what their home range is supposed to smell and look like, too; usually better than most of us deer hunters.

Well, despite our best efforts we never fired a deer slug that opening day even though we heard shotgun slug fire all around us. We met at our trucks at visual dark. We were both disappointed but agreed to hunt each of our stands at daylight again regardless of what our New York weather would bring, and by mid-morning Rick would do his customary deer driving for me. About 9:00 that morning Rick got tired of sitting, and maybe a little cold, too, because the temperature was about in the low twenties and our Lake Ontario winds had started up, also. As Rick walked close to a thick hedgerow at the end of the woods that I was sitting in, out bolted a spooked "monster" of a whitetail buck.

Rick, out of an adrenaline rush, fired one "buck fever" slug at the fleeting monster buck, but it did not find its mark. "As luck only" would have it the "monster buck" ran the length of the cornfield and was still headed towards my trail before it then cut in the woods. When I saw his mass of antlers quickly heading my way, it was all I could do to keep my heart in my chest. "Hey, relax, relax," I thought as I raised my trusty Ithaca Deerslayer at thirty yards and closing. When my shotgun fired at my trophy buck it ran off as if I never hit him. "I know my gun," I said to myself, "and that buck is well hit!" I had been shooting it with open sights for twenty years.

Usually you should wait from fifteen to thirty minutes to give a wounded deer time to expire after a good shot attempt with either a bow or gun. I knew this but could hardly wait to track and find the trophy buck. Despite stiffness from sitting in the cold and the brush I covered that thirty yards to where I shot my buck very quickly and was excited to see a very pronounced blood trail. Rick was still nearly a quarter of a mile away and moving toward me, but it was early morning (8:00) and I could not wait to catch up to and secure my trophy buck, so off I went tracking his blood trail.

The Once in a Lifetime Buck continued

My buck eventually jumped a fence, and then hit the ground and rested, judging from the blood sign, before it gathered itself and then crossed a state parkway. He was almost hit by a car as he crossed that road, as I learned later. He traveled another 350 to 400 yards on the other side of the parkway before I found him in some high grass. His horns gave him away.

With help from some other deer hunters that I happened to meet where I found my trophy whitetail, we were able to get him back to my house using their ATV. True story, I was so excited that I went and got my youngest son (who was in sixth grade) out of school to show him the deer. Then we went and picked up my buck's blood trail just to give my son experience in tracking deer that I would hope he would need some day. The taxidermist weighed my trophy eleven pointer at 201 pounds field dressed. What was special was my son was there, too and was as excited as I was to be a part of it all.

Ron sent us the following recipe to go along with his deer tale above. His note went like this: "Steve, Enclosed is the absolute favorite recipe of our deer crew at my deer camp in New York for venison Slouvaki! This recipe came from a friend over twenty years ago. I would be willing to bet that over the years over seventy-five people have enjoyed this tasty sandwich recipe and everyone has said that this is the best venison recipe they have every tried. In fact, Steve, we have cut up entire deer for venison Slouvaki meat!!" This sandwich recipe is certainly their deer camp tradition!

Ron's Deer Camp Venison Slouvaki (Greek Style)

2	pounds venison steak, cubed (1 to 2-inches x 1 to 2-inches) to be put on skewers for grilling
1	cup olive oil, divided
1	cup red wine, prefer dry and certainly not cooking wine
1½	teaspoons salt, divided
1	teaspoon black pepper, divided
1	teaspoon oregano
1	teaspoon crushed mint or chives
3	cloves fresh garlic, crushed or diced small
¼	cup lemon juice
½	teaspoon parsley flakes
6	ounces feta cheese
1	fresh tomato, diced small
1	(6-ounce) can large pitted black olives, halved
4	thick pita pockets
	Lettuce, shredded optional

Cube trimmed venison steak into cubes large enough for putting on skewers for grilling, 1 to 2 inches. Prepare marinade by combining ½ cup olive oil, red wine, 1 teaspoon salt, ½ teaspoon black pepper, oregano, mint or chives, and garlic in a 13x9x2-inch glass baking dish. Add cubed venison steak to the marinade in baking dish and cover with plastic wrap. Marinate your venison steak cubes in refrigerator 24 hours or longer, turning occasionally when convenient.

While the venison cubes are marinating and before grilling, you will have plenty of time to prepare the special Greek style salad dressing by mixing ½ cup olive oil, ¼ cup lemon juice, ½ teaspoon each salt and black pepper, and parsley flakes in a cup. Set the dressing aside and prepare the sandwich appetizer stuffing by combining the feta cheese, tomato and halved olives in a medium bowl. If using lettuce we suggest adding that to your sandwich just before serving to preserve freshness. Add your Greek style dressing that you set aside to your stuffing mixture, mix well and refrigerate.

Ron's Deer Camp Venison Slouvaki continued

Once your venison steak cubes have marinated for at least 24 hours, fill up skewers and carefully grill steak cubes to medium rare and juicy doneness. While grilling ask for a cook's volunteer to slice 4 whole pita bread pockets around the outside edge and separate them. Place on the oven racks after lightly buttering the inside up. Then bake at 325 degrees for 3 to 4 minutes to lightly brown. Remove them to serving platter.

Once your venison steak cubes are grilled to medium rare or desired doneness add them to the veggie/cheese bowl of stuffing with dressing that you refrigerated earlier and mix well. Now you're ready to have hunters, family, or friends grab their own plate, putting two round pita halves on each of their plates. Suggest they spread ½ of the pita with the grilled marinated venison steak and veggie mixture and top with shredded lettuce, if using, and the other ½ of the pita bread. Now go enjoy one tasty venison steak sandwich! Guaranteed.

Tip: This recipe will make 4 great venison sandwiches. Any left over mixed veggie/cheese stuffing will be gone in minutes, hot or cold, as a side dish or snack. Mm, so good! Depending on the number of your guests this recipe is easily doubled.

Recipe complements of Ron Wilson, one lucky New York deer hunter.
Thanks so much, Ron.

We have heard it, and maybe you have, too, at hunting camp or on a paid hunt, that hunting is America's Family Legacy. Let's not anyone of us lose sight of that from hunting season to hunting season. Support for the National Rifle Association is critical because, what other organization is protecting our hunting or gun owning rights?

We were so pleased at how delicious Ron's marinated and grilled venison kabobs (Greek style) sandwich recipe turned out that it gave us an idea to put a twist on the recipe so that we could have it even in bad weather. You can also enjoy Ron's recipe for venison kabobs sandwich "Italian style" and baked medium rare, tender, and juicy hot from your oven. You talk about one big game tasty sandwich. This is good eating!

Steve's Any Time Tasty Big Game Stuffed Pitas (Italian Style)

2	pounds trimmed big game steaks, cubed small 1 to 2 inches	¼-⅓	cup Italian salad dressing
1	cup olive oil, divided	½	teaspoon onion powder
1	cup dry red wine, not cooking wine	8	ounces shredded Parmesan cheese
1½	teaspoons salt, divided	4	ounces sliced fresh mushrooms
1	teaspoon black pepper, divided	1	cup thinly sliced or finely chopped green bell pepper
1½	teaspoons Italian seasoning, divided	1	medium fresh tomato, cored and diced small
1	teaspoon parsley flakes	4	thick pita bread pockets, split in 2 whole circles
3	cloves garlic, diced small		

Add cubed big game steak to a 13x9x2-inch glass baking dish. Mix ½ cup olive oil, dry red wine, 1 teaspoon salt, ½ teaspoon black pepper, 1 teaspoon Italian seasoning, parsley flakes, and diced garlic cloves in a medium bowl and pour over your cubed steak. Cover with plastic wrap and marinate your big game steak cubes in the refrigerator 24 hours or longer, turning occasionally when convenient.

While the steak cubes are marinating and before baking them, prepare a special Italian style salad dressing in a cup by combining the remaining ½ cup olive oil, Italian dressing, ½ teaspoon each salt and black pepper, onion powder, and ½ teaspoon Italian seasoning. Set it aside while you prepare the big game sandwich appetizer stuffing. In a medium size bowl combine the Parmesan cheese, fresh mushrooms, green bell pepper and tomato. Add your freshly made Italian style salad dressing to your stuffing mixture, mix well, and refrigerate.

Steve's Any Time Tasty Big Game Stuffed Pitas continued

After marinating your chunks of any big game steak and spraying your broiler pan with non-stick cooking spray, it is time to cook! To your broiler pan add all your cubed big game steak. Bake at 325 degrees for 12 to 15 minutes; turn steak cubes. Add 8 lightly buttered pita bread halves to your oven rack, and bake with cubed steaks 2 to 3 minutes. Remove pita bread and steak cubes to serving platter and mix baked steak cubes with your bowl of appetizer stuffing and Italian salad dressing mixture that was refrigerated earlier and mix well.

Have hunters, family, or friends grab their own dish and add 2 round pita halves. Fill 1 pita half with steak/stuffing mixture and top with the other pita half. It is now OK to go and enjoy one big very tasty big game sandwich. Venison is venison, be it caribou, elk, mule deer, or whitetail deer, it will all be delicious!

We Outdoor Enthusiasts
Should Make A Difference

For those of us that want to share their wild game or the fruit of their spoils, they will need to dedicate themselves to sacrifice. They need to hunt, and hunt hard from daylight to dark, if that is what it takes. While I am not the country's best hunter or shooter, I have been there and done that, "hunt from the early morning to chilly or cold night, whether it be

for waterfowl or that big whitetail buck." I have paid my dues in God's great outdoors and have a lifetime of memories with family and friends because of hunting and fishing, too. Try and take a youngster hunting or fishing with you soon; you will more than likely have a good time and maybe make a young friend for life, too.

Pheasant Hunting "Mississippi Style"

Note there are only 9 pheasants taken and we had 10 put out for our hunt. That is because this author clearly missed the last rooster pheasant and could only apologize. Clyde 5 birds and Steve 4. Years later I spoke to Clyde and he asked if I ever found it.

This is a tale about how a Yankee was introduced to "Southern Style" pheasant hunting. Through a donation that was made at our annual Ducks Unlimited banquet in Cordova, Tennessee, a suburb of the river city, Memphis, we had an invitation to pheasant hunt at the Southern Country Outfitter Plantation in Mississippi.

My friend and hunting partner of several past hunts, Clyde, welcomed the chance to join me on this bird hunt of choice and we both agreed on ring neck pheasants only. We both worked a lot of hours during the winter of 1993, but finally on that to be pleasant Saturday morning in February we were in position to hunt.

Now the week-end before our hunt we both took our favorite double barrel shot guns to the trap/skeet range to sharpen our shooting skills. Clyde had not shot much recently but he impressed me. My Ithaca Model 100 12-gauge was as good as ever so I could not wait for next week-end. Clyde would be shooting his favorite double barrel shotgun, also, so there was not much room for error between us if we were to take all of our allotted ten rooster pheasants.

We were both excited about the long awaited pheasant hunt. Our guide and dog handler would be Charles at Southern Country Outfitters, which was located about

Pheasant Hunting "Mississippi Style" continued

an hour south of Memphis, Tennessee. Our dog support would be a Brittany spaniel named Becky. Charles loaded Becky up out of the kennel and into his truck and asked us to follow him by car to the nearby plantation bird fields.

By mid-morning Becky, Clyde and I were in the field and more than ready to hunt pheasants for our families' dinner table. After you have enjoyed some fresh wild game birds, either upland, like pheasants and grouse or waterfowl, prepared correctly, wild game is hard to beat for taste or nutritional value. Both of us knew it and we were counting on each other to shoot carefully so none of our birds got away. It is a matter of pride more than a matter of a bird paid for and not retrieved. I thought to myself, 'a pheasant dinner was promised to my wife for tonight… Just do it!'

Soon after getting out of the truck cage Becky had her tail wagging because she was on a cock bird. Charles said she was a good huntin' dog and he was right. She methodically worked a half of a mile of three grass fields for us for over three hours. She was well disciplined so she listened well to Charles' instructions. One by one we took turns taking the first shot and the partner backing the other up so the pheasant did not get away. Although hunting pheasants for the first time together, we shot like pros, we must admit.

We took nine of our ten rooster pheasants and were giving up when Becky pointed at an unexpected bird. We followed Becky and when the pheasant flushed, it came right at me and over my left shoulder only ten to fifteen yards away. It rattled me so much that I emptied my double barrel at it and it sailed off into another field a hundred yards away. It might not have gotten away if Clyde had been within shooting range, but he wasn't in a position to shoot at it. After this miss I did not feel so great about my previous shooting success…

With having a lot of fun and considerable pheasant bounty we called it a day and certainly an enjoyable hunt outdoors with Mother Nature.

Even though I missed that last pheasant, I still felt fortunate to have brought 4 pheasants home to prepare meals to share with my family. When you are fortunate enough to have a successful pheasant hunt, we encourage you to try this recipe and see if you don't agree with us - that it is delicious!

Clyde's "Memphis Style" Pheasant

¼	cup soy sauce	3	tablespoons apple cider vinegar or dry white wine	
¼	cup cooking oil			
2	tablespoons lemon juice	½	teaspoon black or cayenne pepper	
1	teaspoon chopped garlic clove	2	pheasants, dressed and meat deboned from carcass	

Combine the above marinade ingredients in a large bowl. Soak the pheasant pieces in the marinade in the refrigerator for 12 to 18 hours depending on what meal you are preparing it for, turning it now and again. To your crockpot add marinated pheasant pieces and remaining ingredients below, and stir well.

2	tablespoons butter	1	tablespoon powdered mustard	
½-¾	cup flour	2	cups barbecue sauce	
1	cup chopped green onions	1	(14½-ounce) can stewed tomatoes	
1	cup water	2	bay leaves	
1	tablespoon oregano		A shake of salt and black or cayenne pepper or to taste	

Cook your pheasant mixture on high for 5 to 6 hours or low for 8 to 9 hours depending on eating arrangements. Serve this dish over a favorite rice and add a favorite vegetable for a delicious "Memphis" style meal.

Waterfowling on
Pennsylvania's Lake Pymatuning - 1994

After years of not being in the right marsh or field when it came time to take home some giant Canadian geese to enjoy on our dinner table with family and friends, with the help of friends I was able to find success. It does not get better than this on the marsh!

After another five years passed since my last goose hunt that included two job relocations, we wound up in western Pennsylvania, in a northern suburb of Pittsburgh. The deer hunting would be excellent for me here so I looked forward to the promotion and moving back north while my wife, Gale and daughter, Kelly, did not want to leave Memphis, Tennessee, the warm sunny south.

We arrived in Cranberry Township, a northern Pittsburgh suburb, just before what was a <u>severe winter</u>. Gale and Kelly were ready to leave Cranberry Township by spring, and despite increased job pressures and responsibilities, my only encouragement to them was "fall is coming and the waterfowl, wild turkey, and whitetail deer hunting is great everywhere, so let's not ask for a job transfer just yet."

By the fall of 1994 due to wild game and shooting popularity I had made a number of hunting contacts. Nick called me one Friday evening that I happened to be home and not on the road or at work. He and his friend, John, were planning an opening day waterfowl hunt on the edges of Lake Pymatuning for Saturday morning and I was invited. Jumping at the chance, I said "yes" because we could take either

Waterfowling on Pennsylvania's Lake Pymatuning continued

giant Canadian geese or ducks on a liberal bag limit. This made our joint efforts certainly worthwhile because Nick and John had already been successful on such a hunt on opening day of waterfowl the year before.

You know they say there is always a catch in a plan. The morning hunting catch was two fold this time. First, in order to protect our prime, pass shooting hunting spot on the lake that they had in mind we would have to get there very early to beat other hunters. They shocked me with suggesting breakfast at 3:30 in the morning on Saturday at a local all night restaurant. The second catch, Nick also thought to ask, "what kind of boots do you have to get through the marsh when needed?" My response was "just hip boots." Nick's response was, "that may or may not be a problem, but John and I have waders, so maybe we can help you." Oh, that was a reassuring thought at 10:45 at night and I had to wake up at 3:00 in the morning. "Ok, Nick, see you at the restaurant at 3:30 tomorrow morning," and we hung up.

When I arrived at the restaurant it was easy to find a table for four. To say I ordered coffee is an understatement, but shortly Nick and John arrived. After a great breakfast we were all energized and excited for some of our first of the season's waterfowling. We had many challenging shots ahead of us in order to enjoy waterfowl on our families' dinner tables. Hey, when is the last time the average person enjoyed deliciously, nutritious waterfowl? When is the last time you were able to go and buy wild duck or goose at your local grocery store? Never! It isn't going to happen any time soon, either. Waterfowl hunters earn these tasty meals, shared with family and friends. Despite the "two plan catches," our restaurant meeting at 3:30 in the morning and with only hip high boots, when I should have chest high waders, I was game for waterfowl.

There was all the hunting gear preparation and suddenly it's time to hunt, with whatever gear I had. We ventured one and a half hours north of Pittsburgh to an unknown waterfowl location for me, since I was new to the area. Hey, we are waterfowlers and I had to take these two new hunting friends at their word that our hunting efforts would be worth it! Right?

The plan was to arrive at 5:00 in the morning at the shore line of Lake Pymatuning and secure our ground blind so at daylight, about 7:00 in the morning we would have the best shot at both puddle ducks and Canadian geese that would be coming off the lake and coming into "our" marsh to feed. Nick and John knew what they were talking about from their past experience on the marsh.

Waterfowling on Pennsylvania's Lake Pymatuning continued

By 7:00 that morning the ducks were flying, but the trees to our backside kept them always too high for our best of steel shot. It was about 8:00 to 8:30 that morning that we started to hear the loud honking of the lake's roosting Canadian geese among the squawking mallards and black ducks. All morning we tried to call in both ducks and geese.

It was about 9:15 in the morning and after standing in knee high marsh water for nearly two hours we decided not to call distant flocks of ducks and geese and see if they might land in our marsh anyway. Bingo! What do you know, it wasn't an hour and the probably local ducks and geese on the lake were relaxed and interested in coming into our little piece of marsh "for some piece and quiet that they were used to." Within an hour, separated by camouflage and fifty yards of reeds between us we had all the shooting we could ask for. We all wished we were shooting better, for sure.

The problem was we had to be careful on our duck or goose shots because the marsh was deep in spots and we did not have a boat or a good dog to retrieve our waterfowl. During our morning hunt we pass shot ducks and geese coming over the tree tops of the marsh near Lake Pymatuning. John bagged two ducks, a woodie and a male mallard. Nick took his limit of three ducks, two greenhead mallards and a woodie, too.

Our Lord was watching me because for the first in five years I was able to take two Canadian geese out of a flock. It was a <u>big thrill</u> that, despite the marsh, I was able to retrieve both geese after they hit the water. Thank goodness for my Ithaca shotgun. <u>It was on the mark</u>!

My First Deer

By Ken Hunter

I grew up hunting, as did my father before me and his father before him. I am told that I actually cut my teeth on a gun barrel. It seems I didn't wish to chew on anything else so pop cleaned up the old military pistol barrel for me and let me chew on it until my teeth came in! As you may have imagined by now, we lived way out in the country and money for store-bought beef was not all that common, hence we ate a lot of venison and other wild game. From early on I had a love for the woods and I must have drove my dad nuts begging him for a shell or two to go hunting with. The rules were clear as day, only kill what you intend to eat and kill it as humanely as possible. We lived by a small lake and frosty cold mornings often found me waiting in ambush for a wild duck or traipsing the forest for a ruffed grouse. During the summer I often spent my time fishing for a brook trout for the table.

From the start I was taught firearm safety and drilled to the point that it was instinctive. We raised chickens and shot skunks and things that tried to eat them before we did. It was not uncommon to hear the scream of a cougar in the early evening or the howl of a pack of coyotes. Our little house sat in a valley and there was always something wild nearby. One evening a friend came to the house for dinner and while walking home, he shot and killed a large black bear, about 50 yards behind the outhouse. One learned not to walk around in the dark without a gun.

I hunted with my dad but he shot all of the big game. He did teach me solid values and to respect the land and its creatures. Later we moved to a small town and I grew up somewhat restless. I left home at the age of 17 and soon I was back in the deer woods. This time, I was the one carrying the big game rifle and my first deer came hard. You never forget your first deer and today it is just as clear to me as it was back then. I hunted hard during the early season and never even got a shot at a deer. The late hunt came and was just about over. In fact it was the very last day of the season and I had spent it high in the Cascade Mountains searching for a deer. I was driving a Ford pickup down a mountain in a light snow and my girlfriend was riding quietly and in silence. I was sad because in an hour the season would close and I failed to take a deer. Just then a spike buck ran across the narrow logging road and into the forest. I stopped, grabbed my pump action rifle and ran down the road and then turned parallel to where the deer had gone in. Being familiar with deer behavior I called it right and he came sneaking by me in a tall fern patch that was dotted with large hardwoods. My heart began to pound as I pushed off the safety button and shouldered the heavy weapon. I fired in haste and hit a little low which sent the deer bounding away. I immediately pumped another round into the chamber and when

My First Deer continued

the buck would leap I would fire, pump in another round and fired each time he became airborne. I emptied the rifle and on the last shot he hit the ground. I chambered another round and approached him from behind. I hate to see anything suffer and so I used the last round and ended his short life. I was so excited, I had just taken my first deer on my own but also I was sad that in the last half minute of its life, it had died hard. Although I managed some how not to ruin any of the meat, I felt the deer deserved more respect than that and more humane ending. I vowed never to let myself get too excited again at least until the animal was finished.

I tagged him and said a brief but heartfelt prayer over him. When I got him back to the truck, my girlfriend asked me if I had fought a war? Now my pride was a little wounded but I was very proud of my little buck and by then very adept at cutting and keeping my game in pristine eating condition from field to table. I shared the meat with her family and everyone appreciated tender mild venison.

That was just over 30 years ago now and I recently took a fine whitetail doe for the table. I only bowhunt these days and I am an outdoor writer now. I am blessed with many sponsors and the finest archery tackle available. The thrill is still very great for me and every year I bring home wild game for my wife and me. I still like to share and give my neighbors some of my wild harvest. I hope you like the following "Venison Taco Salad" recipe and may you all be blessed with great hunting.

From those humble beginnings I became determined to be a better deer hunter. I dedicated myself to becoming a respected sportsman who made clean one-shot kills. Now many years later I am amazed to find where that trail has led me. I learned I had a desire to write and became an outdoor writer. You can read some of my articles by logging on to http://edd.alaska.net/ or do a search for ed's archery pages. One thing that I discovered is how much fun it is to get kids started in the outdoors sports. You never know how it will affect them in the long run but it is always a positive step in their development. My good friend Matt is in the Navy and an avid archer. His archery friends got deployed so he asked his 10-year-old daughter if she would shoot archery with him. She said OK, so he got her a compound bow and some starter arrows. After some instruction and some practice, he took her to an archery tournament. She got a medal for fourth place. She also discovered she not only liked winning but liked first place much better. During the next year she won first place in everything. She won every 3-D shoot, every indoor shoot, every marked yardage and safari shoot and so on. She did so well that she got to go to the world's indoor shoot at Las Vegas and took a second place her first time there! She also took a first place

My First Deer continued

bowl at the National Field Archery Championships! The next year she broke almost every state record and won two National titles. The point is this, you just never know what is going to happen when you take a kid with you to share in the outdoors. Every year I help coach kids in the sport of archery. My reward is in their smiles. Taking a kid hunting or shooting can be one of the most fulfilling things you can do. They are the future of our sport... Ken Hunter

Ken Hunter and Olivia Anderson at the
NFAA Nationals in Darrington, Washington

Venison Taco Salad

1	pound ground venison	1	medium cucumber, peeled and thinly sliced
1	(15 to 16-ounce) can black or refried beans	1	avocado, (optional), pitted and sliced thin
1	teaspoon chili powder, or to taste	1-2	cups shredded yellow, taco, or Mexican style cheese
	Corn chips, of choice		
	Lettuce, shredded, approximately 2 cups	1	(16-ounce) jar salsa, your choice of mild, medium or hot, (to put on table for individuals to serve themselves)
1	tomato, 1 cup or so diced small		
1	(6-ounce) can black olives, halved		
1	carrot, peeled and diced or sliced thin	1	(8-ounce) jar taco sauce, (to put on table for individuals to serve themselves)

First brown venison until done and add the black or refried beans and chili powder to taste. Simmer for about 10 minutes. Next, in a large salad bowl arrange your choice of corn chips in the bottom of the bowl until it is covered and put some around the edge of the bowl. Place the shredded lettuce in the bowl and cover with the meat and bean mixture. Next, sprinkle with diced tomatoes, halved black olives, shredded or sliced carrot, sliced cucumber, and sliced avocado. Last, sprinkle your choice of cheese on top. Have salsa and taco sauce on the table for individuals to season their own salad.

This is a fast and delicious dish to prepare and can be done right in hunting camp or it makes a quick and tasty lunch at home. This is a great dish for introducing people to wild game. You may add or delete certain items to appeal to your personal taste.

Ken Hunter

A Deer Season - Short But Oh, <u>So</u> Memorable

A Special Remembrance of Bob Ellsworth

Despite my continued poor health, I was invited to make a personal appearance for a book signing and venison sampling at a gift shop in New York State by the owners Rob and Sue the week-end before the opening of the New York shotgun deer season. I agreed, with only limited hours, because they invited me to deer hunt with their family on their farm on opening day of the up-coming deer season, which was on that following Monday.

Rob, Sue and their staff all helped me to sell a lot of our *Quality Venison* cookbooks and their customers loved samples of my venison dishes. The week-end went fast and soon I was having the usual deer dreams leading up to opening day. With poor health I could only hunt until noon on the first and second day of the deer hunting season. I would then have to return home to recuperate so I would have enough energy to either process my New York deer that I would get on this hunting trip, or try for a deer in my home state of Pennsylvania the following opening Monday morning after Thanksgiving.

Of course I had not been up at 5:00 in the morning in a long time, so the alarm "blasted" me into consciousness. Fortunately experience had taught me to be organized and ready by pre-packing all my needed gear so I could meet my hunting party on time at Rob and Sue's home at just after 6:00 that morning.

During the luncheon book signing and venison samplings at the gift shop I had the privilege of spending some time with Rob's mother and father. They came to see me in the gift shop and Bob, Rob's father, who was a hard worker and now seventy-two years old shared two things with me that I wished I could have helped <u>to change</u>! He described to me his <u>passion</u> for whitetail deer hunting with a bow and a shotgun over his lifetime. In a short time he told me more tales than I could remember. The other important subject that Bob talked about was his years of fighting cancer. I wished by a miracle of God, Bob could have beaten his cancer illness and hunted deer even longer.

Bob, at seventy-two and his sister, Gert, at seventy-five, were the first two hunters to join us in Rob and Sue's kitchen that opening morning. Rob and Sue's college student son would be joining us on the hunt opening and we were all assigned to permanent stands for safety until 12:00 noon. At that time we would come in to compare "deer notes" and have lunch at their house and make a plan for afternoon hunting success.

A Deer Season - Short But Oh, <u>So</u> Memorable continued

Opening morning shotgun fire was heard everywhere, but not a deer crossed within my stand's view. While sitting in my stand at fifteen feet in the air, several times I thought of elderly Bob and his sister making the climb into their assigned stands. They hoped of taking yet another whitetail deer so they could enjoy its healthy and nutritious venison with their family and with the less fortunate people through area food banks. <u>At their age this was inspirational</u>, and I continue to talk about this experience at all of our book signing/venison samplings.

Even though Bob sacrificed his special stand for me, by noon I had not seen a deer, so feeling ill, as expected, the hunt was over for me. The unusually warm weather effected deer feeding and their movement patterns because not a deer was taken by the six of us. Well, I had a need for some food and rest and I told Rob, "if the good Lord is willing I will be back around 6:00 in the morning for yet another morning New York whitetail hunt with your family." "Hey, Steve, tomorrow will be a better hunt," were Rob's encouraging words.

That night I forgot to take my scoped Ithaca 12-gauge Deerslayer shotgun into the motel. On Tuesday the alarm went off early and getting dressed for deer hunting was planned and automatic. This time Bob and his sister were there at Rob and Sue's home before I was. We each had a cup of coffee and wished each other good luck as we ventured out to our same assigned stands. The weather had gotten frosty overnight and while walking to my stand just at daylight I said a little prayer that having made the effort, God would bless me with a deer of either sex.

Then things changed! Shotgun slugs were fired from a neighboring farm woodlot. Going to one knee, anticipating a possible shot, I raised my scoped Model 37 Deerslayer to my shoulder. If a deer came through the woods and crossed this farm road that I was on I would have a shot. Then a doe jumped the fence and was running down the farm road as I aimed my Ithaca to consider a lethal shot. When looking in the scope I could not see anything because moisture from it being in my trunk had fogged it over. It was a costly mistake and certainly a learning experience. There was the cost of my out-of-state hunting license, not to mention, travel expenses, but most importantly, it cost me a supply of farm fed venison for my family and friends by not thinking to take my scoped 37 inside overnight.

The remainder of the morning, once again, no deer came to my stand, but it sounded as if other members of our crew had shot opportunities. By noon I was too sick to hunt any longer, but I felt good because I found out that at least one of those shots I heard was from Rob who had taken a fat six point buck.

A Deer Season - Short But Oh, So Memorable continued

Obviously, I did not have a whitetail to show for my efforts and neither did Rob and Sue's son or Bob, Sr. and Rob's aunt. But the feeling was the deer are here and it is a long season, so the challenge was not over yet among them. Then Sue, Rob's wife made it back to the house and I have never seen a woman so upset. Frustrated and disappointed, she kept saying that deer was near her stand for maybe five minutes and she thought it was a doe that she could take anytime, so she just waited to see if a buck would be joining her. When it finally ran off, she said she could see the horns, but by then, could not get off a shot. She kept saying how disappointed she was.

The happy ending; there was the call a week later when Sue's voice said, "I am calling you to tell you that I got a second shot opportunity at that four point and I made a clean one shot kill." Way to go, Sue! She is one determined hunter. And I later learned from Sue that Rob's seventy-five year old Aunt Gert got a nice eight point buck!

Special Remembrance:

We lost our friend, Bob, to cancer in the summer of 2000
despite our prayers. God bless him; he was a good man and with the help
of his loving wife they raised a good family.

My First 10-Point Buck

By Joel Marvin

Mr. And Mrs. Joel Marvin presently have three boys ages three, five, and seven. His lovely wife and certainly the boys all enjoy venison meals of all kinds. Joel told me, "they'd eat venison dishes three meals a day if we would cook it." Joel's trophy 10-point buck, pictured above, taken with his bow in October, 2001 was a thrill for Joel and a delight for their family's dinner table too.

Maybe I just wasn't meant to kill a double-digit buck I began thinking to myself while sitting in my treestand during the 2001 bow season. After 20 years of chasing deer and killing my fair share, I had a number of nice bucks to my credit, but none of them supported a 10-point or better rack. I had killed a half-dozen nine pointers, which were all trophies in their own right, but I had recently begun to wonder why at least one of them didn't have that extra point, as there is just something magical about a 10-pointer. It started to become almost comical when I would kill a potential double-digit buck and walk up to it only to find it was another 9-pointer. I started to wonder if maybe I was under some sort of unknown hunter's jinx or spell. Or maybe I was destined to follow in my oldest brother's footsteps who, after nearly 40 years and dozens and dozens of nice bucks, killed his first 8-pointer only last year. The most popular rack among whitetail bucks, and he couldn't seem to get one. I was beginning to think that maybe it was something that ran in the family.

I knew the property I was hunting held at least one nice 10-pointer, as I had scouted him since summer and had seen him dining on soybeans on more than a couple occasions. The place was also a natural funnel for other bucks in the area so I was confident that with a little patience, I could get a shot at one of the bigger bucks roaming the area. After filling that part of my freezer reserved for venison with a

My First 10-Point Buck continued

nice, plump doe early in the season, I decided the rest of the year would be spent concentrating on the 10-pointer or one of his equally endowed friends. It was a decision I wouldn't regret.

I had never before focused my efforts on one particular deer, but I soon found it was an exciting way to hunt. Passing on does and smaller bucks opened up a new world to me. Instead of being anxious and ready to let fly at the first valid shot opportunity, watching and waiting provided me with several nights and mornings of entertainment and education. I had deer within 10 feet of me on several occasions, and I had the pleasure of learning from some of the smaller bucks on the property. One of those bucks, a small 6-pointer, was especially entertaining. One morning I watched him act like a 12-pointer with some small saplings before walking to a fallen over tree directly under my treestand to lick and rub his forehead on a place where I had placed some buck lure just an hour earlier. I had let him walk off and then proceeded to grunt him back within range three times that morning. He was a riot to watch, and he never did figure out the game I was playing.

As I began to chuckle to myself at the memory of that deer, a movement just downhill from me got my attention. Two deer, a doe and a buck-fawn, were working their way towards me while feeding on the acorns that had dropped from the mammoth oaks that surrounded my stand. I watched in silence as the two deer not only walked within easy bow range, but also decided to stop directly underneath me to finish their meal. After watching them for several minutes, I decided to have a little fun by dropping spitballs down on them from my perch above. To my amazement, this didn't seem to faze them one bit even when I hit the fawn directly between the shoulder blades with a perfectly placed spitball. Maybe they thought it was beginning to rain. I found myself chuckling and shaking my head again as I watched them finally walk off and out of sight. I think I was laughing not only at the deer but also at myself for doing such a silly thing. I had to wonder if other hunters would have done something like that. I know my dad, who taught me just about everything I know about deer hunting, would either be smiling or rolling over in his grave after watching such an episode.

The rest of the afternoon drifted away taking the silly thoughts that one comes up with while sitting on stand with it. It was time to get serious. The sun was gaining speed in its descent behind the hill so I decided to grunt a few times before getting down. There didn't seem to be any deer in the immediate area when I grunted so it came as quite a surprise when I heard something walking in the leaves behind me

My First 10-Point Buck continued

about a minute after tucking the call into my shirt pocket. A quick glance over my right shoulder verified the noise as a nice buck, and he was closing fast! One quick glance at his rack showed at least five points on his left beam. I don't even remember seeing the other side of his rack because I quickly turned to grab my bow, which was hanging on a limb over my left shoulder. With darkness fast approaching, I made a quick turn in my stand back to my right side where the buck was now within ten yards. Upon drawing the bow back, he stopped broadside at twelve yards. As is usually the case, however, a small tree was directly over the deer's vitals and I couldn't take a shot. I said a quick prayer for the buck to take just one more step. I must have been a good boy that day because I no more than said the prayer in my head when the buck took one more step and stopped again, and I was rewarded with a perfectly placed shot in the vitals.

The buck didn't go far before collapsing, and it didn't take me long to reach him. I still didn't know what the other side of his rack looked like because I hadn't looked at it again after that first quick glance. Needless to say, I was quite overjoyed when the right beam mirrored the left beam's five points. I let out a small whoop before kneeling down to give thanks to the Lord for such a moment — another beautiful day in the wild, a quick and clean one-shot kill, more meat for the family, and my first 10-point buck!!

It only took a sample or two from a teaspoon to realize this barbecue is special. Our home smelled great while this recipe was cooking, so we knew dinner would be delicious and delicious it was, whether plain, with bread or crackers, or over rice or noodles. If it is cold and you are thinking summer, think, "Joel's 'Sporting Tales' Easy Big Game and Bacon Barbecue" to the delight of all who come to dinner, for sure! Just ask my barber shop friends at Harry Spohn's; Harry, Anthony, and Rich, just how good it is. The next time I went in for a hair cut, after giving them all a sample of this recipe the time before, Rich said, 'Oh, Steve, you mean you didn't bring us any more of that venison barbecue?' I said, 'Rich, next time.'

"Joel's Sporting Tales"
Easy Big Game and Bacon Barbecue

1	pound bacon, diced small	1½	cups chopped onions
2-2½	pounds venison steak or big game of any kind, cubed small	1	envelope instant onion soup mix
		1	teaspoon chili powder
½	of a (7¾-ounce) can of jalapeño peppers, diced, (hot) or 1 (4-ounce) can green chili peppers, diced, (mild)	½	cup brown sugar
		½	cup barbecue sauce
		1	(28-ounce) can diced tomatoes
		½	cup red wine, beer, or water

To a large saucepan or Dutch oven with a lid, add bacon, cubed venison, jalapeño, (hot) or green chili, (mild) peppers, and onions. Stir over medium heat 20 to 25 minutes to nicely brown the venison. Add onion soup mix, chili powder, brown sugar, barbecue sauce, tomatoes and other suggested liquid and stir well. Then turn down heat to simmer and cook for 1½ to 2 hours depending on the tenderness of your venison. Enjoy this big game barbecue in bread buns or over rice or noodles. Delicious even as a main meal with family or at hunting camp.

Everyone does not care for "hot" barbecue or chili so this "medium" barbecue dish pleases everyone, and additional hot pepper flakes, hot sauce or cayenne pepper can be added as guests prefer on individual bowls at serving time.

Cooking Tip: Joel tells us that from past experience this tasty recipe can easily be doubled as needed. Also, use other dark meat from wild game if you do not have deer meat and your meal will still be much enjoyed by all.

This recipe is compliments of Joel Marvin, editor of *Sporting Tales Magazine*.

Days of Yore with Bill Arliss, Sr. (Center!)

This photo is now certainly a remembrance of good people and good hunters on days or seasons gone by. This photo of Bill Arliss, Sr. and our deer hunting crew was taken in 1974 after a successful first morning's deer hunt. Most of us used the Ithaca Model 37 shotgun or Model 37 Deerslayer slug guns. It is tradition. They shoot straight, and that means more meat in your freezer.

This is a photo of the "deer pole" after that successful first morning's deer hunt. Steve's spike buck was added to the "deer pole" for aging after his late afternoon's successful hunt. These traditional hunting memories with family and friends with us and thousands upon thousands of hunters across North America will live on for us and among family and friends for years to come, and why not?

Looking Back

It is hard to believe that it was over twenty-five years ago when I heard the always firm voice of Bill Arliss, Sr. say, "before we hang him up let's see where you hit him." I was still a young deer hunter at the time, but it was time for me to begin to understand the importance of an Arliss farm deer hunting tradition of "shot placement" out of respect for our hunting crew and the whitetail deer we hunted in God's great outdoors. Bill liked my one shot to the lungs.

Days of Yore with Bill Arliss, Sr. continued

It was never said, but with some experience, you got the message that if you shot well and always safely to take your deer of either sex, its venison was yours because there were other deer for our crew to hunt. But if you shot badly or needed help in various ways to tag your whitetail, then it was only right that you offered to share your whitetail's venison with others of our deer hunting crew. That is still the right thing whether in the early 70's or after the year 2000. Please consider donating extra venison to area food banks when you have been blessed with abundance. After all, venison from the whitetail deer, no matter where they are hunted, is a nutritious God given gift for our families, friends, and those less fortunate people living around all of us.

We Are Cooking Big Game Chili...

First, we suggest cooking any favorite big game (chunky style) chili a day or two ahead of time and reheating it to enjoy a delicious and nutritious meal with family, friends, or at hunting camp without all the fuss.

Tip 1: Everywhere we do <u>Quality Venison</u> *book signings and venison samplings from our crockpot it seems nine out of ten people want to sample our venison chili because the aroma of the chili permeates the store, and most everyone loves chili. So use elk, moose, antelope, whitetail or mule deer, too, to make chili.*

Tip 2: We suggest making chili "chunky style," or with chunks of venison rather than with ground venison because the chunks give the chili more flavor. Also, we have found that generally people prefer "spicy" chili, not "hot" chili.

Tip 3: Years ago chili was made with kidney beans. There wasn't the variety of beans available in your local food markets like there is today. We suggest experimenting with the various kinds of chili beans in sauces that are available now.

Tip 4: Simmer chili in a Dutch oven for 1½ to 2 hours, once mixed completely, stirring occasionally. Reheating it the next day makes it even better.

After all these tips, whether you use one of our big game/venison chili recipes or your own, get ready for a great meal!

A Tale of Yore Because of Our Friend Ella!

Gale and I talked about how the hunting tale behind this page could possibly have happened, other than, again, help from God. Have we peaked your interest? Then you will have to read our tale to learn more. We really hope you like this "photo" and our tale that follows. It is certainly special by any standards, even Ella's and the Arliss family, too.

Christmas, 2001, Ella sent us a Christmas card with the follow note: *"Steve, Can you believe this? A hunter found this license in the woods down by camp. You might need it again one day.*

They got 6 deer muzzleloader (last day) of 2001 season. Can you imagine? Ella"

Well, I had just finished talking on the phone with Ella Arliss, my other mom, as I like to call her, and once again, in a delightful conversation she had tales to tell me about family and deer hunting this season. The first question she asked was how we liked "the perfectly preserved" New York State Big Game hunting tag of mine that I had lost in 1986 or 1987 in the woods while deer hunting on their farm. We were shocked to open her Christmas card to see my license that one of their many deer hunters had found during the 2001 deer season, some fifteen years later!

Here fifteen years later I can reflect on having to go into Clyde to get a new Big Game back tag instead of eating lunch so I could be back in time to legally deer hunt all afternoon on this important opening day. When I got back to the farm there was a note for me to go sit at the end of the triangle at the edge of the cornfield where it hits the small patch of woods across from camp because our deer hunting crew is driving it to you and other deer hunting watches.

As I hurried to my watch position slugs were being fired. The drivers managed to take a respectable six point buck and a mature doe, too, but no deer crossed the field in font of me. When our crew of drivers came out of the triangle Rog Arliss asked me if any deer got away. I answered by saying that no deer came across the field. Rog then asked me what I wanted to do since it was nearly 3 o'clock. He said that the other hunters were thinking about where they wanted to take their afternoon's silent deer watch after I responded by saying, "after it gets quiet, a watch at the end of the triangle suits me fine. Just come and get me with a truck along the dike near the Old Erie just after dark because there may be a nice deer down and with me, too." Rog then said, "Ok, see you later."

A Tale of Yore Because of Our Friend Ella! continued

The sun never shown and the temperature was in the twenties for those last couple of hours, but on occasion there was some shotgun slug fires to be heard. With water high in the swampy triangle it was hard to find a two hour, comfortable ground blind location near the obvious deer trails. After checking out several, there was one that seemed best, so my tree seat went up and my feet dangled in a foot of icy water. Hey, it's opening day and all New York deer hunters do what they have to do despite harsh weather. We all "just do it" and it helps us enjoy our pride and joy venison meals even more after taking a whitetail deer. You can feel that you did earn this nutritious and delicious venison, too.

My afternoon watch was comfortable because of my layered clothing, well insulated rubber boots and my always dependable Woolrich hunting pants and coat. In my coat's game bag I always carry a hunter orange poncho to keep out the damp snow and wind. That day they helped a lot.

With a constant snow falling and a constant wind, too, the woods were getting very dark, so my watch check of the time kept me aware of the legal shooting time of 4:41 in the afternoon. Despite prayers and chants of "here deer, here deer" seldom a slug shot was heard and not a shot from the crew on the Arliss farm.

Then, as if out of no where, as they say, one of those silent deer appeared feeding along a trail that was to pass right by me. Hey, with both buck and doe tags this deer's venison could be mine. The deer slowly moved feeding closer and closer until at twenty yards my Ithaca 12-gauge Deerslayer was raised and aimed just behind the done deer's front shoulder and the trigger was pulled. The deer went down and never moved. A big cold thank you went up to our Lord for allowing me the opportunity and skill to harvest this whitetail deer.

After waiting ten minutes by my watch and it was getting dark, I moved from my ground blind "to check out my trophy." The deer was a large mature doe without yearlings as I thought, but that is certainly unusual. *I thanked the Lord for blessing me with this venison from the whitetail deer.

About the time the field dressing process was over it was dark and help was on the way because the sound of Rog's farm pick-up truck could be heard coming down the Old Erie's dike toward me. After being out in twenty degree temperatures, and with a wind chill to boot, his truck sounded like good news was coming.

But even better news is to flag down Rog's truck lights and ask his help to get this tagged big, field dressed doe into his pick-up. Harvesting a healthy fat farm fed deer for your family's dinner table or for needy food banks is a good thing.

Hey, make a memory for a youngster and take a kid hunting so they can learn a love of the outdoors and how its bounty can help them provide food for their family's dinner table and even for others, too. The personal rewards can feel great!

Maggie's First Buck

By Karl J. Power
Pennsylvania Outdoor Writer

Maggie Power, standing over her first day/ first hunt/first buck - an Indiana County, Pennsylvania 10-point. Since that wonderful November morning in 1995, Maggie has grown as a woman - and as a hunter, taking at least one good white-tail deer each fall.

As an avid outdoorsman, outdoor writer, and single parent of two daughters, life is not typical in my home. If there was a season, I was out there "working" in the "field office" gathering story material and photos. My daughters, Jessica and Maggie, who I raised myself from the time they were in diapers, grew up with the outdoors sports as an accepted and normal way of life. It was no surprise when they both actively took up fishing and hunting. What was a surprise, however, is their amazing skill - even at early ages.

On Jessica's first hunting season, in 1994, she made an amazing shot that dropped a young buck at more than 300 yards. Her younger sister, Maggie, who always worked hard on deer drives, and helping to get the deer taken out of the woods to the truck, could not wait until the following year when she would turn the magical hunting age of 12 - and actively participate in her own hunt.

It was a long year for Maggie, and she jumped at the chance to take her mandatory hunter safety education course, and a short time later, obtain her very first hunting license - along with a brand-new bright orange license holder. The license hung on her bedroom wall each day until the fall season arrived and squirrel season opened in mid-October. This was Maggie's primer for the upcoming deer hunt at the end of November.

Maggie's First Buck continued

I had already taken my buck in archery season, and Jessica was partnered up with my brother, her Uncle Bill, on a large wooden platform treestand with walls about 100 yards to our side. I was perched in another stand deeper into the wooded hollow with Maggie. It was the first time I had ever seen her so wide-awake before daybreak. She was ready - and her Winchester lever action 30-30 was at her side and within easy reach should a buck come past.

The usual early morning shots rang out, and her anticipation was beginning to peak. Deer were on the move - some of which ran nearly directly beneath our elevated treestand. Between deer sightings, I had her pick out a specific tree, stump, or rock - anything actually, and see how fast she could get the gun sights on it. Knowing sometimes a deer will make it past, without getting a shot off soon enough can be a disappointment. Maggie's rifle had the traditional open sights - which I assumed would eliminate any problems with finding a buck in the scope.

We were in the stand at 6:30 a.m., and within the first hour we had seen at least 20 deer, two of which were bucks. The deer, however, were a little too far off for open sights, and when they did stop moving through the trees - as usual, they were behind large tree trunks. By the end of three hours in the stand, we saw many more does, and another two bucks - that again, she could not get a shot at through the trees.

The fourth hour was moving slowly, with very little deer movement - other than a few does. One small button buck amused Maggie as it fed and slowly passed, within about 20 feet of the base of the tree our stand was positioned in.

Above us, I saw two large deer moving from left to right, and I told her to get ready as I focused the binoculars on them - particularly their heads. Both were does. Her excitement melted as quickly as the deer evaporated into a nearby thicket. Everything was quiet, and Maggie was beginning to look tired. I had her playing the "aim at that tree" game to keep her alert and interested. It worked, because she was not ready to leave the tree stand for an early lunch - and nap. After all, it was only 10:30, and a lot could happen. I kept telling her, "The buck will come through when you least expect it - so always try to expect it."

I noticed two large deer forms in the thick underbrush moving back from our right to the left on the same path the two does took earlier. "Here come a couple," I said. "Probably the two does that just went in there; and they've been turned back." I had Maggie get ready, and to practice setting the sights on both deer as they moved about 80 yards above us. Looking through the binoculars, the first one came into the clearing. "It's a doe. Get your sights on it anyway, but don't shoot," I whispered to her.

Maggie's First Buck continued

The second deer stepped out into the clearing and I could not believe my eyes. It had a huge, white set of antlers. "It's a buck! Get on it," I almost shouted. "Okay, Dad," she said, "I'm on it." Seconds passed, and the silence was incredible. "Should I shoot now?" she asked innocently. "Shoot! - Shoot!" I almost screamed.

"Bang!" the deer hunched, and started running full-steam toward my brother and Jessica's stand. "Bill - There's a big buck running your way - up the hill and behind you!" I yelled.

Suddenly, the large buck came to an abrupt halt. It stood there, head hanging low in a group of small saplings and wild grapevine tangles. The large doe with the buck looked confused. She knew we were nearby from the shot and my yelling to my now-ready brother and daughter, Jessica.

"Holy cow, Maggie - it stopped and it's just standing there," I said, as I repositioned her in the treestand and pointing to the spot where she 'might' get an open shot through the trees. "Get ready, relax, and try to get your sights on the buck's shoulder and squeeze off another shot. Can you see it - it's just standing there - I can't believe it," I said in a very nervous voice. I was actually shaking like a leaf in the breeze. Maggie, on the other hand, was as calm as ever. The shot was a very difficult one to take - almost like threading a needle trying to get the bullet through the tiny tree openings to the buck.

"Bang!" Maggie shot, and the monster buck dropped to the ground so hard, that it looked as though it was pulled down by an invisible force. Now I really was shaking.

I kept my eyes on the exact spot where the buck dropped as Maggie pulled the rope up to the treestand so I could lower the gun. I emptied the rifle and quickly climbed down from the stand. I reloaded the rifle for Maggie as she too climbed down from the stand. I told her that I would carry the rifle up the hill to her, and hand it to her as soon as we saw the buck on the small level bench above us. We slowly and quietly worked our way up the hill to the flat where the buck was last seen. Looking around, we both were confused because there was no sign of the deer.

"Where could it be," we both said at the same time. We were beginning to get frantic, wondering how the buck could have eluded us - after all, I knew it was hit very hard by both shots. Then we saw it, lying behind a tangle of vines. It was down for keeps - and Maggie had just killed what easily could be the biggest white-tailed buck she may ever take. Maggie, unaware of the true trophy value of this magnifi-

Maggie's First Buck continued

cent buck was surprisingly calm. I was surprisingly shaking uncontrollably - and quite surprised, in retrospect that the roll of photos I took on the spot actually all came out clear.

The 1995 Indiana County, Pennsylvania 10-point buck's head is mounted and hangs with all of our pride on the living room wall. We all - sister, Jessica included, will never forget the day. Yes - hunting memories last a lifetime — especially when you are with your kids.

The nearest thing to heaven is a child. A child that hunts understands more about nature - and life as a whole, than most other young people their age. The outdoors breeds wisdom beyond normal years - even for kids.

Author's note: *Each year, my daughters and I look forward to deer season. We all archery hunt, and this past season both of my daughters (both beautiful young women now) took their first archery bucks. Both girls have taken 10-point bucks - and both also have dropped deer with rifles at more than 300 yards. If I sound proud of them - it's because I am.* **Karl Power**

The following is a recipe for venison backstraps that Karl was nice enough to share with us. Enjoy!

Marinated and Grilled Backstraps

When processing your deer, pull the large backstraps (the long strip of meat from which chops are sliced) from each side of the deer's spine. If you remove the front legs of the deer carcass first, you will gain 5 or 6 more inches of backstrap from each side. Trim the venison straps, removing the "silver" layer and any pieces of fat.

I usually freeze the backstraps in plastic zip-lock bags. Just like pre-freezing jerky venison strips before smoking, the freezing will break down the tissues more - allowing better smoke penetration. For marinating meat, the tissue breakdown from freezing also seems to work very well. If you desire to prepare the backstraps immediately, an injector needle will effectively work as a "quick marinade" technique.

Choose your favorite meat or steak marinade and coat the backstraps generously in the solution and keep refrigerated in a plastic freezer/storage container overnight - flipping the meat several times to ensure even marinade coating and penetration.

Remove backstraps and wipe excess marinade from the meat. Melt butter on low heat in a saucepan, and add garlic, chives, seasoned salt, and any other spices you prefer. Coat the marinated backstraps with the herb garlic butter solution and wrap the meat in plastic wrap - and refrigerate for at least 2 or 3 hours. On a hot gas or charcoal grill, place the long backstraps across the grate and sear the meat quickly on each side. The garlic butter will add to the flavor, and at the same time keep the meat from sticking to the grill. Cook the backstraps (depending in size - or age of the deer) from 4 to 5 minutes on each side — or until the desired wellness of the meat is achieved. Venison, being very lean, is preferred by most if cooked rare to medium rare to ensure juicy flavor.

Remove cooked backstraps from the grill and slice into ½-inch thick pieces. Spread them out on a large platter, and serve with potatoes, baked beans, or whatever you are in the mood for - and the platter of meat will quickly disappear before your eyes. If you try these marinated and grilled backstraps, you may never want to eat deer chops again!

Karl Power

Marinated and Grilled Backstraps continued

*Steve and Gale would like to suggest you try one of our dozen or so scrumptious venison marinades in our **Quality Venison II** cookbook when preparing Karl Power's recipe for backstraps. And if you don't already own a copy of our second book, it is a "must have," along with our first book, **Quality Venison,** for all deer hunters, young or not-so-young, to add delicious variety to all your venison meals.*

The Importance of Passing on the Hunting and Fishing Tradition

Although my dad, Harry Loder, did not hunt himself, he knew, as a cub and boy scout, I had a love for the outdoors, so when I became old enough to fish and hunt dad "hooked me up" with his friends who had hunting, fishing, and camping hobbies. Sharing new friendships and new pleasures in God's great outdoors, camping, fishing, and hunting meant the world to me and it will to our youngsters if we make the effort to take them with us. It is also a good idea if we can prepare our catch, either fish or wild game, and let our young people have the opportunity to enjoy "the fruits of our outdoor labor" with us. You can't just go to the local grocery store and buy the wild game or game fish meal we have just very much enjoyed, my friends. You have to go outdoors and earn it!

Nature Laughs in God's Outdoors

Hunting all kinds of wild game with family or friends old and new has made a difference in our lives - both on a personal and spiritual level for our family.

Out in God's outdoors, nature can teach us a lot, regardless of the weather we experience, while seeking our pursuit of wild game or fish. We can feel God's presence in the clean air, the sunshine and often even in the wind rattling the trees or causing the waves.

To me the sunshine I feel in the outdoors gives me a glad heart of thanksgiving even if there are personal or work difficulties. The laughter coming from sunshine and nature works wonders whether I am able to harvest any wild game or fish or not. Taking wild game or fish is the icing on the cake of the outdoors' experience.

We are constantly hearing that the interest young people now have for hunting and fishing, what were our largest outdoors sports, is declining nationally and that is disappointing, to say the least. God wants us to enjoy nature and the legal, ethical taking of his animals or fish from hunting and fishing. It is in God's outdoors that we feel His medicines of sun, air, and His peace. Outdoors, while hunting or fishing, you can often feel being enwrapped in His spirit as we are drawn closer to God from each outdoor experience. Personally, over the years, nature, the outdoors, where I find my God, has been my nurse for my tired soul and often ill, weary body. God bless, Steve

P.S. My health permitting, I will pick you up at 5:00 in the morning and we will enjoy an outdoor hunting or fishing experience together. We are sure to be blessed with a lasting outdoor memory…

A

A Hunter's Small Game Stew 91

A Tasty Venison Corn Chowder 55

An Upland Game Special 94

Appetizers *(also see Dips and Spreads)*

Gerry's Venison Jerky 99

Jack's Marinade
For Big Game Jerky 100

Marie's Marinated Mushrooms 109

Steve's Fish Fillet Appetizer 104

Aunt Lucy's Baked Beans 116

Aunt Marge's Cheesy Venison
and Veggie Bake 60

B

Barbecued "Buck" Burgers 15

Beans and Peas

Aunt Lucy's Baked Beans 116

Delightfully Different
Summertime Salad 103

Dick and Sherman's
Duck Camp Stew 153

Easy "Crocked" Venison Sausage
Creole with Peppers and Beans 46

Easy Venison Sausage
Skillet For Two 33

Gale's Easy Cheesy Potatoes 114

Gale's Green Bean
and Potato Surprise 105

Home Style Italian Chili Soup 49

Lone Brave Venison 57

Louise's Just Right Potato Salad 104

Mexican Style Rice Casserole 116

Mexican Style Small Game
with Venison Sausage
and Fresh Tomatoes 88

Mom's Barbecue Baked Beans 118

Mom's Favorite Venison
Italian Casserole 35

My Mom's Italian Style Sausage
and Two Bean Stew 54

Our Homemade
Barbecue Style Baked Beans 117

Our Masterpiece Venison Chili 56

Rog's Favorite "Slow Cooked"
Venison Chili Soup 162

Slow Cooker Chunky
Wild Game Chili 48

Steve's Italian Style
Goose/Duck Stew 77

Steve's Venison Chili Soup 57

Venison and Bean "Hot" Pot 52

Beef

Denny's Venison Salami 98

Believe It! Wild Duck Stroganoff 68

Big Game

Jack's Marinade
For Big Game Jerky 100

Jerry Molettiere's
Venison Steak Italiano 36

"Joel's Sporting Tales" Easy
Big Game and Bacon Barbecue 197

Steve's Any Time Tasty Big Game
Stuffed Pitas (Italian Style) 179

Bill's Favorite Venison and Pasta 41

Billy Arliss' Duck Breasts
in Tomato Cream Sauce 72

INDEX

Broccoli

A Hunter's Small Game Stew 91

Easy Cajun Spiced
  Wild Game Gumbo 93

Zesty Venison and Broccoli Stir-Fry ... 14

Broiled Venison Steak and Bacon 17

C

Cajun Spiced Venison Steak or Roast 27

Carrots

Loder's Restaurant Venison Ragoût 62

Uncle Dom's Tasty Meatloaf 59

Casseroles

An Upland Game Special 94

Aunt Lucy's Baked Beans 116

Easy Cheesy Onion and
  Zucchini Bake 112

Gale's Cheesy Venison
  Sausage Lasagna 37

Loder's Restaurant Venison Ragoût 62

Loder's Upland Game Special 95

Mexican Style Rice Casserole 116

Mom's Barbecue Baked Beans 118

Mom's Favorite
  Venison Italian Casserole 35

Our Easy Venison
  and Pepperoni Lasagna 38

Our Favorite Potato
  and Veggie Casserole 113

Our Homemade Barbecue
  Style Baked Beans 117

Uncle Dom's Cheesy
  Sausage Casserole 34

Venison and Bean "Hot" Pot 52

"You Just Have To Try It"
  Venison Sausage Casserole 61

Cheese

Cranberry's Cheesy Venison
  and Potato Chowder 101

Gale's Cheesy Venison
  Sausage Lasagna 37

Italian Style Slow Cooker Pheasant
  Stuffed with Pepperoni and
  Black Olives 82

Our Easy Venison
  and Pepperoni Lasagna 38

Our Venison in Mexi-Cheese Dip 110

Steelers Bacon
  and Cheese Dip or Spread 111

Uncle Dom's Cheesy
  Sausage Casserole 34

"You Just Have To Try It"
  Venison Sausage Casserole 61

Clyde's "Memphis Style" Pheasant 183

Clyde's Venison Roast 64

Condiments and Sauces

Deer Hunter's Marinade 24

Garlicky Steak Sauce 18

"Gotta Have It" Venison Marinade 23

Gravy 136

Loder's Restaurant
  Style Pasta Sauce 40

Our Country Kitchen
  Barbecue Sauce 28

Our Peppery Olive Pasta Sauce 39

Spicy Rub 25

Venison Italiano Marinade 24

Venison Teriyaki Marinade 24

Corn

A Tasty Venison Corn Chowder 55

Delightfully Different
  Summertime Salad 103

Gale's Venison and
  Wild Rice Soup 44

Lone Brave Venison 57

Mexican Style Rice Casserole 116

Our Upland Stew 91

Cranberry's Cheesy Venison
  and Potato Chowder 101

Crockpot Recipes

A Hunter's Small Game Stew 91

Clyde's "Memphis Style" Pheasant ... 183

Crockery Cooked Small
  Game Mozzarella 80

Dad's Venison and Pasta Italiano 43

Delicious Wild Duck
  and Wild Rice Stew 69

Easy Cajun Spiced
  Wild Game Gumbo 93

Easy "Crocked" Venison Sausage
  Creole with Peppers and Beans 46

Gale's Venison and Wild Rice Soup 44

Gerry's Deer Huntin' Stroganoff 50

Home Style Italian Chili Soup 49

Italian Style Slow Cooker
  Pheasant Stuffed with
  Pepperoni and Black Olives 82

Jack's Cajun Spiced
  and Pieced Canadian Goose 75

Jocelyne's Marinated
  Waterfowl Supreme 78

Mexican Style Small Game
  with Venison Sausage
  and Fresh Tomatoes 88

New Orleans Style
  Wild Duck Gumbo 73

Our Crockpot Venison Barbecue 29

Our Italian Duck with Mushrooms 71

Rog's Favorite "Slow Cooked"
  Venison Chili Soup 162

Slow Cooker Chunky
  Wild Game Chili 48

Steve's Favorite Venison Stew
  with Roasted Peppers 45

Steve's Italian Style
  Goose/Duck Stew 77

Steve's Wild Duck Stroganoff 74

D

Dad Flack's Special
  Venison Steak for You Two!! 22

Dad's Venison and Pasta Italiano 43

Dan's Southern Style Wild Duck 69

Deer Hunter's Marinade 24

Delicious Wild Duck
  and Wild Rice Stew 69

Deliciously Glazed Venison Kabobs 30

Delightfully Different
  Summertime Salad 103

Denny's Venison Salami 98

Dick and Sherman's
  Duck Camp Stew 153

Dick's "Southern Style"
  Venison Hindquarter 154

Dips and Spreads

Our Cranberry Twp.
  Pepperoni Dip 111

Our Herby Venison
  and Cheese Spread 110

Our Venison in Mexi-Cheese Dip 110

Steelers Bacon
  and Cheese Dip or Spread 111

Duck

Believe It! Wild Duck Stroganoff 68

Billy Arliss' Duck Breasts
in Tomato Cream Sauce 72

Dan's Southern Style Wild Duck 69

Delicious Wild Duck
and Wild Rice Stew 69

Dick and Sherman's
Duck Camp Stew 153

Jocelyne's Marinated
Waterfowl Supreme 78

New Orleans Style
Wild Duck Gumbo 73

Our Duck Eleganté for Two 70

Our Italian Duck with Mushrooms 71

Our Italian Style Waterfowl 76

Steve's Wild Duck Stroganoff 74

Whitetop Wild Duck 140

E

Easy and Cheesy Venisonburgers 15

Easy Cajun Spiced
Wild Game Gumbo 93

Easy Cheesy Onion
and Zucchini Bake 112

Easy "Crocked" Venison Sausage
Creole with Peppers and Beans 46

Easy Does It Veggie Rice Pilaf 115

Easy Venison Sausage
Skillet For Two 33

Ella Arliss' "Farm House"
Venison Steak with Gravy 158

Ella's Farm Raised Venison Roast 64

F

Father's Day Venison Loin Chops 17

Fish (also see Seafood)

Gale's Tasty Italian Fish Fillets 106

Louise's Just Right Potato Salad 104

Our Easily 'Bodacious' Fish Fillets ... 107

Steve's Fish Fillet Appetizer 104

Fourth of July Venison 18

G

Gale's Cheesy Venison
Sausage Lasagna 37

Gale's Easy Cheesy Potatoes 114

Gale's Green Bean
and Potato Surprise 105

Gale's Tasty Italian Fish Fillets 106

Gale's Venison and Wild Rice Soup 44

Gale's Wined and
Dined Venison Meatballs 58

Garlicky Steak Sauce 18

Gerry's Deer Huntin' Stroganoff 50

Gerry's Venison Jerky 99

Goose

Jack's Cajun Spiced
and Pieced Canadian Goose 75

Jocelyne's Marinated
Waterfowl Supreme 78

Steve's Italian Style
Goose/Duck Stew 77

Steve's Lansdale Wild Goose 173

"Gotta Have It" Venison Marinade 23

Grilling Recipes

Cajun Spiced Venison
Steak or Roast 27

Deliciously Glazed Venison Kabobs 30

Easy and Cheesy Venisonburgers 15

Father's Day Venison Loin Chops 17

Fourth of July Venison 18

Herb Grilled Venisonburgers 14

Herb-Rubbed Venison Steaks 19

Leo's Spicy Venison Kabobs 30

Our Spicy Venison
  Steak and Onions 25

Penn's Woods Labor Day
  Picnic Smoked Venison Roast 26

Ron's Deer Camp Venison
  Slouvaki (Greek Style) 177

Grouse

Crockery Cooked Small
  Game Mozzarella 80

Jerry's Tasty Upland Birds 168

Loder's Upland Game Special 95

Steve's Pheasant or Grouse Italiano 81

Steve's Pheasant/Grouse Ranchero 86

Steve's Pheasant/Grouse/Rabbit
  Parmesan 79

Steve's Upland and
  Sausage Stroganoff 87

Upland Game with Fresh Celery
  and Mushrooms 96

H

Herb Grilled Venisonburgers 14

Herb-Rubbed Venison Steaks 19

Home Style Italian Chili Soup 49

I

Italian Style Slow Cooker
  Pheasant Stuffed with
  Pepperoni and Black Olives 82

J

Jack's Cajun Spiced
  and Pieced Canadian Goose 75

Jack's Marinade For
  Big Game Jerky 100

Jerry Molettiere's Venison
  Steak Italiano 36

Jerry's Tasty Upland Birds 168

Jim Trotta's Venison Steak in the Bag 63

Jocelyne's Marinated
  Venison Swiss Steak 20

Jocelyne's Marinated
  Waterfowl Supreme 78

"Joel's Sporting Tales" Easy Big
  Game and Bacon Barbecue 197

K

Kabobs

Deliciously Glazed Venison Kabobs ... 30

Leo's Spicy Venison Kabobs 30

Kelly's Marinated Wild Turkey 144

Kelly's Quick Venison Stroganoff 65

L

Larry's Barbecue Venison Steak 19

Leo's Spicy Venison Kabobs 30

Lockpit Venison Sausage 99

Loder's Restaurant Style Pasta Sauce 40

Loder's Restaurant Venison Ragoût 62

Loder's Upland Game Special 95

Lone Brave Venison 57

Louise's Just Right Potato Salad 104

M

Marie's Marinated Mushrooms 109

Marinated and Grilled Backstraps 206

Mexican Style Rice Casserole 116

Mexican Style Small Game
  with Venison Sausage
  and Fresh Tomatoes 88

Mom's Barbecue Baked Beans 118

Mom's Easy Venison and Veggies 16

Mom's Favorite Venison
    Italian Casserole 35

Mom's Spectacular Venison
    Sauerbraten 136

Mushrooms

Delicious Wild Duck
    and Wild Rice Stew 69

Deliciously Glazed Venison Kabobs ... 30

Ella Arliss' "Farm House"
    Venison Steak with Gravy 158

Gale's Venison and
    Wild Rice Soup 44

Loder's Restaurant
    Style Pasta Sauce 40

Marie's Marinated Mushrooms 109

Mushroom Stuffed Loin Steaks 16

My Mom's Italian Style
    Sausage and Two Bean Stew 54

Our Italian Duck with Mushrooms 71

Steve's Favorite Venison Stew
    with Roasted Peppers 45

Steve's Rabbit Cacciatore 85

Steve's Wild Duck Stroganoff 74

Upland Game with
    Fresh Celery and Mushrooms 96

My Mom's New England
    Clam Chowder 108

N

New Orleans Style
    Wild Duck Gumbo 73

O

Okra

Easy Cajun Spiced
    Wild Game Gumbo 93

New Orleans Style
    Wild Duck Gumbo 73

Onion and Zucchini Bake,
    Easy Cheesy 112

Our Autumn Squirrel Stew 92

Our Cheesy Venison Chowder
    with Green Onions and
    Roasted Peppers 102

Our Country Kitchen Barbecue Sauce 28

Our Country Kitchen's Specialty
    of "The House" 66

Our Cranberry Twp. Pepperoni Dip 111

Our Crockpot Venison Barbecue 29

Our Duck Eleganté for Two 70

Our Easily 'Bodacious' Fish Fillets 107

Our Easy Small Game Soup 89

Our Easy Venison
    and Pepperoni Lasagna 38

Our Favorite Potato and
    Veggie Casserole 113

Our Herby Venison
    and Cheese Spread 110

Our Homemade Barbecue
    Style Baked Beans 117

Our Homemade Venison Manicotti 42

Our Italian Duck with Mushrooms 71

Our Italian Style Waterfowl 76

Our Masterpiece Venison Chili 56

Our "Oven Bagged"
    Priestly Venison Stew 53

Our Peppery Olive Pasta Sauce 39

Our Spicy Venison Steak and Onions 25

Our Upland Stew 91

Our Venison in Mexi-Cheese Dip 110

Our Venison Loin Mozzarella 39

Our Venison Loin Steaks
    with Garlicky Steak Sauce 18

Oven Bag Cooking

Clyde's Venison Roast 64

Cooking Bag Cooking Tips 145

Dick's "Southern Style" Venison
    Hindquarter 154

Ella's Farm Raised Venison Roast 64

Jim Trotta's Venison Steak
    in the Bag 63

Our "Oven Bagged"
    Priestly Venison Stew 53

Sherry Baked Wild Rabbit 127

Spicy Barbecue Venison 55

Steve's Lansdale Wild Goose 173

Whitetop Wild Duck 140

P

Pasta

Believe It! Wild Duck Stroganoff 68

Bill's Favorite Venison and Pasta 41

Crockery Cooked Small
    Game Mozzarella 80

Dad's Venison and Pasta Italiano 43

Easy Venison Sausage
    Skillet For Two 33

Ella Arliss' "Farm House"
    Venison Steak with Gravy 158

Gale's Cheesy Venison
    Sausage Lasagna 37

Gerry's Deer Huntin' Stroganoff 50

Italian Style Slow Cooker Pheasant
    Stuffed with Pepperoni and
    Black Olives 82

Jerry Molettiere's Venison
    Steak Italiano 36

Jerry's Tasty Upland Birds 168

Kelly's Quick Venison Stroganoff 65

Larry's Barbecue Venison Steak 19

Loder's Restaurant
    Style Pasta Sauce 40

Mom's Favorite Venison
    Italian Casserole 35

Our Easy Small Game Soup 89

Our Easy Venison and
    Pepperoni Lasagna 38

Our Homemade Venison Manicotti 42

Our Italian Style Waterfowl 76

Our Peppery Olive Pasta Sauce 39

Quick Pheasant Cacciatore 84

Shotgun Venison Steak 21

Steve's Lansdale Wild Goose 173

Steve's Peppery Venison Meatballs 32

Steve's Pheasant or Grouse Italiano 81

Steve's Upland and
    Sausage Stroganoff 87

Uncle Dom's Cheesy
    Sausage Casserole 34

"You Just Have To Try It"
    Venison Sausage Casserole 61

Zesty Venison and
    Broccoli Stir-Fry 14

Penn's Woods Labor Day Picnic
    Smoked Venison Roast 26

Peppery Squirrel Jambalaya 90

Pheasants

Clyde's "Memphis Style" Pheasant 183

Crockery Cooked Small
    Game Mozzarella 80

Italian Style Slow Cooker
    Pheasant Stuffed with
    Pepperoni and Black Olives 82

Jerry's Tasty Upland Birds 168

Quick Pheasant Cacciatore 84

Steve's Pheasant or Grouse Italiano 81

Steve's Pheasant/Grouse Ranchero 86

Steve's Pheasant/Grouse/Rabbit
Parmesan 79

Steve's Upland and
Sausage Stroganoff 87

Pork

Easy Cajun Spiced
Wild Game Gumbo 93

"Joel's Sporting Tales" Easy
Big Game and Bacon Barbecue 197

Lockpit Venison Sausage 99

Mexican Style Small Game
with Venison Sausage
and Fresh Tomatoes 88

New Orleans Style
Wild Duck Gumbo 73

Peppery Squirrel Jambalaya 90

Rog's Favorite "Slow Cooked"
Venison Chili Soup 162

Steelers Bacon and Cheese
Dip or Spread 111

Steve's Upland and
Sausage Stroganoff 87

Potatoes

A Tasty Venison Corn Chowder 55

Cranberry's Cheesy Venison
and Potato Chowder 101

Ella's Farm Raised Venison Roast 64

Gale's Easy Cheesy Potatoes 114

Gale's Green Bean
and Potato Surprise 105

Louise's Just Right Potato Salad 104

Our Autumn Squirrel Stew 92

Our Favorite Potato
and Veggie Casserole 113

Potato Dumplings 136

Steve's Favorite Venison Stew
with Roasted Peppers 45

Steve's Pheasant or Grouse Italiano 81

Uncle Dom's Tasty Meatloaf 59

Q

Quick Pheasant Cacciatore 84

R

Rabbits

A Hunter's Small Game Stew 91

An Upland Game Special 94

Crockery Cooked Small Game
Mozzarella 80

Easy Cajun Spiced
Wild Game Gumbo 93

Loder's Upland Game Special 95

Mexican Style Small Game
with Venison Sausage
and Fresh Tomatoes 88

Our Easy Small Game Soup 89

Our Upland Stew 91

Sherry Baked Wild Rabbit 127

Slow Cooker Chunky
Wild Game Chili 48

Steve's Pheasant/Grouse/Rabbit
Parmesan 79

Steve's Rabbit Cacciatore 85

Steve's Rabbit/Squirrel Italiano 85

Troy's Upland Surprise 94

Upland Game with Fresh Celery
and Mushrooms 96

Rice

Aunt Marge's Cheesy Venison and
Veggie Bake 60

Dad Flack's Special Venison
Steak for You Two!! 22

Delicious Wild Duck
and Wild Rice Stew 69

Easy Does It Veggie Rice Pilaf 115

Gale's Venison
and Wild Rice Soup 44

Jerry's Tasty Upland Birds 168

Larry's Barbecue Venison Steak 19

Mexican Style Rice Casserole 116

Mexican Style Small Game
with Venison Sausage
and Fresh Tomatoes 88

Mom's Easy Venison and Veggies 16

Our Duck Eleganté for Two 70

Our Italian Style Waterfowl 76

Peppery Squirrel Jambalaya 90

Steve's Lansdale Wild Goose 173

Steve's Pheasant or Grouse Italiano 81

Steve's Upland and
Sausage Stroganoff 87

Upland Game with
Fresh Celery and Mushrooms 96

Rog's Favorite "Slow Cooked"
Venison Chili Soup 162

Ron's Deer Camp Venison
Slouvaki (Greek Style) 177

S

Salads

Delightfully Different
Summertime Salad 103

Louise's Just Right Potato Salad 104

Venison Taco Salad 190

Seafood

Easy Cajun Spiced
Wild Game Gumbo 93

Easy "Crocked" Venison Sausage
Creole with Peppers and Beans 46

My Mom's New England
Clam Chowder 108

New Orleans Style
Wild Duck Gumbo 73

Our Cheesy Venison Chowder
with Green Onions and
Roasted Peppers 102

Sherry Baked Wild Rabbit 127

Shotgun Venison Steak 21

Slow Cooker Chunky
Wild Game Chili 48

Soups, Stews, Chowders and Chili

A Hunter's Small Game Stew 91

A Tasty Venison Corn Chowder 55

Cranberry's Cheesy Venison
and Potato Chowder 101

Delicious Wild Duck
and Wild Rice Stew 69

Dick and Sherman's
Duck Camp Stew 153

Gale's Venison and Wild Rice Soup ... 44

Home Style Italian Chili Soup 49

My Mom's Italian Style Sausage
and Two Bean Stew 54

My Mom's New England
Clam Chowder 108

Our Autumn Squirrel Stew 92

Our Cheesy Venison Chowder
with Green Onions and
Roasted Peppers 102

Our Easy Small Game Soup 89

Our Masterpiece Venison Chili 56

Our "Oven Bagged" Priestly
Venison Stew 53

Our Upland Stew 91

Rog's Favorite "Slow Cooked"
Venison Chili Soup 162

Slow Cooker Chunky
Wild Game Chili 48

Steve's Favorite Venison Stew
with Roasted Peppers 45

Steve's Italian Style
Goose/Duck Stew 77

Steve's Venison Chili Soup 57

Spicy Barbecue Venison 55

Spicy Rub 25

Squash

Easy Cheesy Onion
and Zucchini Bake 112

Our Easy Small Game Soup 89

Our Favorite Potato
and Veggie Casserole 113

Quick Pheasant Cacciatore 84

"You Just Have To Try It"
Venison Sausage Casserole 61

Squirrel

A Hunter's Small Game Stew 91

An Upland Game Special 94

Crockery Cooked Small
Game Mozzarella 80

Easy Cajun Spiced
Wild Game Gumbo 93

Loder's Upland Game Special 95

Mexican Style Small Game
with Venison Sausage
and Fresh Tomatoes 88

Our Autumn Squirrel Stew 92

Our Easy Small Game Soup 89

Our Upland Stew 91

Peppery Squirrel Jambalaya 90

Slow Cooker Chunky Wild Game Chili
48

Steelers Bacon and Cheese Dip
or Spread 111

Steve's Rabbit/Squirrel Italiano 85

Troy's Upland Surprise 94

Steve's Any Time Tasty Big Game
Stuffed Pitas (Italian Style) 179

Steve's Favorite Venison Stew
with Roasted Peppers 45

Steve's Fish Fillet Appetizer 104

Steve's Italian Style Goose/Duck Stew 77

Steve's Lansdale Wild Goose 173

Steve's Peppery Venison Meatballs 32

Steve's Pheasant or Grouse Italiano 81

Steve's Pheasant/Grouse Ranchero 86

Steve's Pheasant/Grouse/Rabbit
Parmesan 79

Steve's Rabbit Cacciatore 85

Steve's Rabbit/Squirrel Italiano 85

Steve's Upland and
Sausage Stroganoff 87

Steve's Venison Chili Soup 57

Steve's Wild Duck Stroganoff 74

T

Tomatoes

Dad's Venison and Pasta Italiano 43

Easy Cajun Spiced
Wild Game Gumbo 93

Italian Style Slow Cooker
Pheasant Stuffed with
Pepperoni and Black Olives 82

Jim Trotta's Venison
Steak in the Bag 63

Mexican Style Small Game
with Venison Sausage
and Fresh Tomatoes 88

Our Italian Style Waterfowl 76

Slow Cooker Chunky
Wild Game Chili 48

Steve's Venison Chili Soup 57

Troy's Upland Surprise 94

Turkey

Kelly's Marinated Wild Turkey 144

U

Uncle Dom's Cheesy
Sausage Casserole 34

Uncle Dom's Tasty Meatloaf 59

Upland Game with
Fresh Celery and Mushrooms 96

V

Venison

Burger

A Tasty Venison Corn Chowder 55

Barbecued "Buck" Burgers 15

Easy and Cheesy Venisonburgers 15

Gale's Wined and Dined
Venison Meatballs 58

Herb Grilled Venisonburgers 14

Home Style Italian Chili Soup 49

Loder's Restaurant
Style Pasta Sauce 40

Lone Brave Venison 57

Mom's Favorite Venison
Italian Casserole 35

Our Cheesy Venison Chowder
with Green Onions
and Roasted Peppers 102

Our Easy Venison
and Pepperoni Lasagna 38

Our Herby Venison
and Cheese Spread 110

Our Venison in Mexi-Cheese Dip ... 110

Steve's Peppery
Venison Meatballs 32

Steve's Venison Chili Soup 57

Uncle Dom's Tasty Meatloaf 59

Ground

Denny's Venison Salami 98

Lockpit Venison Sausage 99

Venison Taco Salad 190

Hindquarter

Dick's "Southern Style"
Venison Hindquarter 154

Roast

Cajun Spiced Venison
Steak or Roast 27

Clyde's Venison Roast 64

Ella's Farm Raised Venison Roast 64

Gale's Venison and
Wild Rice Soup 44

Mom's Spectacular
Venison Sauerbraten 136

Our Crockpot Venison Barbecue 29

Penn's Woods Labor Day
Picnic Smoked Venison Roast 26

Sausage

Barbecued "Buck" Burgers 15

Dad's Venison and Pasta Italiano 43

Easy Cajun Spiced Wild
Game Gumbo 93

Easy "Crocked" Venison
Sausage Creole with
Peppers and Beans 46

Easy Venison Sausage
Skillet For Two 33

Gale's Cheesy Venison
Sausage Lasagna 37

Home Style Italian Chili Soup 49

Loder's Restaurant
Style Pasta Sauce 40

Mexican Style Small Game
with Venison Sausage
and Fresh Tomatoes 88

Mom's Favorite
Venison Italian Casserole 35

Our Cheesy Venison Chowder
with Green Onions
and Roasted Peppers 102

Our Easy Venison and
Pepperoni Lasagna 38

Our Herby Venison
and Cheese Spread 110

Our Homemade
Venison Manicotti 42

Our Venison in
Mexi-Cheese Dip 110

Steve's Peppery
Venison Meatballs 32

Uncle Dom's Cheesy
Sausage Casserole 34

"You Just Have To Try It"
Venison Sausage Casserole 61

Shoulder

Easy Cajun Spiced
Wild Game Gumbo 93

Gerry's Venison Jerky 99

Loder's Restaurant
Venison Ragoût 62

Steak

A Tasty Venison Corn Chowder 55

Aunt Marge's Cheesy
Venison and Veggie Bake 60

Bill's Favorite Venison and Pasta 41

Broiled Venison Steak and Bacon 17

Cajun Spiced Venison
Steak or Roast 27

Cranberry's Cheesy Venison
and Potato Chowder 101

Dad Flack's Special Venison
Steak for You Two!! 22

Deliciously Glazed
Venison Kabobs 30

Ella Arliss' "Farm House"
Venison Steak with Gravy 158

Fourth of July Venison 18

Herb-Rubbed Venison Steaks 19

Jerry Molettiere's Venison
Steak Italiano 36

Jim Trotta's Venison
Steak in the Bag 63

Jocelyne's Marinated
Venison Swiss Steak 20

"Joel's Sporting Tales"
Easy Big Game and
Bacon Barbecue 197

Kelly's Quick Venison Stroganoff 65

Larry's Barbecue Venison Steak 19

Loder's Restaurant
Style Pasta Sauce 40

Mom's Easy Venison and Veggies 16

Mushroom Stuffed Loin Steaks 16

Our Country Kitchen's Specialty
of "The House" 66

Our Crockpot Venison Barbecue 29

Our Masterpiece Venison Chili 56

Our Spicy Venison
    Steak and Onions 25

Our Venison Loin Mozzarella 39

Our Venison Loin Steaks
    with Garlicky Steak Sauce 18

Ron's Deer Camp Venison
    Slouvaki (Greek Style) 177

Shotgun Venison Steak 21

Zesty Venison and
    Broccoli Stir-Fry 14

Stew Meat

Easy Cajun Spiced
    Wild Game Gumbo 93

Gale's Venison
    and Wild Rice Soup 44

Gerry's Deer Huntin' Stroganoff 50

Gerry's Venison Jerky 99

Loder's Restaurant
    Venison Ragoût 62

My Mom's Italian Style
    Sausage and Two Bean Stew 54

Our Masterpiece Venison Chili 56

Our "Oven Bagged"
    Priestly Venison Stew 53

Rog's Favorite "Slow Cooked"
    Venison Chili Soup 162

Slow Cooker Chunky
    Wild Game Chili 48

Spicy Barbecue Venison 55

Steve's Favorite Venison Stew
    with Roasted Peppers 45

Venison and Bean "Hot" Pot 52

Tenderloin

Deliciously Glazed
    Venison Kabobs 30

Father's Day Venison Loin Chops 17

Herb-Rubbed Venison Steaks 19

Leo's Spicy Venison Kabobs 30

Our Country Kitchen's
    Specialty of "The House" 66

Venison and Bean "Hot" Pot 52

Venison Italiano Marinade 24

Venison Taco Salad 190

Venison Teriyaki Marinade 24

W

Whitetop Wild Duck 140

Y

"You Just Have To Try It"
    Venison Sausage Casserole 61

Z

Zesty Venison
    and Broccoli Stir-Fry 14

Zucchini *(see Squash)*

Quality Venison

Homemade Recipes and Homespun Deer Tales

A complete field to freezer guide for preparing venison that is lean, tender and not "gamy." Follow the author's instructions for preparing your venison and you're assured of great tasting meat!

You've been reading about the original *Quality Venison* cookbook in this book, and here's how to buy a copy of your very own. We don't want you to miss any of the great recipes in the first book (all are different form the recipes in *Quality Venison II* and *III*) and we know you'll enjoy the deer tales and great article reprints, so be sure to add this book to your collection.

You'll love the deer tales - straight from the author's hunting journal. The cover is a full color reproduction of wildlife artist Jack Paluh's painting, "In Thanksgiving," a reverent rendering of Native American hunters and their spiritual ties to the whitetail.

Contains 150 family tested recipes in 5 sections:

- Grilling Venison
- Crockery Style
- Family Favorites
- Italian Style
- Traditional Style

Published in 1998, 186 pages, 6x9, comb bound with a hard cover.

Quality Venison II

All New Recipes and Deer Tales Too

Quality Venison II contains 150 new recipes plus two new recipe sections - Cooking Venison Southern Style and Preparing Venison Marinades and Sauces. Put together with the same care and attention to detail as the first book, this title will expand your collection of mouth watering venison dishes. To start, you'll want to try: Easy Deer Camp Venison Roast, Appalachian Mountain Sauce, Rebel Yell Hot Barbecue Sauce and Chunky Venison Pasta Bake. There are so many great tastes here, you'll be in the kitchen for days and your family and friends will applaud the results.

Published in 1999, 192 pages, 6x9, comb bound with a hard cover.

Order your copies today by using the handy order form on the facing page, or simply send $14.95 plus $3.50 shipping and handling per copy (Pennsylvania residents add $1.11 sales tax) to:

Loders' Game Publications

PO Box 1615 • Cranberry Township, PA 16066

Photo courtesy of *Centre Daily Times*

Loders' Game Publications, Inc.

P.O. Box 1615, Cranberry Township, Pennsylvania 16066
Phone: (724) 779-8320

Please send _____ copies of *Quality Venison III*   @ $14.95 each _____

Please send _____ copies of *Quality Venison II*   @ $14.95 each _____

Please send _____ copies of Quality Venison   @ $14.95 each _____

Postage and handling   @ $ 3.50 each _____

Pennsylvania residents, add sales tax   @ $ 1.11 each _____

Total _____

Make checks payable to: Loders' Game Publications, Inc.

Name _____

Address _____

City _____ State _____ Zip _____

Phone (day) _____ (night) _____

❏   Please keep me informed of future wild game publications

- -

Loders' Game Publications, Inc.

P.O. Box 1615, Cranberry Township, Pennsylvania 16066
Phone: (724) 779-8320

Please send _____ copies of *Quality Venison III*   @ $14.95 each _____

Please send _____ copies of *Quality Venison II*   @ $14.95 each _____

Please send _____ copies of Quality Venison   @ $14.95 each _____

Postage and handling   @ $ 3.50 each _____

Pennsylvania residents, add sales tax   @ $ 1.11 each _____

Total _____

Make checks payable to: Loders' Game Publications, Inc.

Name _____

Address _____

City _____ State _____ Zip _____

Phone (day) _____ (night) _____

❏   Please keep me informed of future wild game publications

Names and addresses of bookstores, gift shops, outdoor gear stores, and hunting supply stores, etc. in your area would be appreciated.

- -

Names and addresses of bookstores, gift shops, outdoor gear stores, and hunting supply stores, etc. in your area would be appreciated.